£8.95

Welfare and Youth Work Practice

Welfare and Youth Work Practice is the second book in a series of three dealing with youth issues. The first book, *Youth Work*, was published in conjunction with the British Association of social workers. The third book will be *Young People, Inequality and Youth Work*. All three books are edited by Tony Jeffs and Mark Smith.

Welfare and Youth Work
Practice

Edited by

Tony Jeffs and Mark Smith

**MACMILLAN
EDUCATION**

First published 1988

Published by
MACMILLAN EDUCATION LTD
Houndmills, Basingstoke, Hampshire RG21 2XS
and London
Companies and representatives
throughout the world

Printed in Hong Kong

British Library Cataloguing in Publication Data
Welfare and youth work practice.
1. Social work with youth — Great Britain
I. Jeffs, Tony II.   Smith, Mark, 1950 –
362.7'0941   HV1441.G7
ISBN 0–333–40981–7 (hardcover)
ISBN 0–333–40982–5 (paperback)

Contents

v

List of Tables

List of Figures

List of Abbreviations

ACC Association of County Councils
ACW Association of Community Workers
ADC Association of District Councils
ADSS Association of Directors of Social Services
AMA Association of Metropolitan Authorities
APTC Administrative, Professional, Technical and
    Clerical (related to local authority pay scales)
BYC British Youth Council
CAB Citizens' Advice Bureau
CDP Community Development Project
CETYCW Council for the Education and Training of Youth
    and Community Workers
CNAA Council for National Academic Awards
CP Community Programme (MSC)
CPRS Central Policy Review Staff
CQSW Certificate of Qualification in Social Work
CPF Community Projects Foundation
CSE Conference of Socialist Economists
CSS Certificate in Social Service
CSV Community Service Volunteers
CYSA Community and Youth Service Association
CYWU Community and Youth Workers' Union
DE Department of Employment
DHSS Department of Health and Social Security
DOE (NI) Department of Education (Northern Ireland)
D of E Duke of Edinburgh's Award Scheme
FE Further Education
GRE Grant Related Expenditure

GREA	Grant Related Expenditure Assessment
HE	Higher Education
HMI	Her Majesty's Inspectorate (Education)
ILEA	Inner London Education Authority
IMF	International Monetary Fund
INSTEP	In-service Training and Education Panel (CETYCW)
INTEP	Initial Training and Education Panel (CETYCW)
IT	Intermediate Treatment
JNC	Joint Negotiating Committee for Youth Workers and Community Centre Wardens
LEA	Local Education Authority
MAYC	Methodist Association of Youth Clubs
MSC	Manpower Services Commission
NABC	National Association of Boys' Clubs
NACRO	National Association for the Care and Resettlement of Offenders
NACYS	National Advisory Council for the Youth Service
NAYC	National Association of Youth Clubs
NAYCEO	National Association of Youth and Community and Education Officers
NAYLEA	National Association of Youth Leaders in Local Education Authorities
NAYLO	National Association of Youth Leaders and Organisers
NAYPCAS	National Association of Young People's Counselling and Advisory Services
NAYSO	National Association of Youth Service Officers
NCVYS	National Council for Voluntary Youth Services
NI	Northern Ireland
NISW	National Institute of Social Work
NUT	National Union of Teachers
NVYO	National Voluntary Youth Organisation
NYB	National Youth Bureau
PHAB	Physically Handicapped and Able-Bodied Clubs
PSBR	Public Sector Borrowing Requirement
PSI	Policy Studies Institute
RAT	Racism Awareness Training
RTPI	Royal Town Planning Institute
SCEC	Scottish Community Education Council

SCOYO	Standing Conference of Youth Organisations (Northern Ireland)
SED	Scottish Education Department
SSCVYO	Scottish Standing Conference of Voluntary Youth Organisations
TAG	Training Agencies Group (Initial Training)
TUC	Trades Union Congress
TVEI	Technical and Vocational Education Initiative
URDD	Urdd Gobaith Cymru
UVP	Unified Vocational Preparation
VPP	Voluntary Projects Programme (MSC)
VSU	Voluntary Services Unit (Home Office)
WOED	Welsh Office Education Department
YMCA	Young Men's Christian Association
YODU	Youth Opportunities Development Unit (NYB)
YOP	Youth Opportunities Programme
YSA	Youth Service Association
YSIC	Youth Service Information Centre
YSU	Youth Service Unit (DES)
YTS	Youth Training Scheme
YWCA	Young Women's Christian Association

Preface

This is the second of three books on contemporary youth work which, we hope, will collectively go some way towards stimulating the construction of a grounded theory and debate around youth work practice. Each of the three shares common elements, but they focus upon different facets of youth work. The first, largely written by practitioners, addresses theory and practice. The third is concerned with young people and inequality and the ways in which disadvantage is simultaneously reproduced and addressed within practice. In this middle book, youth work and the Youth Service are examined as an element of welfare.

The scale of the task means we have accumulated a number of debts. Firstly, we must thank the contributors, all of whom have been supportive and willing to endure rewrites. Secondly, a special thank you is needed to Jackie Kelly and Leslie Patrick for typing a number of manuscripts. Thirdly, we are indebted to Marion Leigh for providing a much needed critique of the text that focused our attention on a number of important areas. Fourthly, we must express our thanks to Jackie Apperley and Chris Rogers for their support and lack of any willingness to massage the pretensions of the editors. Fifthly, we are grateful to Alistair and Andrew Jeffs for being totally unthreatening and untroublesome adolescents (as far as we know), a constant and pleasant reminder that normality is the norm. Lastly, mention must be made of Alex and Christopher Rogers, who have, on occasions, had to put up with delayed meal-times, postponed outings and disrupted sleeping arrangements – victims of our anxiety to complete these books. The odd visit to McDonalds, we sense, hardly compensated for the disruption, but did at least spark serious debate concerning the ideological correctness of the editors in one respect – a debate that has now been resolved following the introduction by the Wimpy Bar of beanburgers to their menu.

TONY JEFFS
MARK SMITH

Introduction

Optimism and a sense of excitement at the potential of youth work to make a positive contribution to welfare and educational practice and thinking was a central theme throughout *Youth Work* (1987), the first of these linked texts. This, the second of the three books, tempers that with a critique which questions the very future of the Youth Service, whilst still being positive regarding the activity of youth work. A regard which is underlined in the last book, *Young People, Inequality and Youth Work* (1988), where the focus is upon the impact of social division and the possibilities for effective practice.

Youth work is something of an enigma. Not only to the general reader who may be puzzled as to precisely what it is, where it comes from, and where it fits into the tapestry of welfare; but also to many full-time youth workers and students of youth and community work. The problems, in part, flow from the paucity of literature and research relating to this area of social policy. What follows will, hopefully, fill in a number of the gaps, but any such discussion of youth work ought to begin by recognising that the problem is not merely one of an absence of empirical research and data. The gaps also relate to deficiencies in theory and structural analysis.

Firstly, there has been a traditional reluctance within youth work to locate contemporary practice within a continuum. The price extracted for this oversight has been high. Notably those elements of continuity and tradition, as powerful in their own way as the dynamics of change, have been all too easily forgotten. Similarities thus become lost along with differences. It needs constantly to be stressed that youth work has a substantial history.

Yet only recently has this attracted the attention of serious historians (Gillis, 1974; Springhall, 1977; Springhall *et al.*, 1983; Dyhouse, 1981; Blanch, 1979). However the available material remains patchy, for example only recently has the history of work with young women emerged from the shadows and begun to acquire a literature that reflects its achievements. Now a serious gap that remains is the total void concerning early black youth work. Compared to other areas of welfare work, the Youth Service still lacks a systematic sense of its own past. This is reflected in the content of training which is largely ahistorical apart from the obligatory lecture on the Albemarle Report (HMSO, 1960) and a limited number of key Acts, Circulars and Reports. Perhaps more disturbingly, an active sense of history is missing from debates relating to the construction of policy at all levels. For example, the re-emergence of mass youth unemployment since the 1970s graphically highlighted this failing. The response of the Youth Service to youth unemployment was, and remains, both woefully inadequate and belated. The solutions eventually offered by the Youth Service to a large extent unknowingly reproduced those which had in the main been tried, and found wanting, in the 1930s and earlier.

Secondly, and related to this lack of a sense of history, there is so often an absence of any clear understanding within youth work of the dynamic of change. In particular the ways in which not only the tasks of youth work have been restructured, but also the workers themselves. There are constant references to change in the language and literature of youth work. The message is that youth work must continually adapt to the ever-shifting needs of young people as expressed in often dramatic and strident language such as that surrounding drug usage, homelessness, violence, crime, prostitution and the impact of discrimination. A consequence of this, as Marsland has noted, is that the Youth Service is all too easily 'engulfed in the fashionably extraneous concept of the moment' (1978, p. 143). It is difficult to convey the sense in which the Youth Service is simultaneously in a state of constant flux, yet still possesses a pervading air of timelessness. Caught in the noise and ferment of the moment youth work so often dances to a rhythm selected by others, barely aware from whence the music came, and too entranced to appreciate either the past or the future. An impression of timelessness and constancy lingers; partly this is because change is the continuous order of the day, but also because the rapidity of the apparent change is such that it barely touches the actual rhythms of practice. The demands of the daily round, stocking the coffee bar, organising the part-time rota, booking the minibus, opening and closing the building, setting in motion the time-honoured activities, and attending meetings, these can combine along with other pressures to close the circle. Reinforcing the historic *modus operandi* of youth work, part of which embraces the idea that the issue of the moment must be addressed. This is ritualised and compartmentalised within activities such as training, area team meetings and support groups. The implications contained within this for youth workers are substantial. At one level the individual worker is expected to be flexible, continuously able to adapt and meet changing expectations. To make and remake themselves in a new image according to the dictates of fashion. Having been equipped with little theory either about the essential purpose of their work or about how that purpose has arisen, they have only a narrow basis upon which to make informed decisions regarding the validity of the shifts they are expected to undertake (Jeffs & Smith, 1987, pp. 1–9). The result is rhetoric without substance, a resort to tried and tested ways of operating but often with a superficial gloss of modernity, and traditionally high levels of staff turnover and dissatisfaction amongst both full- and part-time staff.

What is youth work?

This question is almost never asked. For practitioners, managers and trainers the answer is either assumed to be self-evident and obvious or, given the anti-intellectual tradition within youth work, is dismissed out of hand as irrelevant navel-gazing. At times, however, the question has been posed, not as a consequence of intellectual enquiry, but rather as a means of justifying the exclusion or incorporation of a particular activity or organisation. Examples of the former would be the non-recognition of youth groups associated with the political parties and the exclusion for funding purposes by some authorities of work with young people under fourteen. A group such as the Woodcraft Folk (a uniformed organisation associated with the Co-operative Movement) expressing as it does such ideas as fraternity, co-operation and non-violence has fallen foul of both central and local government 'regulations' concerning the transfer of grant-aid. In relation to incorporation, it is sufficient simply to point to numerous examples of Youth Service agencies attempting to expand their sphere of influence, income and safe-guard their future by claiming that aspects of their work such as Junior Clubs for the under fourteens, preventive work in relation to the juvenile justice system and the development of various sporting activities equate with youth work.

Faced with the confusion and rag-bag of activities and organisations that constitute the Youth Service it is perhaps tempting to answer the question 'what is youth work?' by saying it is what the Youth Service does. Certain institutions such as Scout and Guide Groups and youth clubs are taken as the paradigms. Thus what happens within them is youth work. Others are then to be measured against the template of those paradigms to ascertain their legitimacy.

An alternative way of approaching this definitional problem is to label particular ways of doing things, that is to say the process, as youth work. Thus youth work may be seen as the provision of opportunities for 'informal education, social intercourse and the creative use of leisure through the membership of a group' (Hall, 1965, p. 264). It is of course possible to use the notions both of institution and of process to arrive at a definition. For example many youth club workers will describe some aspects of their programme as youth work, whilst others for example, are dismissed as being mere 'redcoating' (Foreman, 1987).

The aim of a particular piece of work could be a further element of a definition. However even the most cursory examination of the expressed aims of those who consciously describe their engagement with young people as youth work yields a wide range of intentions. These may encompass religious conversion, self-actualisation, enjoyment, self-development, consciousness raising and the building of character (Jeffs & Smith, 1987).

The client group appears superficially to be an attractive definitional tool. Unfortunately the concept of youth is itself problematic. Is it a physical state or attitude of mind? If it is the former what age ranges does it encompass? Within organisations in receipt of Youth Service funding we find the term used to describe those that admit to membership people of between ages 7 and 30. If it relates to an attitude of mind, what sort of tests do we administer to ascertain an individual's or group's 'youthfulness'?

Possibly the nature of the provider could be utilised as the definitional agent. Certainly the literature of youth work is strewn with references to 'sympathetic adults', people of 'good character' or 'the caring listener'. What such references overwhelmingly reflect is the idea that young people would benefit from spending time in the presence of hand-picked adults. That is those who possess qualities that are deemed to be unavailable in the household, family or immediate environment.

The nature of the relationship between provider and user is yet another possible way of securing a definition. Here we might consider the fact that young people choose to be the objects of youth work, and indeed often pay for the privilege. Thus many would argue that the moment attendance becomes compulsory the relationship can no longer be considered as being located within the context of youth work. For example, a number of youth organisations based their opposition to any involvement with Intermediate Treatment on the grounds that it was in the final analysis an instrument of punishment. As such it was deemed to be incompatible with youth work for it impuned the whole question of voluntary attendance (Blackmore, 1973, p. 10).

The concern with the principle of voluntary attendance may just be another way of saying that youth work takes place in a space of time known as leisure. Most, if not all, definitions offered build upon the concept of leisure. Again as with so much conceptualisation in this area the term leisure along with youth and other key ideas is overwhelmingly viewed as being unproblematic. Unfortunately even a passing acquaintance with an introductory sociology textbook would offer adequate warning as to the disputations surrounding the use of the concept (Rojek, 1985; Clarke & Critcher, 1985).

It is possible to define youth work using all of these elements. Thus youth work is portrayed as a certain type of process, in a specified range of institutions such as youth clubs, with particular aims and targeted at a group defined as young people and within time designated as leisure. This process is to be facilitated by adults possessing respected qualities or qualifications within a voluntary relationship that may often involve a cash transfer. The problem with such approaches to a definition of youth work is, as has already been hinted at, that each constituent element is the focus of dispute. We therefore have to turn to other mechanisms or means for delineating our area of study.

For the term youth work to have a meaning it would be reasonable to assume that those who call themselves youth workers or youth leaders have something in common with each other and can be distinguished in significant ways from other welfare workers. Faced with an officer of the Army Cadet Corps, a feminist worker with young women, an outdoor pursuits instructor, the manager of a youth house, a detached youth worker, a school youth wing tutor and a neighbourhood youth and community worker, it would be difficult to ascertain what qualities are shared and what sets this group apart. However difficult it is to define, there does exist a commonality, even if this is as minimal as the fact that they may describe themselves as working with young people.

The boundaries that are drawn can perhaps be best understood in relation to symbols embodied within the major traditions of what is known as youth work. In other words to make sense of youth work we must explore the ideas, behaviours and artefacts that people make reference to both when asked to explain what they think youth work is and that are alluded to in the normal course of practice. What must be stressed concerning this route of analysis is that as with concepts such as style and culture, youth work has been refracted through decades of usage and as a consequence 'has acquired a number of quite different, often contradictory, meanings' (Hebdige, 1979, p. 1). These meanings along with the traditions from which they have both emerged and have sustained are both discrete and interlocking. Indeed they retain a presence by reference to each other. The existence of the competing traditions contributes to each's identity, unique character, *raison d'être* and sense of wholeness. Although this communality and interdependence is often denied all parties require it. For that reason if for no other the disparate list of workers already noted and many others still tenaciously cling to the epithet 'youth worker' and seek to give a meaning to the term 'youth work'. The generic terms 'youth work' and 'youth worker' may be embellished, enhanced or clarified by the use of such labels as 'leader', 'enabler', 'social educator', 'counsellor', 'tutor', 'instructor', 'warden', 'officer', 'organiser' and 'secretary'. The importance of each of these titles is that they help to codify the sub-groups and the competing and complimentary traditions. As such they cannot be dismissed as mere labels, for they represent in almost all instances a living and vibrant tradition within youth work. Yet at the risk of repetition it is important to stress that they form the constituent elements of a wider entity which, for the want of a better or more explicit title, both they and we will call youth work.

In the introduction to a book that is fundamentally concerned with the relationship between the state, welfare policy and youth work it is not feasible adequately to examine in any depth the unique and common elements of the key traditions within youth work. Nor is it possible to delineate their contemporary spheres of influence and inter-relationship. Partly it would be a superfluous exercise as one of the co-editors has explored this area at much greater length elsewhere (Smith, 1988), and also because it would in many ways merely serve to obscure the debates that need to be addressed.

Youth workers and social divisions

It is necessary to set youth work within a context. Subsequent chapters are criss-crossed with references, oblique and open, to entities such as class, gender and ethnicity. These realities cannot be wished away and it is crucial to address them from the beginning.

Youth workers live and operate within a class society. Their conversation is littered with coded references to class, be it their own or that of the young people with whom they work. For as Marshall has observed, 'the institution of class teaches the members of a society to notice some differences and to ignore others when arranging persons' (1950, p. 159). What appears, however, to be missing from the bulk of youth work literature is both an acknowledgement of the centrality of class and the realisation that being a youth worker of itself locates one within a class structure. Clearly class is a highly contested concept both in an academic context and at the level of everyday discourse. As such it is the repository of many theoretical traditions. Historically, though, the debates have been dominated by two great traditions which have emanated from the work of Marx and Weber. Both these emerged in the period immediately following the appearance of mass industrialisation. Given the common root it is not surprising that although subsequently it has been the differences in analysis that have been stressed, they have much in common. Amongst these are a belief in the significance of class as a tool of analysis.

Our starting point is that classes comprise groups of individuals 'defined principally but not exclusively by their place in the production process' (Poulantzas, 1975, p. 14). Although this may be a Marxist position, it is one which, according to Parkin, has 'affinity with those bourgeois models of class that demarcate social boundaries by reference to the arrangements of positions in the division of labour' (1979, p. 4). Social researchers have conventionally taken occupation as an indicator of class position. However, difficulties arise in relation to those who are outside the formal labour market such as school students. The traditional solution of locating them via the 'head of household' has inherent weaknesses; the same as those which have contributed to the invisibility of women in much sociological writing on class (Roberts, 1981; Morgan, 1985). With the growth of mass youth unemployment and the expansion of further and higher education, more and more young people cease to have a class location independent of their parent(s). The bulk of the actual and potential Youth Service clientele are in this position. Such difficulties may also relate to part-time youth workers, those in training and women youth workers who live in a household of which they are not the 'head' for the purposes of social research. However, when we consider the occupation of 'youth worker' itself, the definitional problems shift.

The categorisation of occupations and their allocation to class groupings by the Registrar General and other influential codings such as the National Readership Survey (Marsh, 1986) and the Hall-Jones scale (1950) are not uniform. Differing labels and titles are used but the youth worker is unambiguously placed alongside such white-collar semi-professionals as teachers, social workers, bank cashiers and lower-managers. Within this frame of reference youth workers are viewed as being middle class, even though in terms of income they are barely distinguishable from skilled manual workers. For Marxists the location of groups such as youth workers may be problematic. Some Marxists would simply categorise youth workers as members of the proletariat on the grounds that they have only their labour to sell and possess no controlling ownership over the means of production (Slaughter, 1985, pp.

22–8). Others would see them occupying 'contradictory locations within class relations' (Wright, 1978, p. 61). This would place them uncomfortably between the bourgeoisie and the proletariat, having limited influence over the allocation of resources whilst possessing an apparent degree of control over the use of their own and other's labour. This is a position which Parkin's development of Weberian theory explores through the notion of closure (ibid), wherein relations between and within classes are portrayed as being in permanent tension as different groups attempt to usurp and exclude others.

If youth workers sometimes display a measure of confusion and express ambivalence when trying to understand where they are located in a class society it is hardly surprising. Some will perceive themselves as middle class, some as working class and still others will experience confusion; emotionally committed to one class whilst finding themselves defined into membership of another. For the individual this may pose a dilemma. However, beyond the level of individual angst, how youth workers define themselves in respect of class is significant for it has always divided them. As Bernard Davies shows in Chapter 10, the debates relating to unionisation and professionalism reflect this fundamental conflict over class definition and affiliation. The debates cannot be dismissed as an academic exercise. Equally it is a conflict that should not be seen in personal terms, however tempting both options may be. For the disputes arise from the reality that youth work takes place and youth workers operate within a class society. As a consequence not only are relationships between workers mediated by class, but also their engagement with young people and employers. The reality of class relations is such that youth workers must continually make choices, choices that will bring them into conflict. For a class society is one in which conflict is the norm and not an unpleasant aberation like a Wimbledon cloudburst. Two major classes are in competition and workers are consequently forced, often against their will, to choose which side they are on. This is frequently manifested in what often appear on the surface to be mundane decisions such as those concerning the allocation of the worker's time, the distribution of resources, the use of plant and even things like opening hours.

Conflict over resources cannot be explained simply in terms of class. Youth workers operate in a context where it is not merely the balance of class forces which determines the allocation of resources or the experiences encountered. Patriarchy pre-dated the rise of capitalism (Humphries, 1980) and has been successfully incorporated within its social structure and relationships. The history of welfare, has been inextricably linked with the desire to reinforce the oppressive elements of patriarchy. As Wilson shows, 'one way of looking at social policy would be to describe it as a set of structures created by men to shape the lives of women' (1983, p. 33; Gittins, 1985; Wilson, 1977). Youth work, as a number of writers have argued, is no exception to this rule (Dyhouse, 1981; Nava, 1984). Although there is an important if somewhat hidden history of working with young women in order to ameliorate some of the disadvantages they experience, youth work as a whole has disproportionately devoted its resources and attention towards the needs of young men (Smith, N., 1984). Consequently the staffing of the Youth Service has reflected not merely the traditional elements of patriarchy found within welfare employment per se, but also the particular orientation of the work itself. If the focus was on young men and the medium of intervention was largely, but not exclusively, through a masculine view of activity, then little space existed for a female presence. As research has shown, a masculine view of the world continues to hold sway over much youth work (Hanmer, 1964; ILEA, 1984). There is conflict concerning this between workers; between workers and managers; and between workers and young people; not only around resources but also over attitudes, language, behaviour and the activities of youth work. As with class the conflict may often be presented or interpreted in terms of personality or age (Little, 1984). This is understandable but mistaken, for the origins of the conflicts, large and small, lie within the economic and political structure. Consequently although youth work may offer some opportunities for interventions that challenge patriarchy, the pace of change will always be constrained by the operation of those structures. As Gittins comments:

> Family ideology has been a vital means – the vital means – of holding together and legitimising the existing social, economic, political and gender systems. Challenging the ideology thus means challenging the whole social system, but it would not mean that as a result people ceased living and interacting together (1985, p. 168).

Faced with the enormity of that task youth work clearly can only make a restricted contribution and nothing more. Youth workers who imagine that they can go beyond that are doomed to disappointment, frustration and, possibly, rejection. It is no more possible for workers to build within the walls of the youth club a mini-society free of sexism or racism than it is to exclude class.

Youth work can be seen as a haven into which it is possible to retreat – where reactionaries may isolate themselves from the winds of change, and reformists construct models of what might be. Like early Owenite socialists, some radicals and reformers may even see in youth work an opportunity on the fringes of welfare, a site for the construction of a 'New Lanark', wherein 'the outline of our future proceedings then becomes clear and defined' (Owen, 1969, p. 106). As Barker has commented, Owen's scheme was unconsciously designed to destroy a working-class culture that seemed unsavoury and uncivilised (1986, p. 6). Over 150 years later many youth workers still operate from a standpoint that is centrally located within that tradition. As widely noted, youth work is prey to moral panics regarding the norms and behaviour of young people. It would be mistaken to imagine that such panics are the sole prerogative of the moral majority. Radical welfare workers can and do fall into the trap of constructing working-class folk devils, of acquiring a belief in 'the primacy of a particularly narrow form of idealism over materialism' (Jones, 1983, p. 61). It is a dangerous and damaging exercise in which workers attempt to impose the 'right' set of moral values with scant regard to the material experiences of young people. All too comfortably it is overlooked that patriarchy is not confined to the council estate nor racism to the working class.

Successive new orthodoxies have emerged within youth work and much of welfare during the last decade. Most recently the icon of anti-racist practice has become enshrined in the language of youth work. Countless sins may be committed and excused in its name but undoubtedly many youth workers have learnt to appreciate the legitimate demands of black young people and recognise the racist nature of their own practice (Popple, 1988). Unfortunately much of the anti-racist effort has been introspective, concentrating upon the feelings of the workers and providing them with an appropriate vocabulary. Learning has therefore often hindered, rather than aided, the development of effective and positive practice. By again focusing on the individual such approaches often leave the worker immobilised. A generation of white youth workers have seen their practice exposed as racist. But like rabbits frozen in the glare of headlights they have all too often become mesmerised by the illumination; lacking an adequate theory by which to interpret their situation, they remain transfixed. The naive and simplistic analysis embodied within such jingles as 'power + prejudice = racism' has acquired a deified presence of sufficient force almost to stifle serious discourse. The concentration on the individual has been reflected in the wholesale adoption of Racism Awareness Training (RAT) as a means of cleansing the Youth Service of racism via personal conversion. The inherent weaknesses of RAT, which have been graphically highlighted (Gurnah, 1984; Sivanandan, 1985; Jervis, 1986), have only slowly eroded the strength of RAT and its equivalents within the Youth Service. This reluctance to abandon the personal and the worker's self has helped ensure the recalcitrance of the Youth Service towards work which enables black young people collectively to address racism. The reasons are not difficult to ascertain. The weight of tradition and the power of training have combined to make youth workers particularly receptive to personalised explanations of individual and group behaviour. This applies as much to racism as a phenomena as to patriarchy. But again to blame youth workers for responding in this way is as much to personalise the problem as to hold young people solely responsible for attitudes that originate within their relationship with the social and economic structure.

Within youth work it is not possible to wish away or lightly ignore questions of class, gender and race and elements of division. These must always be acknowledged and recognised as forming the backcloth for any analysis of practice. This means that they cannot be neatly packaged and stored away in the loft to be taken out and dusted down like an unwanted wedding present whenever the hapless donor comes to call. They must be integrated within an analysis that will enable us to create a construct that offers us an understanding of the central character of the welfare activity to which we and the other contributors have given the generic title of 'youth work'.

The book

This book and its companions have no pretensions to be the all-embracing texts on youth work. They represent an – albeit limited – attempt to fill some of the significant gaps in the literature regarding the relationship of youth work and youth workers to social policy and the state. At this point it is important to note that we have focused upon youth work rather than the often aspirational title 'youth and community work' adopted by many local authorities and initial training courses following the Fairbairn-Milson Report (DES, 1969). Whilst the change in title may have occasioned some restructuring, the attitudes and practices of the DES and many youth organisations remain rooted in the different traditions of youth work. Given that it is youth work, rather than community work or even some hybrid version of the two, that overwhelmingly occupies centre stage in the experience of this area of welfare, the choice of focus requires no further comment.

1

Youth Work, Welfare and the State

TONY JEFFS and MARK SMITH

The state, both local and central, has long involved itself in the daily lives of young people. Indeed, one of the principal motivations underpinning both the creation and the maintenance of the Welfare State has been a desire to secure the future well-being of the nation via the production of a fit, educated and socially responsible new generation. Within the context of the contemporary world, with its interweaving patterns of competition, both military and commercial, no nation state dare risk entrusting the education, health or moral training of the 'new generation' to the uncontrolled whims and vagaries of the family, the voluntary sector or the market. As Tawney so eloquently expressed it, this function is crucial, for:

> Historians tell us that decadent societies have been revivified through the irruption of new races. In England a new race of nearly 900,000 souls bursts upon us every year. They stand on the threshold with the world at their feet, like barbarians gazing upon the time-worn plains of an ancient civilisation (1914).

Ten years earlier G. Stanley Hall, possibly the most influential figure in the field of adolescent psychology during its formative years, had from a different perspective delivered a similar message. Warning his audience that for those interested in 'the future of our race . . . the field of adolescence is the quarry in which they must seek to find both the goals and means. If a higher stage is ever added to our race . . . it will come by increased development of the adolescent stage, which is the bud of promise for the race' (Hall, 1904, p. 50). The omens were clear and oft stressed, the new industrialised societies had little option but to respond by creating a network of policies that addressed themselves to those areas of 'concern'. Tawney's 'barbarians' had to be civilised as a matter of some apparent urgency.

Those concerns have neither evaporated with the passing of time, nor been erased through the application of liberal doses of welfarism. Just as the 'poor seem always to be with us', so do the hooligan and the troublesome youth. The youth problem may, on the surface, possess an apparent continuity. For example, it is the case that as Pearson argues 'the predominance of young people in the criminal statistics has certainly been one of the strikingly consistent features for more than half a century' (1983, p. 224). However, although youth may be a constant topic of discourse and focus of expressed public concern, the parameters and epicentre of the 'youth problem' is in a state of constant flux. At one moment the problem is getting the kids to stay at school, the next it is persuading them to enter employment, then it is that they have too much surplus cash, then too little; always it seems one difficulty supplants another, to tax and challenge the ingenuity of the policy-maker or the youth worker.

Obscured by the apparent cavalcade of fresh manifestations of the 'youth problem' is an almost timeless reality. Concerns regarding the irresponsibility, criminal behaviour, moral degeneracy and self-destructive habits that threaten the well-being of young people are motifs that occur and re-occur. Within these accumulated vexations lies a tendency to use 'youth' as 'a metaphor of social change, a vehicle for the articulation of a broader set of fears about the quality of "society" and troubling issues' (Mungham, 1982, p. 30). Since the 1950s this has had a special significance when considering the way in which the youth problem has been interpreted and re-interpreted with reference to young blacks. At one level we are furnished with erroneous pathological models of the 'cultural conflict' between Asian parents and their children, or the 'negative self-image' or 'weak' family structures of Afro-Carribeans. Such pictures of pathological black households and behavioural norms help to sustain racism and fit 'only too well with common-sense racist imagery' (Lawrence, 1982, p. 95). This imagery, however, also contributes an important ingredient to a lethal cocktail, one that with deft sleight-of-hand connects such disparate social 'problems' as street crime, drug abuse, alienation, prostitution, unemployment and poor educational performance, giving them a recognisable personna in the shape of Black Youth. This group is capable of being portrayed as being doubly dangerous and threatening because it is simultaneously not only young but can also be designated as 'alien'. Such a construct builds carefully upon the historic fears of Tawney's 'young barbarians' whilst encapsulating and articulating the irrational racist fears embodied and given succour in the following comment of Mrs Thatcher that:

> people are really rather afraid that this country might become swamped by people with a different culture. And, you know, the British character has done so much for democracy, for law, and done so much throughout the world, that if there is fear that it might be swamped, people are going to react and be rather hostile to those coming in (quoted in Gordon, 1983, p. 143).

Via the mechanism of integrating this view with traditional fears concerning the threat posed by young people per se, black youth, in particular, have come to symbolise deep-seated and longstanding fears. Fears around such issues as youth unemployment and law and order wherein the young black, and in particular the young male black, on the street has become 'a sort of personification of all the positive social images – only in reverse: black on white'. As Hall *et al.* (1978) stress, 'it would be hard to construct a more appropriate Folk Devil' (p. 162).

The 'commonsense' continuity concerning the youth problem can, as has been implied, be explained and de-coded in ways that are simplistically misleading and dangerous. It is all too easy to overlook the extent to which common sense serves as the 'folk wisdom of the ruling class', defining and re-defining problems in a way that coincides with the world view of those who control the levers of power. This does not mean that 'ordinary' people, as opposed to the 'extra-ordinary', who overwhelmingly possess the power and influence, are not worried about juvenile crime or youth unemployment. On the contrary it is almost inevitably the case that it is from amongst the ranks of the 'ordinary', rather than the extra-ordinary, that the victims of such phenomena will be drawn. For example, young people feel intensely concerned and worried by the appearance of mass youth unemployment (DES, 1983: Kirkman, 1985). However, concern is one thing, but whether that concern is or is not translated into a policy response is another matter. Inevitably the social location of the observer changes in crucial, but often subtle, ways the parameters and definition of the problem itself. For those with jobs, position, property and power, the problem of youth unemployment can all too easily be translated into predominately one of social control: how can 'they' be usefully occupied; how can 'they' be trained so that one day 'they' will, if required, be fit for work; how can 'they' be kept out of the shopping precinct, off the streets; from having the children 'they' can't afford? It takes little imagination to see that the problem viewed from the 'bottom-up' acquires a very different shape and set of solutions.

A catch-all such as the 'youth problem' is not neutral. Within it are located powerful symbols, assumptions and messages. These change over time and inevitably are simultaneously decoded in contradictory and contrasting ways by various professional and social groups, and to an extent by generations. Yet again after acknowledging this it is essential to note salient continuities, not least because the 'youth problem' has historically been framed overwhelmingly with reference to young males. Like adolescence itself, youth has overwhelmingly been a masculine construct. Predominately the images of policy making, as well as those of popular discourse, embrace and reproduce sexist language and assumptions whenever youth is the subject. For as Hudson (1984) notes, 'all our images of the adolescent . . . the restless, searching youth, the Hamlet figure: the sower of wild oats, the tester of growing powers – these are masculine images' (p. 95). As the predicaments have been framed in predominantly masculine terms, so the solutions are likewise male-orientated, as are the practices that arise (Springhall, 1977; Hendrick, 1986). This should not be interpreted as saying that young women have been absent from youth work, or their problems ignored. There has been a considerable, although often overlooked, tradition of work with young women and girls (Stanley, 1890; Pethick, 1898; Rooff, 1935; Dyhouse, 1981; Carpenter & Young, 1986). Yet despite these contributions the overall emphasis upon the 'needs' of the young male ensures that the space for both young women and girls is severely constrained and has continually had to be justified. The staffing, clientele, activities and the very conception of the youth work task bear testament to the dominance of men (N. Smith, 1984; ILEA, 1984). Youth work and the Youth Service, however, are not hermetically sealed from the impact of wider changes taking place within society. The re-emergence of the women's movement; the transformation of the labour market; shifting expectations within education as to the abilities and potential of young women; all these have contributed to the implantation of an alternative reference point to the established male view of youth work. In addition, these movements have created a new corpus of knowledge, experience and consciousness amongst women workers in all areas of welfare, a corpus that youth workers have both contributed to but perhaps more importantly have been able to draw upon (Dale & Foster, 1986). The growth within youth work of a commitment to 'working with girls' and the rejuvenation of single sex provision; the space secured within training; and changes wrought in the language; all these must not be underestimated, but there remains a real danger that form will be mistaken for content. For once the veneer of much 'anti-sexist' or 'non-sexist' rhetoric is removed and practice itself interrogated, then much of the optimism and talk of progressive practice appears distinctly premature. Firstly, the shift of resources into the treatment of young offenders has invariably redirected the attention of workers and policy-makers towards young men. Secondly, the unbroken preoccupation with moral panics, unemployment, crime, hooliganism, drugs, AIDS and homelessness leads workers to focus their energies and resources towards catering for boys and young men. Even where girls acquire a presence in this issue-based scenario, for example in relation to concern over teenage pregnancy, intervention tends to run a serious risk of re-asserting traditional gender roles. Finally, youth work in the mass is still ensnared within its own history, traditions, buildings and practices, all of which bespeak a male orientation and emphasis. An accumulation of these factors means that young males are both seen as, and see themselves as the pre-eminent client group. As we note elsewhere, no evidence exists that the gender profile of the client group has tilted to a significant degree in favour of young women and girls. As a consequence and given the historic constraints it is inevitable that much so called 'anti-sexist' and non-sexist' work has been orientated towards changing the attitudes of boys, rather than the lives of young women. If any further evidence of the limited advances achieved in this area is required, then the effective disappearance of girls' work from the agenda of the National Youth Bureau by the mid-1980s and the closure by the NAYC in 1987 of its pioneering Girls' Work Unit provides it.

The youth problem, although ever-present in its various guises, was never the sole or even the pre-eminent one taxing social reformers and politicians during the nineteenth and early twentieth centuries. High death rates eroded the stability of the labour force; ignorance created a shortage of skilled labour; radicals, socialism and trade unions were causing 'dissatisfaction' amongst the lower orders; epidemics threatened the health of the nation states; crime sapped the moral cohesion of society; and by the turn of the century falling birth-rates already seemed to cast a spectre over the ability of the colonialist and industrialised nations to sustain their empires and economic domination. Faced with that array of challenges it was inevitable that within the context of free-market capitalism the policy responses were pragmatic and wide-ranging. They were also at times contradictory and even counter-productive. Nevertheless, there gradually emerged a set of agencies, both statutory and voluntary, that engaged with such problems, not least the task of inducting the 'youthful barbarians' into society. Those agencies, voluntary and statutory, many years after they had individually been initiated, acquired a collective epithet – the welfare state.

The state

Before proceeding to a discussion regarding the relationship between the welfare state and youth work it is important, albeit briefly, to acknowledge the extent to which the use of the term 'state' is value-laden and the subject of fierce controversy. The idea of the state as a public realm, apart from and beyond the individuals who manage and hold office within it, is central to any discussion concerning the contemporary function of youth work and the role of the Youth Service. The state is at one and the same time a territorial and a spatial concept. It is also a configuration of social structures whereby control 'is exercised through a complex set of institutional arrangements and offices, which is distinguished from the largely localised and particularistic forms of power that preceded it' (King, 1986, p. 31).

As King implies, the state has expanded alongside the unfolding of industrialisation. It is thus common to talk of the modern state, which is involved not merely in collective activities such as the management of health, education and housing, but 'becomes the veritable arranger of the process of consumption as a whole' (Cassells, 1977, p. 459). The links between early youth work and the state were tenuous, and where they existed were often embodied in the activities of identifiable individuals. These held positions of power within the state and simultaneously were involved in an apparently voluntary and individualistic fashion in youth work. As a consequence of the then prevailing social order inevitably the dominant national figures were both male and bourgeois. Whilst women often played a key role in welfare organisations this was in part a by-product of their exclusion from the political arena (Dale & Foster, 1986, pp. 21–38). It is still possible to identify a number of leading figures who are members or affiliates of the governing bodies of major voluntary organisations, however the relationship overall between youth work and the state has over time self-evidently become more complex and formalised.

Explaining what youth work is can be difficult; offering an account of the state is infinitely more so. Yet it is essential, if contemporary youth work is to be understood, that some grasp of the role and function of the state itself is set alongside any analysis of contemporary youth work practice and the functioning of the Youth Service. Any attempt to understand the state more clearly as an entity is not made easier by its seemingly inexhorable expansion throughout the twentieth century, a growth that in the UK and elsewhere has barely been checked by the attempts of some contemporary politicians to 'roll back the state'. Not surprisingly as the size and importance of the state, as well as the range of its activities, has increased, so political scientists, amongst others, have sought to offer an account of its structure, role, boundaries and the linkages with other societal groupings and seats of power. In so doing they have understandably been unable to conjure up an exhaustive definition. Yet the literature that has emerged is of immense relevance to youth work in particular, and welfare in general.

In the context of welfare, much recent discussion has centred upon the extent to which welfare services are constructed in the interests of those who control the means of production and the degree to which consumers and electors can, and do, shape and control those services (Ginsberg, 1979; Taylor-Gooby, 1985; Croft & Beresford, 1986). At a theoretical level this discussion has tended to be located around an attempt to determine the degree to which the apparatus of the state possesses autonomy of action. Discussions regarding the nature of power relationships within and around the state are legion (see for example King, 1986; McLennan, 1984; Leys, 1983; Middlemas, 1979). It is crucial to note that in recent years these debates have broadened out to encompass an analysis of the contribution of the state to the maintenance of patriarchy (see for example McIntosh, 1978; Wilson, 1983; Dale & Foster, 1986). Likewise the extent to which the state sustains racism, and is racist of itself, has been a topic which has generated fierce controversy (see for example Scarman, 1982; Sivanandan, 1982; Gordon, 1983; Ben-Tovin *et al*; 1986; Gilroy, 1987). We have no desire to enter into a lengthy regurgitation of these debates here. But the unavoidable reality is that the state is an active agent in the maintenance of oppression. Oppression not only linked to class, gender and race but also reflecting the discrimination and disadvantage that have historically been linked to age, sexuality, disability and religion. Manifest, for example, in the structuring and operation of immigration laws, the income maintenance and tax systems, employment policies, policing practices, health care and education. All welfare, therefore, not least youth work and the sectors focused upon young people, is a transmitter of disadvantage and consequensially sites of resistance (Jeffs & Smith, 1988).

Given the centrality of the role of the state it is necessary to offer some limited account of how we apply the term – the state – in subsequent discussions. We take the state to be a set of institutions over which any specified government at any specified time has only a limited measure of both formal and actual control. It comprises those agencies which implement government policy such as the civil service and the inspectorates, and those who may enforce such policy, such as the police and the judiciary. Further, such a formulation must include other agencies, many of which are more loosely linked to the machinery of central government. Agencies such as schools, the nationalised industries and statutory welfare agencies, many of which are controlled by local authorities or funded indirectly through grant-aid and the like, all these and others must be included within this category. The amalgam, which at first glance may appear simply as the collective agencies of government, is in fact, an entity which government must always struggle to control. As any MP or local councillor is aware, the bureaucracy is not a cipher that will unyieldingly do the bidding of the elected representative. Just as youth and other welfare workers seek a meaure of autonomy in the control of their working environment, so will bureaucrats and others who operate the machinery of the state. Yet the state is not simply a collection of semi-autonomous individuals. It has direction and it possesses an in-built dynamic, yet like a giant tanker it can be, and is, turned and manoeuvred. There is a rudder – the question is who or what determines the overall course of the super-tanker state. In a society where power is unevenly divided, control over that rudder will inevitably be in the hands of a privileged group. They will be happy to forgo the discomfiture of standing permanently in the wheel-house, but when it is in their interests they will, perhaps reluctantly, leave the captain's table to take the helm. In the meantime the knowledge that they are capable of doing so is sufficient to ensure that the overall direction of the state coincides with their wishes and interests.

Thus, in a capitalist society where the means of production are controlled by a small elite, the state can never be neutral. It is an instrument of class rule which, in its own interest, is obliged to play a major role within the accumulation process. To ensure its own survival, the state will seek not only to provide the conditions under which accumulation can take place, but as a consequence will also endeavour to meet the needs of capital. Yet the relationship is not one of simple servant and mistress, for the state is also subject to a range of popular pressures and demands. Collective struggles for legal, political and social rights mean that it must also take some account of the wishes of other constituencies besides those who control the means of accumulation. This does not mean that there exists an unbridled pluralist bear-garden of competing interest groups, each of which given good fortune and a fair wind may grasp control of the state or policy area. For power is so unevenly spread that the ability of these groupings is constrained and marginalised. However, the potential of labour and other groups to disrupt the accumulation process and the tenacity with which certain long-fought rights have been, and can be, defended means that the state must always endeavour to carry a substantial proportion of the population with it, rather than drive them like geese to the fair. Such endeavours may also be clearly seen to enhance both the legitimacy and the efficiency of the state. Finally, it can never be assumed in the short-run that those who have control over the means of accumulation share a common purpose and aim. Indeed, in the normal course of events they are often engaged in atavistic conflict one with another. This conflict however far from merely weakening the state, can provide a unique source of power. For, as a consequence, the responsibility for securing the long-term interests of capital, such as the value of the currency or the rule of law, is delegated to it. Included within these is the need for a 'special institution "alongside and outside bourgeois society" . . . which at the same time provides, on the undisputed basis of capital itself, the imminent necessities that capital neglects' (Altvater, 1978, p. 41). Thus the state has thrust upon it and may take unto itself the responsibility for taming the 'barbarians' and nurturing the 'bud' of adolescence in the wider interests of capital and accumulation. A limited degree of autonomy exists as to how the state approaches and engages upon that task. However, those individuals who opt to challenge the orthodoxy and the parameters within which welfare must operate face certain risks, especially when they stand in opposition to the norm that both youth work and welfare services should, in essence, seek to formulate and develop the interests of capital (Taylor, 1987). The configuration of these forces and factors mean that in sum,

> the state has to operate in the 'space' left to it by capitalist pressures on one side and popular resistance on the other. In times of rapid capital accumulation and/or working class passivity, that space can be quite wide; but the inherently unstable nature of the accumulation process means that the boundaries of that space are perpetually in flux and inherently prone to close in times of recession (Coates, 1984, p. 227).

It must be acknowledged that at all times the state is endowed with a degree of autonomy, but there are several limitations constraining that autonomy. The pressures hinted at by Coates have not been solely experienced within the UK. The state in all industrialised societies is in a constant state of flux, buffetted by forces it has only limited powers to manage and control. The changing nature of production and ever-evolving technologies, when set alongside the shifting balances of world military and economic power, combine to impel states in certain directions. There is a danger in undue generalisation, but as Scase argues in a comparative analysis of the role of the state in Western Europe, a number of significant trends are discernible. Most prominent amongst these are that:

- the state has increasingly taken over functions necessary for the maintenance and reproduction of labour power;
- the state has become explicitly more repressive, reinforcing its functions of control and surveillance;
- the functions of the state have become more centralised, with the 'rationalisation' of local and regional state activities, and their integration within centralised, national bureaucracies;
- a growing trend towards the direct intervention of the state within the productive process; and
- a growing contradiction between the internationalisation of capital and the maintenance of national states (1979, pp. 16–18).

Each of these trends, and in particular the first four, has been self-evidently present in the re-structuring of youth policy during the post-war years. Further, they have led to both the creation of new youth work agencies and the re-shaping of much daily youth work practice. These then are not abstract trends taking place on a distant plane, but intrusive and pervasive. They have led to the massive injection of funding into agencies such as the MSC and to the ever more direct management of schooling, post-school training and juvenile justice (Davies, 1986). At the same time, after initially encouraging the expansion of the Youth Service, they have subsequently operated to weaken it as a welfare agency. As a consequence they continuously intrude into discussions concerning youth policy, and hence youth work, in this and subsequent chapters.

Before leaving this discussion of the modern state it is important to consider briefly some aspects of how that state is structured, not least because it operates at a number of levels. Firstly, as a civil association – overseeing the whole community, whilst endeavouring to maintain the general arrangements whereby individuals may pursue their own interests and activities. Secondly, it also embodies an ethical ideal, wherein membership of the nation transcends membership of other groupings within the civil society, demanding loyalty to the state over and above all other loyalties. Finally, as already implied, the modern state is an apparatus of domination. As has been emphasised by a number of writers, 'it is the mark of a civilised society that private violence be forbidden, and that violence, the power to compel by physical force or constraint, be a monopoly of the government' (MacPherson, 1966, p. 39). This monopoly, especially within in the context of an advanced technological society, places in the hands of the state an awesome array of physical, moral and legal weaponry for the purpose of maintaining and securing its authority, power that within a class society will, in the final analysis, be put at the disposal of the dominant class. For youth work and youth workers the state is thus not merely a set of administrative arrangements, or an abstract entity that may elicit willing or begrudged loyalty, but is the final arbiter that constructs the boundaries within which they must operate. Those boundaries certainly allow space for individual and collective manoeuvre, but this is severely constrained. For the state has access to the means to determine what youth workers as welfare workers, may or may not engage in. In a welfare sector that has long held dear the notion of partnership between voluntary and statutory agencies, the role of the state must always be recognised as the managing agent of the latter and, crucially, the licensee of the former.

Young people and welfare policies

What constitutes a welfare state (or even a welfare service for that matter) is problematic, not least because 'the concept of the welfare state is considered to be both empirical and normative' (Kaufmann, 1985, p. 44). However in an earlier work Kaufmann (1982) did offer a possible route out of the empasse by classifying what may constitute welfare policies:

- public interventions granting and protecting social rights (legal form of intervention);

- public interventions influencing the income situation (economic form of intervention);
- public interventions to improve the material and social environment (ecological form of intervention);
- public interventions to improve directly the competence of individuals (educational/advisory form of intervention).

In the British context public interventions that fall within each of these four categories and which relate directly to young people can be traced and isolated from the mass of welfare policies. For instance it is possible to cite numerous legal interventions relating specifically to young people. The introduction of legislation aimed at protecting young people from excessive exploitation within the workplace, such as the procession of Factory Acts between 1802 and 1898, is a case in point. These gradually came to be augmented by the curtailment of parental power over young people. Commencing with the Prevention of Cruelty and Protection of Children Act (1889), later legislation embraced safeguards against sexual exploitation. For example, incest was finally made illegal with the passing of the 1908 Children's Act. Cumulative and complex legal intervention, ostensibly to safeguard the interests of young people both within the workplace and the home, has led to often contradictory outcomes. For as Ives (1986) points out, the laws that protect also bind. So that the growth in public intervention in these spheres, as in others, has both protected and safeguarded young people from exploitation, but also self-evidently denied them fundamental rights and reinforced dependency (Franklin, 1986). For young women in particular welfare legislation has embodied these Janus-like qualities, wherein the protective elements have tended to reflect the 'prior agreements between capitalists and working class men, whose interests converged in keeping women out of well-paid, skilled work and who both benefited from women's service and dependence as wives and mothers' (Gittens, 1985, p. 135).

In terms of the second category, income transfers, the state has interceded in a number of ways using both the fiscal welfare system, which operates through the medium of taxation, and the social welfare system which operates largely via the transfer of payments and the provision of free or subsidised services. In particular, it has included the use of tax abatements for parents with dependents under sixteen or in full-time education introduced in the 1909 Budget; direct payments in the form of Family Allowances first paid in 1944; grants to young people wishing to enter Higher Education which first appeared in a limited form in 1902 with the introduction of Municipal Scholarships; and for those denied or unable to secure employment, but who were too young to have made any contributions to the State insurance schemes, provision was included within the Income Maintenance structure following the 1934 Unemployment Act. However, the direct transfers of cash pale into insignificance when set besides those embraced within free or subsidised services. Predominant amongst these are education, which became compulsory in 1880 and free in 1891; and health care, which spreading outwards from the 1907 Act that first required LEAs to 'provide for the medical inspection of their schoolchildren', came to cover, through the National Health Service founded in 1946, the whole of the population young and old alike.

Ecological intervention, in the form of Public Health, Housing and Planning legislation, is clearly much less age-specific than other areas of state welfare. Although it must be acknowledged that it was often a concern regarding the health and welfare of young people that provided a significant motivation for reform. The history of youth work during the nineteenth century bears testament to this close linkage. For example, housing reformers such as Octavia Hill and the Barnetts were influential in advocating and establishing youth facilities for the purpose of alleviating some of the worst effects of slum housing. Later we see a close relationship between youth work and environmental issues, initially encompassed with the emphasis laid upon the rejuvenating effects of the 'great outdoors' by influential youth workers such as Smith, the founder of the Boys' Brigade and Baden-Powell, who launched the Scouting Movement. The mass youth movements they, and similar innovators, created prior to the first World War helped to sustain the pressure not only for urban planning in the interests of the health and well-being of young people, but also for the protection of a rural heritage as a resource for health-giving and improving recreation. During the inter-war years this concern was translated into a 'contest over public access to land and traditional rights of way which continued with real intensity through the twenties and thirties, and in organisations like the

Federation of Ramblers Clubs, the Woodcraft Folk and even perhaps the proletarian-taming Youth Hostels Association it had a recognisably working class base' (Wright, 1985, p. 54). This pressure eventually contributed to the creation of National Parks, rights of access and the passing of the 1937 Physical Training and Recreation Act. The latter, for the first time – it should be noted – within a national structure, allocated state funds in the form of grants to youth organisations for the express purpose of building and maintaining youth centres.

Finally, public interventions designed to improve the competence of young people clearly embrace much that is currently included within the remit of the Health and Personal Social Services. These services have inherited responsibility for the care, training and education of significant numbers of young people for whom they are often given a legal responsibility. The origins of this responsibility can, to a large extent, be traced back to a key piece of legislation, the 1908 Children's Act. This was aimed at reinforcing 'responsible parenthood' and sought to reduce the impact of deprivation during childhood and adolescence, to prevent the abuse and accidental death of young people and to control criminal and anti-social behaviour. This particular piece of legislation represented an important milestone, not least because the Act expressed the determination of the state to ensure that it, rather than parents, would take unto itself the final responsibility for young people. It was a mandate that directly applied only to a relatively limited number of young people. The socialisation and education of the overwhelming majority was to be entrusted to the family, the school system and the burgeoning voluntary youth organisations. The family was to be increasingly supported via the already mentioned income transfers of various kinds and monitored by a growing army of professionals such as Health Visitors, Children's Officers, Midwives and Social Workers who possessed both supervisory and educational roles in relation to young people.

With regard to schooling, intervention was to be strengthened by compulsion, expansion and the professionalisation of those entrusted with pedagogy and management. The slow but continuous growth of schooling was highlighted in the unremitting appearance of Education Acts which succeeded the first intervention of the state in this arena in 1833. Initially such interventions appeared in the shape of the support and minimal supervision of voluntary provision but after 1870 through the medium of local School Boards and following the 1902 Act, Local Education Authorities. More recently this control has been yet further centralised by the enlistment of the MSC, which is unambiguously dependent upon central government funding, and moves towards the imposition of a centrally determined core curriculum. Clearly, given the interruption of two world wars and the fluctuating fortunes of the national economy, nothing has proceeded within welfare without serious disjunctures. It is, nevertheless, possible to illuminate key long-term trends in relation to education. One has been that the length of the educational experience of young people has extended in both directions, further down into infancy and upwards through and beyond adolescence. Secondly, it is not merely the length but the breadth of the educational experience that has changed. It has tended to radiate increasingly outwards to embrace an ever more encompassing remit. Pastoral systems not only link 'home and school' but intrude into the latter as well as monitoring the leisure of school students. Likewise the curriculum, under the dubious and ill-defined epithet of 'social education', has been used to justify the school taking responsibility for the instruction of young people in almost every aspect of their actual or potential experience; nothing it seems is to be left to chance. It is within this arena that the Youth Service has retained a tenuous but official presence on the fringes of the welfare structure.

All these interventions have to be placed within the context of the historical development of the British welfare state which, as has already been implied, grew in a piecemeal fashion. Although to a degree pre-figured by Poor Laws and similar legislation dating back to the fourteenth and fifteenth centuries, it was with the emergence of mass urbanisation and industrialisation during the late eighteenth and early nineteenth centuries that the modern welfare state first began to take shape. The creation of a welfare state has not been a uniquely British experience, for the involvement of the state in these areas is one of the great unifying features of all modern industrial societies. Its over-arching presence lends superficial weight to the arguments of the convergence theorists who believe that the logic of industrialism and economic development impels different societies towards the adoption and acquisition of institutions that over time share a basic ethos and structure (Kerr *et al.*, 1960). However, the strength of that assessment has been undermined with the somewhat belated emergence of an extensive literature flowing from the comparative study of social policy. Writers such as Bendix (1964), Wilensky (1976), Maddison (1980) and Heidenheimer, Helco and Adams (1975 and 1983) have shown this analysis teeters upon the simplistic. Convergence theory gives insufficient weight to crucial structural differences between societies, and in particular, the variety of forms, scope and content of their welfare programmes. For, as Mishra notes, industrialism's structural constraints may limit the potential variations within social structures but that still leaves 'plenty of room for diversity' (Mishra, 1973, p. 556). A great deal of that diversity flows less from the desired end product of welfare and more from the chosen mechanisms for delivery. Building upon the analysis of Titmuss (1968) it is possible to show that a key variable flows from the weighting assigned to the three principal modes of welfare delivery. These three different delivery systems of 'social service', namely fiscal welfare, operating via the taxation system; social welfare in the form of transfers of cash or kind; and occupational welfare linked to employment, wherein employees receive benefits in the form of company pensions, health care and the like; combine to create a welfare structure or welfare state. But it is one in which, according to Titmuss, the three agents of delivery come 'to operate as virtually distinct stratified systems' (ibid., p. 53).

In comparing the welfare structures of different nations it is possible to perceive the differences primarily in terms of the balance and emphasis laid upon each of these modes of delivery, the relationship between them, reflecting not only cultural and historic elements but also crucially the balance of class forces. In Britain during the last decade the defeats inflicted upon the working class and the erosion of its power has been reflected in a changed balance between the modes of delivery. Changes that have with few exceptions amplified already established patterns of social division and disadvantage. Fiscal welfare, for example tax relief on mortgages and occupational welfare, has been expanded and strengthened at the expense of social welfare. Given that less than 40 per cent of those aged 16–19 are in waged employment (Drake, 1986), few are the beneficiaries of the improvements in occupational welfare. A combination of falling incomes amongst young people linked to exclusion from the labour market ensures that even fewer benefit, including those who have dependents, from the fiscal welfare system. Yet it is always important to remember that a sizeable number of young people have reaped considerable benefit from the shifts that have taken place in recent years. They have experienced higher living standards as the tax burden has been shifted from the better off onto the lower paid, they have enjoyed the benefits of private schooling and health care. These beneficiaries are a minority but a significant one. For the majority dependent upon benefits, training allowances, grants, parental handouts and low paid jobs, the movement away from social welfare towards fiscal and occupational welfare has lead to a worsening of their relative positions. Such an erosion in living standards and life chances is not of it itself a 'youth problem' in the normally accepted meaning of the term and rarely posed as such. Private misery yes, but a public problem rarely.

The youth problem and welfare analysis

It can be argued that all nation states share a youth problem of one sort or another. In the Soviet Union the concern may be centred upon the issue of the alienation of young people and the attractiveness to them of bourgeois culture (Riordan, 1987; 1987a); in the EEC youth unemployment may be classified as 'the most serious problem with which governments, society and the Community institutions will have to grapple' (EEC, 1983, p. 51); elsewhere or at other times it may be drugs or crime which is viewed as the pre-eminent manifestation of the problem. Whatever the precise nature of the malaise, this is in a sense immaterial, for what remains crucial is that, as Pearson (1983) argues, it is 'crisis' that is constant. So that it seems as if always in 'today's world, concern grows for young people. Child abuse, drug abuse, unemployment and discrimination make life a living hell for many. Many more find even "normal" growing up hard in a harsh environment' (Cattermole, 1986). Although the shopping list of problems may change at the edges, outpourings such as this have a 'timeless' quality. They reflect not only the lack of any sense of history or coherent understanding of youth 'problems' and policy during the last hundred years on the part of the countless perpetrators of such nonsense, but also the degree to which such 'problems' have become the common coinage of discourse in this welfare sector. It is vital that the element of continuity should be borne in mind, but this should not lead to a dismissal of each successive manifestation of the crisis as an artificial creation. As merely another in an endless stream of 'moral panics' conjured out of thin air by an irresponsible media hungry for copy, by youth workers and agencies using shock tactics to secure improved funding; or by a cynical government anxious to re-direct the attention of the voters from the 'real problems' that are beyond its capacity or will to solve to artificial ones.

Such an interpretation of the re-occurring panics concerning young people is not without a certain basis within reality. For example, this is found in the manipulation of the debates around the abuse of welfare (Middleton & Golding, 1982) and the dangers posed by the criminal activity of the young (Chibnall, 1977; Hall *et al.*, 1978; Porteous & Colston, 1980; Smith D. M., 1984). However, such an interpretation may also be damaging, especially where it is allowed by youth workers to shape policy and practice. Either it can be translated into a pitch of concern that merely leads to the Youth Service appearing ridiculous, for there is a limit to how many times the crisis can be pronounced before the audience grows restless. Alternatively, in their understandable desire to correct the balance of public opinion in favour of their clients and also to defuse the situation, youth workers can drift towards a position approximating to moral abdication. Culling, in an often crude fashion, theories from such areas of sociology as deviancy and labelling theory, what is so often constructed is a pseudo-justification for arguing, that, for example, youth crime is 'marginal' and 'unimportant' and that ergo intervention must inevitably be dangerous and stigmatising. The risk with a stance which juxtaposes the 'trouble with kids today' with a jaunty 'the kids are o.k. and worry not they are great survivors' is that it can both under-play a real problem and in the process 'talk-out' effective intervention. Equally it verges on the naive as it risks destroying the credibility of those workers with all parties, young and old alike. Firstly, it ignores the felt needs and concerns of those young people who are the victims of crime, or unemployment, or poverty. Secondly, it nihilistically either ignores the 'problem', or comes to accept it as immutable and therefore resistant to effective intervention. This is wrong, because it fails to acknowledge the extent to which policies exist, and have been shown to work, which can dramatically improve the life-chances and lot of young people both individually and collectively.

In part alternative policies are understandably obscured by their distance. For instance, it is rarely acknowledged that certain other European nation states have, through the adoption of more dynamic and interventionist labour market policies, held both adult and youth unemployment at levels which by British standards would render the problem invisible (Therborn, 1986). Equally, juvenile crime levels can be influenced positively, as can educational performance levels or recidivism rates (see for example King & Petit, 1985). In the context of all these, comparative policy analysis has considerable potential for bringing about an improvement in service delivery. Comparative analysis should not be seen to embrace solely an international perspective. Within the UK cross-regional and authority studies can highlight remarkable variations in performance. For example, the graphic variations between incarceration and recidivism rates amongst young people between areas (R. Smith, 1987) and regions (Powell, 1984; Adler & Dearling, 1986).

Youth work, in line with a number of other welfare sectors, urgently needs a more substantive comparative element, not one based – it is essential to add – upon sight-seeing tours and exchanges of dubious value and high cost to limited budgets, but upon a comparative dimension grounded in structured research. Although more effective solutions do exist, the disturbing evidence suggests that few youth workers at any level are aware of their existence; that they have scant conception of what might be done even to initiate policies capable of tackling the real problems encountered by young people (Garner & Gillespie, 1986). The challenge, therefore, for youth workers is to re-orientate welfare policies and to engage in a re-structuring that favours their clients rather than disadvantages them. However, in conjunction with the possession of a clear set of policy objectives such a process would, in addition, require a clear understanding of the dynamics of welfare and the delicate balance between its constituent elements.

The contradictory role of the welfare state

The possibility of re-directing policy in relation to young people lies within the ability of youth workers and others to 'exploit' the underlying contradictions of the welfare state. These contradictions are not the end product of mere administrative confusion and over-load, but spring, to a large extent, from the duality of roles laid upon both the welfare state and youth work. This duality and much confusion emanates, as O'Connor argues, from the structural constraints which bind the state within a capitalist system, a context that demands that the state fulfil two 'basic and often mutually contradictory functions – accumulation and legitimation' (1973, p. 6). These roles are such that the state must seek to create and sustain the conditions which enable profitable capital accumulation to take place whilst ensuring 'conditions for social harmony'. For 'a capitalist state that openly uses its coercive forces to help one class accumulate capital at the expense of other classes loses its legitimacy and hence undermines the basis of its loyalty and support' (ibid., p. 6). These twin imperatives create a tension that must be absorbed. In part this may be achieved by the depoliticisation of social problems. For example by the transposing of social problems into questions appertaining to administration, management and technical expertise.

The Youth Service, alongside other welfare agencies, has experienced a long history of such attempts to re-formulate the structural problems that have beset it in those terms. For the Albermarle Committee (HMSO, 1960), the solution to the 'youth problem' lay to a large extent in heightened professionalisation and the injection of expertise; more recently the Thompson Committee (HMSO, 1982) in similar fashion attempted to pull the managerial rabbit from the hat. However well intentioned these attempts were to solve the problems of the Youth Service, in the end they met with little or no success, for no other reason than that they were running from, rather than confronting, the structural problems. They were searching for non-political solutions to fundamentally political problems. Another strategy for the depoliticisation of social problems has been that of defining politics out of the debate. This approach has been clearly visible within governmental responses to the inner city disorders of the early 1980s. These events have been 'branded as "criminal acts", "senseless outbursts" or the work of "drug barons". Thus avoiding, at least in the medium term, the introduction of economic and political reforms directed at the structural causes' (Solomos, 1986, p. 15). Further, this de-politicisation may also be achieved, at least in the short to medium term, via the individualisation of a given social problem, whereby, for example, youth unemployment is translated into an end-product of personal inadequacy. To the extent that 'for a long time, the view that youth unemployment was due to faulty supply, rather than lack of demand, and could be solved by educational rather than by economic means went virtually unchallenged' (Cohen, 1984, p. 105). There are of course limitations to these strategies and the state has been continuously forced to intervene in a more direct fashion despite the underlying tendency for a capitalist free-market system to resist the expansion of the state welfare sector. Ultimately, as Mishra (1986) chillingly reminds us, another alternative always exists for a cornered capitalist state, in the shape of militarism and imperialism. Accumulation and economic expansion can be encouraged as much by investment in the warfare state or as Davis (1985) terms it, 'the motherlode' of the Defense Department, as in welfare. This shift has clearly been reflected within both Reaganism and Thatcherism which incorporate a bellicose foreign policy, increased military investment and anti-welfare policies and rhetoric on the domestic front.

State intervention within the welfare sector and within other areas is, as already has been noted, not without its contradictions. Different component parts have to be identified if we are to avoid seeing it in overly simplistic terms. State expenditures have within them a duality that relfect 'the capitalist state's two basic functions: social capital and social expenses' (O'Connor, 1973, p. 6). The first of these, *social capital*, is essential for profitable private accumulation and can further be seen to comprise two elements. These are social investment and social consumption. The former of these comprises projects and services that serve to enhance the productivity of labour and by implication the rate of profit. Within this category, for example, will be found the expenditure devoted to Skill Centres, and YTS. The latter, social consumption, incorporates those projects and services that lower the reproduction costs of labour, such as Child Benefits and general educational provision. *Social expenses* encompass those elements of state intervention which are seen as necessary to engender social peace and harmony, which seek to curtail class conflict and which serve to sustain the legitimation function of the state. Under this heading would be found expenditure on provision for 'non-productive' groups as the retired, the long-term sick and the disabled, as well as the funding of law and order agencies.

Discrete areas of social policy such as education, housing and health do not fall neatly into one or other of these compartments. The dual role of the state in a capitalist society is such that within each and every sector of welfare are found both accumulation and legitimation functions. Equally, expenditure upon young people can be located and identified within projects and services designated either as *social capital* or *social expenses*. The confusion that arises concerning, say the role and function of the Youth Service, is not inevitably the end product of faulty analysis or theory-making, but may flow from the contradictory nature of state intervention and welfare itself. This can be illustrated from a cursory examination of the MSC. The MSC is involved in directly financing industrial development with grants for equipment; in lowering the costs of labour for employers by socialising the expenses involved in training, transferring those in part or in whole from the budgets of the individual employer to the state; finally, it is a social expense, a legitimating agent. Firstly, by publicly conveying through its activities a largely erroneous impression that the state is concerned about the problem of unemployment and anxious to eliminate it. Secondly, it helps to allay public concern by hiding the scale of unemployment through a massaging of the unemployment figures, via the simple act of re-designating those engaged on MSC schemes as employed. Finally, it removes the young unemployed from the home and public spaces to occupy, entertain, educate, train, oversee and control them.

Viewed from this perspective it is possible to clarify and identify many of the conflicts surrounding policy initiatives such as the Community Programme(CP). Certainly CP may marginally raise the overall productivity of labour through the output of goods and services; perform a training function valued both by the individual and by some prospective employer; and simultaneously occupy potentially disruptive elements within society. Once the paradoxes within the very nature of CP are recognised in this fashion, it becomes easier to understand why, within youth and community work, the Community Programme has led to such vociferous debate and engendered deep divisions within organisations such as CYWU, ACW and the public sector unions. It also places in a context those debates which have been replicated at the unit level, where workers have utilised the Programme to increase the 'productivity' of the centre 'for the benefit of the clients' and to offer some opportunity to secure training, experience and a marginally higher income for an unemployed person. The gains have to be set against the negative elements such as the naked exploitation of CP workers (Dooney & Watson, 1985); the dishonest use of CP budgets to bolster the flagging finances of some organisations and units with the consequent growth in dependency upon those budgets that results; the deleterious impact upon the process of youth work itself, not at least as a consequence of the transference of a growing proportion of face-to-face work into the hands of untrained and ill-prepared CP workers; the de-skilling effect of such programmes; and the broader political question of the Youth Service being seen publicly to collude with a programme that has been, and is being, cynically used to hide and contain the unemployed. The contradictory role of the state thus can be seen to be encapsulated and reflected within not only welfare itself, but mirrored within both agencies and policies at all levels.

Where does youth work fit in?

The Youth Service may overwhelmingly be categorised as lying within what Kaufmann classifies as those 'public interventions to improve directly the competence of individuals'. However, when one analyses the function, rather than the location, of the Youth Service and seeks to interpret youth work in relation to the accumulation/legitimation continuum then many of the contradictions locked within the role and function of the activity come to the surface.

A clear point of access is the examination of youth work as a legitimating activity. It unambiguously contributes towards a generic demonstration of the concern and commitment of the state towards helping and supporting young people enmasse and individually. In particular, it has sought to reinforce this by claiming a special concern for those young people with 'special needs'. Certainly the rhetoric and tone of the contemporary official and quasi-official pronouncements on youth work consist, in great measure, of exhortations to help and promises to assist those young people with 'special needs'. The definitions of 'special needs' can become so elastic as to be meaningless, indeed to the point that one could legitimately ask the question 'does there exist a normal young person?' The categorisation can embrace within one DES document the young unemployed, girls, ethnic minority youth, young people with disabilities and young people at risk (a group which, after mentioning drug addiction and 'deviant behaviour', proceeded to include 'alcohol addiction, neuroses, e.g. agoraphobia, anorexia, the lonely and the neglected' (NACYS, 1986c)). Another shopping list from the same source, after calling for 'guidelines which would help in identifying the young people whose need is greatest', proceeds to draw special attention to the following examples:

(a) Isolation, which may have any of a range of different causes – scattered rural communities, in urban areas where travel and communication is difficult; it may effect young people 'disabled' in conventional senses, and other young people lacking the social competence or confidence to mix freely with their peers.
(b) Alienation, in communities characterised by social disruption, high crime rates and disaffection through chronic unemployment, poverty or racism.
(c) Disjunctures in personal development such as those caused by youth unemployment in a society which has come to expect the fact and processes of employment to aid and signal transition in adult status.
(d) Cultural impoverishment in narrow, but not necessarily materially poor, home backgrounds.
(e) Discontinuities in family life and stable parenting (NACYS, 1986e).

Such catch-all lists, which could embrace the offspring of every family from Buckingham Palace to Coronation Street and back, although quite useless in terms of constructing a realistic policy agendas, do in fact serve a purpose. Firstly, as already indicated, they serve to legitimate the role of state. They help to convey the impression of a society that cares, whilst obscuring the reality that the problems that are identified flow from an economic and social system that in the interest of profit has no intention of seriously tackling the structural causes of those problems, unless or until they directly threaten the rate of accumulation of profit. Secondly, such approaches are mutually advantageous for both the state and national youth work agencies such as NYB and NCVYS, enabling them to project an image of disabling adolescence. The young person as the preordained victim serves to justify the existence of such agencies, secure their funding and sanction their activities. This of course applies not only to national agencies but also to local youth work units and projects.

In addition to being portrayed as vulnerable, young people are also commonly perceived by significant groups, as already noted, in terms of posing a threat to the stability and well-being of society. By attempting to keep young people 'off the streets', 'out of harm's way' and by proffering an opportunity for 'purposeful leisure activity' the Youth Service provides a symbol of the determination of the state to 'do something about' troublesome youth. But it also offers evidence of something far greater. As for the state

> to contain and control deviance, and thereby master it, is to supply fresh and dramatic proof of the enormous powers behind social order. The visible control of deviance is one of the most effective mechanisms by which a social order can tangibly display its potency. The act of harnessing things which are dangerous helps to revitalise the system by demonstrating to those who live within it just how awesome its powers really are (Scott, 1972, p. 29).

This role in both its symbolic and its concrete forms clearly contributes to the process of accumulation. However, in a more positive manner the majority of youth workers would lay claim to an educational role. Since its earliest manifestations youth work has sought to synthesise the divergent elements from the arenas of leisure, instruction, rescue and control. Over time the balance between these competing roles and the *raison d'être* for intervention have shifted. The readily identifiable education content within youth work has been obscured, if not eliminated. There has occurred during this century a consistent, but not necessarily unimpeded, transferrence of the instructive component of youth work to the school, training centre and college. Similarly the rescue function has been professionalised and codified within the medical, probation and personal social services. Remnants of these two have, of course, lingered in the corridors of youth work, surviving principally in the form of counselling, advice work and the attempted injection into activity of an educational content, real or illusory. Above all else, the rhetoric of youth work has clung tenaciously to the argot of the improver and child saver. As a consequence much mere activity becomes invested with a higher purpose and veneer of moral righteousness which it rarely if ever warrants. The key to unravelling this process lies within the exposure of such notions as 'social education' and 'group work' for the sham that they so often are. Further it will entail recognising honestly that the bulk of youth work is largely activity for activity's sake and that the educational content intrudes more by chance and accident than by design. To do this may be uncomfortable but it will at the very least allow those within the Youth Service to comprehend needs and enable the workers to set themselves and others realistic objectives and goals. The time span for this process to be undertaken may be severely limited, for even the residual role of leisure provider to the young is being increasingly threatened by a pincer movement comprising commercial provision on the one side and the expanding presence of local authority leisure departments on the other. It can therefore be seen that the Youth Service's contribution to sustaining and creating the conditions for profitable capital accumulation whilst ensuring the conditions for 'social harmony' is limited and virtually only understandable when placed in the context of total welfare provision.

2

The Youth Service and the Threat to Welfare

TONY JEFFS and MARK SMITH

The predicament of the Youth Service concerning its future capacity and purpose has, to an extent, been obscured for many practitioners by their perception of an overarching threat to the long-term stability and even survival of public sector welfare per se. With the determination of the Conservative Government elected in 1979 to 'roll back the frontiers of the state' and to control and reduce public sector expenditure there was a understandable outpouring of anxiety amongst many practitioners and within agencies over the maintenance of funding levels within all branches of welfare. This was reflected within the Youth Service where the tenor of the early 1980s was generally one of despondency and nervousness concerning long-term prospects (Smith, 1980). A feeling that the statutory Service was 'getting back to the 1950's . . . when the Youth Service had diminished in some areas to the point of actually disappearing' (Nichol, 1981, p. 13) was not uncommon. Certainly, like other welfare sectors the statutory Youth Service found it difficult to come to terms with often significant reductions in the size of budgets and rate-capping. The voluntary sector, much of which had become either partially or wholly dependent upon public funding, also found the lessons painful. However, given the miniscule size of the Youth Service in comparison to the big battalions of welfare, concern over the reductions in expenditure within this sector generated little in the way of public sound and fury. The trimming of public sector welfare expenditure that marked out the late 1970s and early 1980s

41

was, as has already been implied, not simply a matter of economic expediency. Such policies also reflected an ideological shift from 'welfarism' towards a professed faith in the free market and a desire to resuscitate the 'night-watchman state of classical liberal theory limited to the functions of protecting all its citizens against violence, theft, and fraud, and to the enforcement of contracts and so on' (Nozick, 1974, p. 26). For the individual this meant a requirement that they embrace the competitive individualism which in the words of Margaret Thatcher entailed acquiring:

> The sense of being self-reliant, of playing a role within the family, of owning one's own property, of making one's way, are all part of the spiritual ballast which maintains responsible citizenship, and provides a solid foundation from which people look around to see what more they might do for others and for themselves (1977, p. 97).

Those critiques of welfare which flow from the ideological tradition embodied within this view of the world and of the place of the individual within it, have, when addressing it, directly displayed a contradictory approach to the Youth Service. In part, as an agent of the state both local and central, it has been castigated along with all sectors of welfare as a failure both in terms of its inefficiency and as a dispenser of 'bureaucratic serf-dom' (Marsland & Anderson, 1981). Yet the Youth Service has also in contrast been the recipient of plaudits. For as Marsland argues, in his contribution to a key text within this tradition, the Youth Service, despite its flaws, can be viewed as:

> a realistic, small, specialised service, attending to relatively modest and relatively clearly defined objectives through methods which are relatively well specified and established. I believe all the evidence suggests that such a service is essential and that it is doing its work with a remarkable degree of effectiveness com-pared with some others, particularly schools and social work (1980, p. 25).

The attraction of some of the most outspoken and unyielding critics of welfarism to the Youth Service as an agency, although at first surprising, is not difficult to ascertain. For here they find, albeit on the periphery, a sector that apparently demonstrated how mass voluntary effort and commitment could be mobilised to offer a welfare service: also, although flawed, it nevertheless could be characterised as a living embodiment of the practicability of developing a partnership between statutory and voluntary provision; and finally, as for instance the Thompson Report was at pains to demonstrate via its analysis of Youth Service funding, it could be portrayed as an example par excellence of what might be 'achieved' by the exploitation of voluntary labour, charity, sponsorship and a levying of charges. Thus the Youth Service acquired friends in what at first glance might have been seen as unexpected quarters. Their defence and advocacy was, however, muted, for as they were ever anxious to stress, they sought to reverse the trend towards ever greater state involvement in all areas of public life. This trend, it was argued, had encouraged the Youth Service to wander dangerously down the 'primrose path which has been beaten across the wilderness of the "welfare state" by health, schools, and social services' (ibid., p. 13). The solution to the ills that had befallen the Youth Service, therefore, was readily at hand and lay in the termination of the partnership and the removal or diminution of the statutory element. Thus the campaign for 'real voluntarism' advocated that in future

> instead of voluntary associations going cap in hand to the state, expecting funding as of right, and torturing their own principles in order to conform with state controls and orthodox fashions to ensure funding, instead of this, why not genuine independence seeking its own support and funding in the open market of ideas and value for money (Marsland & Anderson, 1980, p. 12).

Fine rhetoric and even possibly good theory, but there is scant evidence that this view appealed to the hardened operators of the voluntary sector as a good guide for practice. They have exhibited no desire in the interests of ideological purity to wander in 'the market place of ideas and value for money' rattling a collecting box if it can be avoided. For them a much more attractive proposition was the welfare pluralist model that underpinned the Barclay Report on the Personal Social Services (NISW, 1982). Although one suspects the members of the Thompson Review Group on the Youth Service were unfamiliar with the concept of, let alone the literature relating to, welfare pluralism they certainly grasped the potential of the model. Not least the extent to which support might be forthcoming within the climate prevailing at the time for the 'mixed economy of welfare' approach advocated by writers such as Weale (1983), Hadley & Hatch (1981) and Gladstone (1979). As far as the Youth Service was concerned this, like all other alternatives, foundered upon an inherent weakness, namely that without the intervention of the local state the Service was unlikely to survive let alone develop. The state had to a significant extent reluctantly taken a hand precisely because the voluntary sector was in a sickly condition. It did so with little apparent enthusiasm as was the case with other welfare provision. Such state provision developed:

> only because people had signally failed to provide these services for themselves – for the simple reason that they could not afford to do so. Demand did not evoke supply because it was not, and could not be, backed by the necessary financial bait (Wootton 1983, p. 286).

If you require an exception to demolish that thesis it would be a waste of energy picking over the history of youth work. For within it, the story of the relationship between voluntary and statutory youth work during the course of this century is open to no other interpretation other than that the former was incapable of providing a comprehensive service. What the voluntary sector even at its height sustained was largely provision for those who were fortunate enough to live in the more prosperous regions and who were not amongst the most deprived. No subsequent evidence has yet appeared to indicate that a return to voluntarism would surmount its historical limitations, and as a consequence, it is therefore dangerously naive to argue otherwise. The same is overwhelmingly true of all sectors of welfare and perhaps for this reason, as much as any other, all the evidence supports the belief 'that the public are loath to give up easily benefits which they have gained over the years' (George, 1983, p. 29: also Judge *et al.*, 1983; Taylor-Gooby, 1982, 1985 and 1985a; Mack & Lansley, 1985). This reluctance should not be dismissed as some manifestation of innate and unthinking conservatism, but rather as a realistic assessment of the capacity of the voluntary and commercial sector to cope. For employees, as opposed to consumers, of a particular

service such a response can equally be derived from an un
standing that the apparent cost-savings which it is often argued
flow from voluntarisation and privatisation are merely 'regressive
income transfers resulting from inferior conditions of pay and
service imposed upon lower-paid, subcontracted, ancillary workers' (Robinson, 1986).

The widespread public support for the key elements of welfare
may well be eroded over time. The survival of large-scale state
welfare simply should not be taken for granted and youth workers,
for example, would be ill-advised to place excessive faith in the
confident assertions of writers such as Offe who claim that whilst
capitalism may encounter difficulty in co-existing with the welfare
state, 'neither can it exist *without*, the welfare state' (1984, p. 153,
emphasis in original). Partly caution is required, for the oft
vaunted commitment of the electorate towards the maintenance of
public welfare structures must not be allowed to deflect attention
from the expressed support for what free-market advocates term
choice or the right of individuals to have the 'freedom to contract
out of state education and health services' (Harris & Seldon, 1979,
p. 59). Such findings inevitably lend credence to the conclusion of
Judge *et al.* (1983) that it is essential to acknowledge the ambivalence within public attitudes towards the funding and management structures of welfare. Further caution should always temper
optimism in these matters for, as Taylor-Gooby (1985a) clearly
delineates, the depth of expressed support for public sector welfare varies substantially from sector to sector. Youth workers
cannot, therefore, assume that apparent generalised support for
state welfare provision either will, or does, embrace a commitment
to a statutory Youth Service, or that welfare is seen by any party as
an holistic entity, a Harrod's hamper, the contents of which may
only be purchased in toto never, in part. Indeed within the UK the
gradual but unchecked abandonment of those policies designed to
sustain full-employment and, therefore, defeat the fifth of Beveridge's Five Evils blocking the road to progress – idleness –
provides ample evidence of the extent to which the welfare state
can and has been parcelled-up, enabling once key elements to be
neatly discarded. It would be wrong to view this as merely swings
and roundabouts, the end product of political tweedledum and
tweedledee. The shifts in fashion within youth work and the changing
occupancy of ministerial posts may lend a certain credence to that

fact that beneath the surface; structural
...tantive and long-term nature may be taking
...r history of youth work neatly dissected by
...a degree totally predictable, reports such as
...Thompson can be interpreted as the very model
...and incremental development. Of course, the cur-
...at fails to see behind the façade belies the reality.
Whe... ...emarle attracted resources, indeed it was produced in part to justify monies already allocated (Jeffs, 1979), the others served very different ends. They failed to winkle resources from a reluctant Treasury and indifferent governments because they were designed to obscure the reality that the government had no intention of doing more than the minimum required to sustain a barebones Youth Service. Thus, on a much smaller scale, the retreat from the Youth Service reflects similar moves to re-commodify housing, withdraw from the subsidisation of public transport, and reject a cheap fuel policy. Such shifts entail costs; in the case of the more substantive examples, it has largely been 'purchased' via the enormous expansion of means-tested benefits which have driven up the Income Maintenance bill to the point that it now stands at treble that for either education or health services. In the case of the Youth Service the costs entailed have amounted to little more than a trimming of the MSC programme and the pumping of funds into juvenile justice provision that already offers the promise of high cost-effectiveness. Overall the trends relating to the Youth Service do not augur well for the future.

In relation to the welfare sector, priorities change over time. However, as Davies notes, within a capitalist society it is 'the requirements of the labour market and of its imperatives which provide the ultimate, and the hardest edge' (1986, p. 22) in the structuring of youth policy. How that requirement is translated into hard policies is not an incidental, but is crucial, not least for the Youth Service. It is ironic, yet inescapable, that it is liberalism with its commitment to the free market that necessitates vast state intervention 'because the state is the only institution available within liberal society for expressing public purpose' (Crouch, 1979, p. 49). Thus in order to restructure the labour market, the MSC must be created and re-created by governments whose avowed public intent is to deregulate labour and remove themselves from that arena. In this sense Offe is correct in his assertion that 'the welfare state is indeed a highly problematic, costly and disruptive arrangement, yet its absence would be even more disruptive' (1984, p. 288). However, as has already been argued, this 'necessity' cannot ensure either the survival of a statutory Youth Service or the indefinite funding of a voluntary sector incapable of sustaining itself.

The Youth Service, youth unemployment and crime

Both external supporters and practitioners alike have long justified the Youth Service as an essential protector and confidant of the young as they negotiate the 'storm and stress' of adolescence. Simultaneously the Service has been portrayed as a redoubt, holding in check the ever present tide of 'threatening youth'. To a significant degree, therefore, the survival of the Youth Service must depend upon its ability to deliver in both these respects. It must convince those who hold the purse strings that it has a serious contribution to make in terms of containing these problems.

The phenomenon of youth crime has long been an area of concern. To a great extent the origins of contemporary youth work including the innovatory work of Robert Raikes and Hannah More during the late eighteenth century owe much to fears relating to the 'lawless state of the younger class' (Raikes quoted in Curtis & Boultwood, 1960, p. 6). That preventative role was continuously emphasised during the formative years of both voluntary and statutory youth work. It featured as a justification for the legislative involvement of the state in this sphere of welfare. Later, particularly during the expansion of statutory provision in the post-Albemarle period, it was again given a high profile. The argument was simple, if not actually simplistic. It promised that the Youth Service and youth workers were capable of diverting significant numbers of young people from involvement in criminal and disruptive behaviour. Albemarle in particular promised so much. In a purple passage it argued that:

the Youth Service can do much to make the appeal of the good society stronger than the dynamic of wickedness. Reformed and enlarged and supported in the manner in which we sketch it in succeeding chapters, it should be far more capable of granting new and adventurous opportunities to the young than are at present possible and should engage the energies of many more young people in the acquisition of personal skills, or the delights of good social life, and in forms of service to the community. As it grows it will draw, not only more of the good and law-abiding, but also more of the critical and restless and those who are natural but perhaps reckless leaders of their age groups (1960, p. 19).

That promise could not of course be fulfilled. Worse it offered a clear hostage to fortune whereby the performance of an enlarged and re-equipped Youth Service staffed by a new cadre of professionals would be judged and measured against criteria over which it had, and has, fundamentally no control and precious little influence. Inevitably the Youth Service 'failed to deliver the goods'. However flimsy the evidence throughout the post-Albemarle years, the impression was abroad of a substantive increase in juvenile crime (Muncie, 1984, pp. 58–94). In the face of that 'evidence' it was assumed that the Youth Service card had failed. Within less than a decade of Albemarle, new initiatives designed to halt the 'tidal wave' of juvenile crime were being formulated. These all fitted neatly into the 'traditional approaches to young people and crime. . . . in convenient shorthand, punishment, welfare and treatment' (Rutherford, 1986, p. 12). Whatever the varying traditions to which they owed allegiance, they all had in common a distance from the Youth Service. In relation to the control of juvenile crime the Youth Service no longer possessed either a role or function. The emergence in particular of IT, which although a generalised term that 'covers a rather heterogeneous range of community-based, but mainly individual-orientated, interventions' (Rutter & Giller, 1983, p. 346), nevertheless created a national and local network of provision for targeted young people outside the boundaries of the Youth Service. Its continued growth not least as a result of direct nurturing from central government has marked the almost total and final removal of the Youth Service from any involvement in the area of juvenile justice. Indeed the chasm that has developed is such that it has become a necessity for practitioners to argue for even the most minimal Youth Service involvement in the juvenile justice system (Teasdale & Powell,

1987). The Youth Service no longer sees itself as playing either a substantive preventative role or a curative role in relation to juvenile delinquency. A long tradition has finally, it appears, come to rest. This may be in part the end product of the erosion of the resources available to the Youth Service, as Davies (1986) implies, but this hardly explains the overall trend, for the funding was readily available during this period for both new IT initiatives and the much-clamoured for punitive interventions so beloved by Tory Party conferences. The reasons were that the Youth Service simply lacked the expertise, proven success and capability to deal with the growing volume of young offenders. Worse, it could produce no evidence of any success in staunching the 'flood' of youthful criminality. As Barnard notes, research does indicate that an 'absence of leisure facilities in the areas with highest crime rates is clearly a factor leading young people into petty criminal acts' (1986, p. 29). It is not without significance that the need is seen as being for leisure facilities not a reinvigorated Youth Service.

The advent of mass youth unemployment on a scale certainly not experienced since industrialisation in the nineteenth century clearly posed both a challenge and a threat to the Youth Service. Here surely was if not the actual appearance, at least the harbinger, of the 'generalised crisis of youth' (Marsland, 1986, p. 88) which so many writers and commentators have for so long predicted. The real and tangible challenge posed to the Youth Service by youth unemployment has, however, only succeeded in placing a larger question mark against its future. For like Salvationists fleeing from the Day of Judgement, here was the Youth Service, for all to see, seeking refuge from rather than engagement with the challenge of youth unemployment. In displaying neither the will, nor the inclination, nor the intellectual or physical capacity to profer a serious response at any level the Youth Service has, as a consequence, experienced a damaging assault upon its credibility. As the problem of youth unemployment has grown in scale, so the presence of the Youth Service within the cockpit of youth policy-making has been perceived as being of ever-diminishing relevance. In particular, any residual pretension on the part of the Service to cater on any scale for those in the post-16 age-bracket has been shattered. The hope articulated by Albemarle, that the Youth Service would 'remain always what it intended to be, a Service primarily to help young people who are out in a world which lacks the wealth of community provision and personal contacts of the school' (HMSO, 1960, p. 43) is no longer even on the agenda. The Service has been elbowed aside from any substantive engagement with what Albemarle and others termed the 'transition from school to work' or, alternatively, from school to higher education. Other agencies better structured and endowed to carry out this role, either wholly or in part, have taken the responsibility to themselves. As a consequence of this, there exists an eerie disjuncture between the official and semi-official literature of the Youth Service and the experience of the vast majority of practitioners. The former retains a touching affiliation to the fiction that the Service is addressing the problems of young people located within the upper end of the designated age group. Meanwhile, the latter encounter the reality of clubs, centres, units and projects catering predominantly, and sometimes exclusively, for those of compulsory school age.

The failure of the Youth Service to acquire a significant presence in governmental responses to youth unemployment was not totally of its own making. The historic linkage of the Service to the DES and its predecessors undoubtedly disadvantaged it during the period in which the early responses were formulated. A long-standing weakness of the DES with regard a number of other major Whitehall departments resides in its relationship with local authorities who control the bulk of educational expenditure. The DES, as Broadfoot has noted, is as a consequence obliged to depend to a great extent upon 'informal channels of influence to affect policy debates' (1986, p. 61). Certainly this perceived weakness of the DES became a factor during the debates that preceded the launching of YOP, the first major initiative constructed to counter rising levels of youth unemployment. As Short notes, it was during this point of time

> authoritatively rumoured . . . that a battle raged in the Cabinet before the decision was made between the DES and the DE about which of them should be given the money to provide for the young unemployed. We are told that DE won because it could guarantee to produce places very quickly. . . . The DES could promise much less because it would have to make grants to LEAs and simply exhort them to deliver (1986, p. 42).

The inability of the DES to retain dominant, let alone exclusive, control over what after all was a key area of responsibility for it, and the onset of the seemingly inexorable rise of the MSC was not entirely unrelated to the almost total absence of any response to youth unemployment from either the Youth Service or main-stream sectors of education. These agencies were, it appeared, clueless as to how a coherent policy response might be constructed and it showed. The incursions into the school curriculum, FE, social education and HE by the MSC were thus barely opposed, not merely because the MSC controlled the 'resources', but also because those who might have mustered a resistance to this in-truder had neither an alternative strategy nor a vision. The Youth Service was not alone in this, but it was the most exposed of the LEA agencies working with this age group, lacking the clear public role and *raison d'être* of the schools and colleges, and as such its weakness and inadequacy was perhaps the more ruthlessly re-vealed.

What was remarkable on reflection is the ease with which the Government and the DE were able to impose their solutions and also the degree to which mass youth unemployment has not and did not precipitate a 'generalised crisis of youth'. From the per-spective of the state the management of youth unemployment has been so far little short of a major success. From the onset as the unpublished, but widely circulated, Central Policy Review Staff (CPRS) report emphasised, the national response to youth unem-ployment embodied a strategy aimed at excluding an ever greater proportion of young people from the labour market and simulta-neously lowering both their income levels and expectations. To quote from the original CPRS document:

> The essence of the proposal is to reduce the size of the labour force by raising to 17 the age of entry to the normal labour market . . . young people would receive a modest allowance well below the normal wage. It would be possible, in time, to prescribe a lower training wage for those being trained by their employer (including apprentices) . . . a particularly desirable objective (quoted in Walker, 1986, p. 173).

Approximately a decade on, it is apparent that tangible ad-vances have been made towards the attainment of these goals.

Fewer than 40 per cent of young people aged 16–19 are in the labour market proper; youth wage levels have overall been reduced; the real value of the YOP/YTS Allowance has been lowered in 7 years by 38 per cent; the removal of those under 21 from the remit and protection of the Wages Councils is further encouraging a lowering of youth wages and eroding working conditions; and as a consequence of the 1986 Social Security Act single claiments under 25 without children are to receive £6.60 less than older people in similar circumstances. The combined impact of these and other measures has been to gnaw away at the relative living standards of the majority of young people, whilst narrowing to the point of irrelevance the margin separating those unemployed, in HE, on special employment schemes and the bulk of those in employment. In particular, working-class young people are being shaped and trained for their slot in a dual and segmented labour market. As the recession has gathered pace so the parameters of a dual labour market have grown more sharply delineated. Within this two industrial sectors co-exist, the core (or monopoly) sector and the periphery (or competitive) sector. The core is composed of industries or firms characterised by:

> Large numbers of employees, high capitalisation, large profits, and large yearly yields. Most important, such firms control their markets and operate as price-setters because of the oligopolistic or monopolistic nature of their markets. These firms also tend to employ advanced technologies and to have high productivity and high rates of unionisation. The periphery sector is characterised by low levels of capitalisation, small size, regional or local marketing, and single-product lines. These firms operate in highly competitive markets. Further, they employ little advanced technology, tend to be labour-intensive, and have low rates of productivity, profit, and unionisation (Hodson, 1983, p. 20).

For the growing proportion of young people destined for the labour-intensive peripheral sector, low wages must be set alongside low benefits and low expectations. The potential for educational experiences to upset this and generate dissatisfaction, therefore, must be minimised. So the world of low status and often repetitive work is thrust ever downwards into the school curriculum via such entities as work experience and TVEI. Simultaneously parental poverty and unemployment have fed young recruits into the expanding market of part-time low paid work for those of school age. This gives an experience of the labour market that helps to reinforce the messages of the school-based programmes, and which offers 'a learning experience which, whilst the particular kind of work might be rejected, makes for a continuity between pre- and post-school economic life, and ensures an early exposure and subjection to the rigours of the labour market' (Finn, 1984b, p. 44). Young people earmarked for the periphery by their class, lack of educational achievement and to a degree by their race (Lee & Wrench, 1983; Brah, 1986; Cross, 1987) and their gender (Wharton, 1986; Cockburn, 1987, 1987a) may, given the narrowing divergence between their potential earnings and/or benefits, come to perceive the impact of unemployment less acutely. In measuring themselves against their neighbours, kin and peer groupings the absence of 'paid' work, although felt may not impose the degree of relative financial deprivation that might impair an acceptance of their lot. This acquiesence in the face of long-term unemployment is recounted by a number of authors who stress the extent to which it dulls and anaesthetises the sense of anger whilst personalising and internalising the problem (Seabrook, 1982; Campbell, 1983; Stokes, 1983; Coffield *et al.*, 1986; Henderson *et al.*, 1980). Such a response is clearly one that operates to the advantage of a government that is either incapable or unwilling on ideological grounds to provide the necessary employment. However, the advantages that may accrue must be set alongside the risk of creating a 'reserve army of labour' subsumed within a 'culture of poverty' incapable of work, even if required to do so. For such a social grouping could both damage the longerterm prospects for growth and entail a risk of staunching the essential flow of cheap labour to the secondary labour market. Consequently, various agencies of the state have become embroiled in a delicate balancing operation whereby CP, Restart Programmes, Re-settlement Centres, Claimant Advisers and DHSS Fraud Officers are brought into play in order to monitor the young unemployed and periodically thrust them back into some form of work. Their avowed intention is to augment the work ethic so carefully implanted by the school, part-time work during school years and YTS or an earlier variant.

It is persuasively argued that youth unemployment has many

deleterious side effects. For example, that it contributes to a growth in juvenile delinquency (Rutherford, 1986); increases the incidence of mental and physical illness amongst the young (Stokes, 1983:); encourages drug abuse (Auld *et al.*, 1984); and increases suicide (Platt, 1986), racial harassessment and prejudice (Cochrane & Billig, 1983) and homelessness (Brynin, 1987). Clearly the quality of the evidence to support such assertions may be variable but few would question a degree of correlation. These side-effects of youth unemployment, although of great import for the individual and those around them, are in fact still in terms of their overall impact marginal. As with unemployment itself these outcomes are unlikely to be experienced by the majority of young people, not least because unemployment is highly concentrated spatially within regions and localities. The overwhelming majority of those in their early twenties are in secure employment and are, for example, adequately housed. The scars of youth unemployment like those of adolescence fade for all but a minority.

Mass youth unemployment appears to have had a significant and continuing impact in one direction. It has bred in the young a new political conservatism that has been commented upon in relation to both the UK (Elcock, 1983) and the USA (Norris, 1985). Other writers have preferred to label this as amounting to a new realism and pragmatism (Manaster *et al.*, 1985). Whatever the nomenclature there has been a marked decline in certain manifestations of 'youth radicalism' and a resistance to the political message of the Left. As Cohen notes, there exists a 'large and growing number of young workers, trainees, unemployed young people and early school leavers who . . . are consistently refusing even to consider voting Labour' (Cohen, 1984a). In a similar vein it has engendered a diminished faith in the future (DES, 1983) and growing indifference to the machinery of politics. In the USA, for example, this shift in mood is expressed in the dramatic decline in the number of 18–20 year olds casting their vote in elections, with a fall from 48.3 per cent in 1972 to 35.7 per cent in 1980 (US Bureau of Census, 1980). The conclusion must be that just as mass unemployment has curbed the combativeness of the trade union movement, so has it disciplined young people and brought them into line. Where it has illicited a response it has almost invariably been an individualised one, in the form of crime, or illness. In no way should this be interpreted as a denial that youth unemployment has contributed towards serious street disorders; it has. But those disorders have always been ignited by other crucial elements. In both 1981 and 1985 in localities such as Brixton, Handsworth and Toxteth it was policing practices and racism (Field & Southgate, 1982; Gordon, 1983; Hutchinson, 1985); in Derry and Belfast in 1981 the deaths of hunger strikers; and in 1986 in the Loyalist areas of Ulster the imposition of the Anglo-Irish Agreement. A high proportion of those involved, even possibly a majority, were unemployed, but given the spatial distribution of youth unemployment that was almost inevitable, and there are scant grounds for saying that those outbreaks would not have occurred if the levels of youth unemployment had been 10 per cent, 20 per cent or 30 per cent lower. Youth unemployment may have contributed to outbreaks of street violence but it has neither produced nor sustained a coherent or substantive reaction from amongst its victims. It should not simplistically assumed that this will remain the case. If, for example, YTS became totally discredited as YOP was before it, or policing practices become even less acceptable to substantive sections of youth, then the situation could rapidly alter and a brush fire of youth rebellion break out. That is always the risk. So far the assessment of governments has, on the available evidence, been proved correct. It appears to have found in large scale youth unemployment and within the workings of a re-structured labour market, a far more effective agent of socialisation than the Youth Service ever was.

Conclusion

During the last decade or so, governments can hardly have perceived themselves as being confronted by a youth problem of any magnitude, whatever the self-appointed youth 'experts' might have told them to the contrary. Indeed, with a certain smugness ministers may reflect on the undoubted success, within their terms, secured in this policy area at least. Even with the apparently intractable challenge of youth crime, the figures give grounds for guarded optimism. Success achieved in relation to any youth 'problem' after a decade of minimalist investment in the Youth Service is bad news for the service. In an era in which, for a decade at least, the tide has flowed against welfarism and may well continue to do so for some time, and in which 'the future cannot be sensibly viewed as an extrapolation of the past' (Klein & O'Higgins, 1986, p. 223), those services which are unable to deliver will certainly not grow and some will undoubtedly expire. Elements of what currently constitute the Youth Service may well therefore be extracted, re-structured and relocated. However, for large sections of the Service, the future holds little promise when viewed from the perspective of governments anxious to ensure that welfare services make an effective contribution towards both legitimation and accumulation.

3

The Political Economy of Youth Work

TONY JEFFS and MARK SMITH

Little has been written about the economics of youth work. Scattered amongst local authority policy documents, government reports and research papers we can find fragments of information. Nowhere are they drawn into the sort of comprehensive analysis one would expect for an area of welfare which consumed over 130 million of public money in 1985–6 in England alone. Why is this?

It might be that the range of sources that such an analysis would have to draw upon is so wide that the task would become inordinately difficult. The fact that similar exercises are undertaken in other welfare fields with the same or a higher degree of complexity indicates that it is not beyond the realms of practicability. If it is not the technical difficulty of the task, then perhaps there are ideological problems relating to the collection of such information within youth work? Again it is difficult to see what might mark out youth work from other welfare fields in this respect. Certainly it is clear that this task has not been seen as important by the agencies and personnel most likely to undertake such analysis. Resources have not been committed on any substantial scale by the DES, NYB, NCVYS or by academics within institutions associated with youth work training. This failure to attend to 'hard data' is no doubt associated with the general lack of intellectual rigour within youth work and the tendency towards an unthinking acceptance and application of ideas and approaches that value the 'subjective' as against the 'objective' (Jeffs & Smith, 1987). However, there is more than an undercurrent of anti-intellectualism operating in youth work.

Youth work has developed in an incremental manner with the initial sponsorship of the work being primarily conducted through the medium of middle-class voluntary organisations. Relative to parallel welfare services such as formal education, intervention by the State was late. Voluntary organisations still sponsor the bulk of Youth Service provision and they still seek to establish and maintain a separate identity. As a consequence it is often more helpful to ignore the generic category 'The Youth Service' and to view the area as a loose collection of different organisations and practices. A lack of attention to the global allocation of resources within the youth work field can be seen as a by-product of the emphasis upon the discreteness of youth work organisations. Absence of attention to economic analysis means that fundamental questions concerning the allocation of resources and power relationships within youth work have until now been only partially addressed.

In a chapter such as this it is clearly not possible to undo years of neglect. What we have attempted to do is develop some key themes. The chapter focuses on the allocation and consumption of resources within youth work but does so in a specific way. It is a political economy because we are 'essentially concerned with the relationship between the economy – the way production is organised – and the political and social institutions and processes of society' (Gough, 1979, p. 10). More specifically we are interested in the relationships between the institutions and processes known as youth work, the nature of the resources given to the work, the means of making such allocations and the prevailing, capitalist, mode of production. However, before we can begin to construct a political economy, we have to draw together what we know of the nature of the resources utilised by youth work. A lack of any serious analysis of resource allocation within youth work has impeded a holistic understanding of this area of welfare.

Youth work organisation

The first impression that one gets of youth work organisation is of the size and number of units. For instance the largest non-uniformed organisation, NAYC, has 6012 affiliated clubs with a claimed membership of 655 270 in the United Kingdom (NAYC, 1984–5). The biggest uniformed group, the Scouts, has 12 155 groups with 479 081 members (Scout Association, 1984–5). The smallest youth work unit may have less than twenty members with only two or three workers, whilst at the other extreme can be found those with a membership in excess of 1000 young people with a staff of 30 or more. There are also massive differences in the turnover and complexity of the units. Figures produced by NCVYS suggest that the costs of the average voluntary youth work unit are between £2000 and £4000 per annum (quoted in HMSO, 1982, p. 105). Such figures are inevitably tentative. The accounts of some of the organisations we examined show costs as low as £200, whilst at least one showed annual costs in excess of half a million pounds. In addition, whilst there may be national standard financial arrangements within the major voluntary youth organisations, local authorities have very different funding policies and structures which again make generalisations difficult (Leat *et al.*, 1986, pp. 149–174).

A second feature is the nature of the labour force. Within Scouting, for instance, the 92 933 uniformed leaders are voluntary. Only headquarters staff are paid. In a recent survey of LEAs, Harper found that there were approximately 3020 full-time and 28 300 paid part-time youth and community workers in provision wholly or partly funded by local authorities in England and Wales (1985, p. 5). It appears that 97 per cent of face-to-face workers are part-timers, two-thirds of whom are unpaid. Harper's definition of a 'youth worker' basically applied to those involved in clubs, detached work and projects. Figures compiled for the Review Group on the Youth Service in England included the uniformed organisations and other voluntary provision. These figures suggest that there are over half a million unpaid volunteers involved in local authority or voluntary sponsored youth work (HMSO, 1982, p. 88).

Third, if we then turn to the organisations themselves, it can be seen that the local unit is reasonably self-contained. Frequently it will have individual charitable status and in the vast majority of cases a separate legal status and associational structure, i.e. its own officers such as chair, secretary and treasurer. This means that substantial areas of decision-making are effectively decentralised. Whilst a Guide group, for instance, has to abide by the rules of the national organisation, it has considerable discretion as to how it conducts its affairs. In addition, the geographical dispersal of units means that there are effective barriers to centralised control. However, perhaps the most significant feature is the extent to which resources are generated by and within the local unit. Figures given for the total local authority expenditure on youth work considerably understate the financial costs of the work. Part of the reason for this is that such figures are usually based solely upon the dispersion of monies through education budgets. Also as NCVYS, in the evidence quoted above, estimates there are 100 000–140 000 units in the voluntary sector. The Youth Review Group notes that 'If these estimates are likely [sic], the voluntary sector must be able to draw on funds of at least £200 million per year' (HMSO, 1982, p. 105). In other words over double the amount spent by LEAs on youth work. Given that there has only been limited research in this area, such estimates must be approached with extreme caution.

Fourth, an important feature of youth work is its market orientation. Two aspects of this require noting here. First, attendance by young people is voluntary – they therefore have to be attracted to provision. Second, the bulk of the income of youth work units derives from customers and their families. This is most obvious in the case of the uniformed organisations and small voluntary provision such as village and church based youth clubs. In this sense, youth work is 'in the market' in a material way.

Fifth, funding also has to be attracted from other sources. Again, in relation to the bulk of provision, the state plays only a minor role. There are considerable hidden subsidies from community organisations such as churches and community associations in the form of cheap or low rent accommodation. In addition, many voluntary organisations derive a significant proportion of their income from industry and commerce and trusts. This is, perhaps, more noticeable in the accounts of the national bodies.

Sixth, the financial environment in which youth work units operate can be particularly uncertain. This uncertainty appears to contribute towards difficulties with, and a consequent lack of attention to, forward financial planning. There are reasons for such inattention including the absence of appropriate skills and, perhaps more importantly, a worker ideology in some traditions of work which sees financial and administrative competencies as unimportant. But these are not the only reasons, for one of the major obstructions is local authority budgeting processes. For example, units tend not to get details of their grants or the scale of contribution to their costs until well into a given financial year.

All of this means that the local unit will be the key reference point for the bulk of those involved in youth work. Even where membership is closely identified with a distinctive movement such as Guiding or the YWCA, the focus for activity remains the 'front-line'. This is a familiar phenomenon within social work and welfare (G. Smith, 1979). However, the combination of a high degree of initiative held within the front-line unit, the relative autonomy, the multiplicity and dispersion of units, the nature of the labour force and the market orientation all combine to make youth work something of a special case.

Youth work, along with other welfare services, has experienced pressures for an increased division of labour and a centralisation of some controls. In a number of places, local authorities have sought to take power away from voluntary committees. However, the tradition of autonomy, the identity that the separate organisations provide and the relative strength of local groups in terms of the resources they generate have limited the extent of such moves. As we will see, instead of direct control, financial inducements are often made to front-line units in order to encourage them to follow policy lines 'favoured' by external funding agencies.

To understand how youth work may respond to the deeper workings of the economy it is necessary to focus on the operation of the front-line unit. It is here that the nature of youth work practice is finally decided. Two initial points require noting. First, as has already been suggested, state bureaucracies have a limited but growing role in relation to the front-line. Second, it is necessary to note the scale and nature of direct interventions by capital in youth work and debates about youth policy. Examples of this include the establishment of direct training programmes such as the Boys' Clubs' 'Adjustment to Industry' courses, the sponsorship of various forms of activity at both a local and a national level by industry and commerce and the debates concerning the establishment of a national scheme of community service for young people (Jeffs, 1984). However, such direct intervention is most usually found at the national and regional levels of youth organisations and then only within limited areas of work. This is not to say that local units don't have relationships with local companies, but that these mostly take the form of the provision of resources, rather than any direct participation in organisation. What we will see is that, to a significant extent front-line youth work organisations respond to the deeper workings of the economy, because they are part of that economy and cannot insulate themselves from to its imperatives.

What follows is based upon a limited investigation of the resourcing of a small number of uniformed organisations and youth clubs and projects. Whilst the scale and nature of the survey was restricted, the commonalities which emerged, when considered alongside the limited amount of published evidence concerning front-line resourcing, suggested five themes for study:

1. the scale of 'hidden' resource transfers and the implications this may have for the work of the units;
2. The significance of young people when seen as paying customers;
3. the overall level of funding and regional variations within this;
4. the effect of restrictions and cutbacks in funding; and
5. the impact of a multiplicity of resourcing arrangements and sources.

We will examine each of these in turn.

Hidden transfers

The type of financial arrangements historically made within youth work and the scale of voluntary effort contribute toward a somewhat misleading picture of resourcing at the front-line. As we have already seen, the payment of staff is far more likely in club, project and detached forms of youth work. Harper's figures show that 99 per cent of the youth workers paid by local authorities are in these forms of provision (Harper, 1985, p. 16). Where staff are on the payroll of youth organisations, their wages are likely to be the largest item of expenditure, often dominating the accounts. Whilst detailed national figures for LEA expenditure are not available, DES figures show that local education authority expenditure on salaries in England was between 60 to 65 per cent of net recurrent expenditure on the Service (HMSO, 1982, p. 108). Equivalent figures for Wales show that 62 per cent of LEA resources devoted to youth work were spent on personnel in 1981–2 (HMI Wales, p. 14).

The practice of seconding local authority employees to individual units gives their accounts a high degree of unreality as wage costs are not shown. Figures detailing the extent of secondment by local authorities are not available, but it is our impression that when MSC-funded posts are excluded from consideration, the vast majority of paid workers are now directly employed by local authorities. The practice of grant aiding local units in respect of employment costs, whilst still significant, does appear to have been discouraged by a number of authorities in favour of seconding or direct management arrangements.

A second feature of accounts is the extent to which accommodation costs are under-represented. For instance, around 80 per cent of Girl Guide groups and Girls' and Boys' Brigades meet in premises of which they do not have exclusive use. The figures for the Scouts and clubs affiliated to NAYC are around 50 per cent (Thomas & Perry, 1974, p. 44). The bulk of uniformed organisations are affiliated to churches and frequently use church premises. It is rare to find any reference in the accounts of such groups to items such as heating, lighting and rent. In a number of examples we analysed donations were given to the host church, but the amounts, which ranged from £10 to £150, could in no way be a reflection of the true cost of accommodation. The same position holds for many youth clubs associated with churches. Village and neighbourhood youth clubs that do not have their own premises and that do not use church halls are more likely to pay rent. But again, there is evidence in the accounts we have seen that there is a high likelihood of their being located in subsidised premises. Village halls, community association halls, schools, and other council premises generally have special rates for recognised youth groups. Many educational premises are available free for use by recognised youth groups. A further important element with regard to premises is the mandatory rate relief which voluntary youth organisations have received up until now. At present that rate is set at 50 per cent, with a number of authorities granting further discretionary relief of up to 50 per cent of the balance, although in some instances this is dependant upon the organisation having charitable status (King, 1986, p. 10).

Those organisations that do have their own premises may also not show the actual costs in their accounts. Here local authorities may provide certain maintenance and caretaking services. In addition use has been made of the Community Programme by both uniformed and non-uniformed groups in order to undertake maintenance and building work.

Many other costs may not be truly reflected in accounts. Here we might consider the use of subsidised minibuses and people's cars, the provision of materials and space for events such as camps and the gift and discounting of materials and equipment by local firms and local authorities.

Lastly, note must be made of the voluntary contribution of time by workers, leaders, and others involved in the organisation and delivery of youth work such as the members of management committees. Harper has shown that 65 per cent of the total face-to-face work force in England and Wales is unpaid (1985, p. 6). His data does not appear to take account of uniformed organisations, where the figure would be nearer to 100 per cent (although payment is made in organisations linked to the armed forces). The scale of the voluntary contribution in youth work is fairly unique within UK welfare. The Wolfenden Committee's survey of voluntary work in social service areas showed that some 14 per cent of the national sample had reported undertaking some voluntary work in the previous year (1976). Around 10 per cent of the sample had worked with a recognised voluntary organisation. The Report notes that this was equivalent to about 400 000 full-time workers (on average people reported that they spent about six hours a week on such work) and, that this would be equivalent to 10 per cent of the total staff time employed in all the social and environmental services at the time (Glennerster, 1985, p. 107). Subsequent research has shown rather higher figures for volunteering. The 1981 General Household Survey found that 23 per cent of those that they interviewed had undertaken some unpaid work of service to others beside their family and friends in the preceding 12 months (HMSO, 1984). Humble (1982) came up with a figure of 44 per cent with a somewhat broader definition, which included social and sports clubs, political and trade union activity and involvement in community organisations such as churches. However, such differences do not disturb the significance of the scale of volunteering in youth work which, in terms of overall staffing, is much higher than the norm.

The somewhat unreal nature of many front-line organisations' accounts has a number of significant outcomes. Here we want to comment on two. First, although the local organisation may well have responsibility for plant, the day-to-day deployment of workers and the nature of the programme, the basis upon which decisions concerning resources are made can be somewhat skewed. The classic example here concerns staff time. The cost of staff is not a matter of significant interest to many managers at the front-line as it does not show in their balance sheet. As a result staff can be used in highly inefficient ways – undertaking all sorts of trivial tasks.

Second, from the comments received to our enquiries, it would appear that youth organisations are particularly prone to financial crises at the point when 'hidden' subsidies become 'actual' costs to the organisation. Payment for accommodation was frequently mentioned here, where financial problems in host or renting organisations are exported to the youth group in the form of higher rents or contributions. Within the local authority sector problems have occurred when, for instance, community schools have transferred to 'budget financing' and youth work activities have been forced into shouldering substantial additional financial responsibilities in order that other areas of community provision may be resourced. Another area cited is the cutback in the number of paid part-time youth work sessions that local authorities allocate to units. In order to maintain the level of work, other resourcing options have to be considered by the unit.

This raises again the question of the dependency of the front-line unit either on the state or upon voluntary organisations such as churches or national youth organisations. Many 'voluntary' organisations derive a very high proportion of their resources from the state. This is particularly so where they employ paid staff or are responsible for the upkeep of substantial plant. For instance in the UK some 59 per cent of community workers are employed by the voluntary sector, but funding for 85 per cent of all voluntary sector workers comes from the statutory sector (Francis *et al.*, 1984, pp. 5–6). Unfortunately comparable figures are not available for youth work. Voluntary organisations which receive higher levels of grant-aid are more likely to perceive a loss of independence as a disadvantage of such aid. However, as Brenton shows, the nature of alternative sources of resources and the consequences of not receiving such funding may involve a greater loss of freedom

(1985, p. 66). Whilst hidden transfers are an essential element of many front-line organisations' resource strategy – and allow the provider some potential influence over policy and practice – many decisions are taken largely on the basis of overt finances. The relative neglect of 'hidden transfers' contributes to an adoption of an overt market orientation.

The paying customer

What is apparent from the accounts we examined is the importance of the financial contribution made by young people. Posnett, when examining the income of voluntary welfare organisations in the UK, found that some 65.9 per cent of their income came from fees and charges (1984). Fund-raising and donations, and rents and investment income, contributed a further 12 per cent apiece. Grants from statutory bodies amounted to just under 8 per cent. However, a very high proportion of the fees and charges are actually paid from government funds. The contrast with youth work is marked. Leat *et al.* comment, 'many youth organisations exist solely on the basis of member subscriptions' (1986, p. 150). In the uniformed organisations we examined, the two major sources of income were fund raising and customer payment. In smaller youth organisations, perhaps where premises were provided free or at low cost, then subscriptions and items such as coffee bar receipts were the major source of income. Where there are buildings to maintain and major activities to finance such as camps, a substantial fund raising effort is required. Some respondents mentioned that such efforts usually meant getting money from the households of the young people involved under a different guise from subs and payments for goods and services. This was confirmed by the HMI review of Youth Service Provision in Wales (1984, p. 16).

As much of the resourcing for club and project work is 'hidden' to the unit, income from people also plays a major role, especially where the unit is susceptible to fluctuations in attendance. Smaller neighbourhood or village youth clubs can hover precariously around a break-even point and quickly eat up any reserves when the warmer weather invites their customers out to the open air. A substantial number of clubs have been dependent on income from events like discos, which are peculiarly liable to sudden movements in attendance. Such fluctuations can also severely affect hidden resourcing in that the allocation of staffing by local authorities is often specifically tied to attendance figures.

The size of membership is also a significant factor in the finances of the national organisations. Where units are affiliated the level of payment is usually based upon the size of membership. Within non-uniformed organisations the per capita contributions has traditionally been fairly low. Most of the income for those organisations is derived from other sources such as DES Headquarters Grants, national fund-raising efforts, trading activities, legacies and sponsorship deals. The bulk of the local unit's payment to the central organisation is often attributable to various forms of insurance cover. However, a different picture emerges in the uniformed organisations, where members bear a higher proportion of the cost of the central organisation. As a consequence emphasis is placed upon capitation fees within such organisations. In some units that we examined they comprised up to 15 per cent of the local unit's costs, in others 2–3 per cent. They paled into insignificance when compared with the cost of annual camps, however, which were frequently a focus for complaint by the workers and leaders within units.

Second, the fact that young people (and their households) have to pay for all or part of the services they consume has serious implications for who can afford to take advantage of them. This is perhaps most clearly articulated in the uniformed movements, who both receive significantly lower levels of state funding and impose upon their members substantial additional costs in the form of uniform. A number of troops have set up special uniform funds, or do not enforce certain elements of the uniform. Uniform is particularly important because it is, in effect, a joining or initiation fee, although the material benefits don't necessarily go to the organisation. The initial period of attendance can therefore be expensive. Further, one of the largest elements both in the finances of the organisation and in the payments that young people make in uniformed groups is for special activities such camping (or 'The Camp'). A substantial proportion of the cost has to be borne by the people attending. The cost can discriminate against young people in low income households.

Third, it is also important to explore the way in which young people have been given the role of 'customer' within many organisations. This is perhaps most apparent where there is not an emphasis upon the idea of membership, nor any sense of the organisation's structures being open to those involved. In most youth organisations there is an emphasis on 'paying your way'. Sometimes this forms part of a conscious educational programme, particularly where there is an attempt to develop young people's ability in, and commitment to, running things for themselves. The economics of the unit are therefore opened up and the implications for programming and costing worked on by those involved in the organisation (Lacey, 1987). Where there is not this sense of association or the concern to develop young people's organising abilities, then 'paying your way' becomes a means of separating the 'provider' from the 'consumer' and retaining control in the hands of the former – 'If you pay, we provide'. Over the years workers have also gained much from an acquaintance with marketing techniques, designing products and then selling them. This view has been strengthened by the increased emphasis on youth work as a form of leisure provision rather than a form of education.

Such commonsense views of the world are the very stuff of subordination. They reflect and reproduce the idea that things have to be paid for by the consumer. In this way, relationships between young people and youth workers can come to resemble employment situations where the only tie that bind workers and employers is the payment of wages for work done. This cash nexus depersonalises the relations between youth workers and young people by turning them into simple financial transactions which are located in the marketplace. It is rare to find workers actively helping young people to understand the political and economic systems that determine the financing of the unit.

Overall funding and local variations

The resourcing of youth work has to be set in the general context of welfare funding. The UK devotes a relatively low proportion of its Gross Domestic Product, to welfare, some 26 per cent in 1986–7 (HMSO, 1987). Educational expenditure was 5.25 per cent of GDP (ibid). In turn youth work consumes only a very small proportion of the education budget. In 1982–3 expenditure on the Youth Service was 0.94 per cent of the total expenditure on education in England (D. I. Smith, 1985, table 6).

Within youth work, from the highly speculative figures that have been assembled it is possible that for every pound of state expenditure on youth work through education budgets, some two pounds is raised from the levying of fees and charges and the receipt of gifts and donations. When the giving of skills, time and resources in kind is taken into account we have a resource base which is unique in UK welfare. But does this amount to a relative under resourcing of this area of work by the state?

The Review Group on Youth Service Provision in England comments that they could find no method of establishing whether current resources are sufficient to meet needs (HMSO, 1982, p. 113). Constrained by their terms of reference they make only general, recommendations concerning resources.

> First, the Youth Service is worth funding at a high level because of its potential for meeting crucial social needs. Resources should be as readily available for a Service which helps prevent young people from getting into trouble as for those services, such as Intermediate Treatment, which provide a rescue operation once that point has been reached. Secondly, funding of the statutory sector should be channelled through the usual policy making network of local authority department responsible for the Youth Service, and the growing inequality in funds reaching different areas should be reduced (ibid.).

However, the Government has been less restrained regarding its ability to assess the appropriate level of resourcing. Following the 1980 Local Government Planning Act major changes were made in the structure of the rate support grant. In particular the grant was to be distributed on the basis of detailed standard expenditure figures set by central government for each service. These figures, the 'grant related expenditure' (GRE) for each service, are 'an assessment of the cost to that authority of providing a comparable standard of service to other authorities, allowing for differences in the characteristics and needs of different areas' (HMSO, 1983a).

When D. R. Smith analysed the GRE assessment figures for the Youth Service and the actual expenditure by local authorities in England he could find little relationship between the two. This he attributes to local resistance to being told what to do by central government and his assertion that such estimates were rarely seen outside the Treasurer's Office.

> Analysing the movement in GREA and expenditure over the four year period highlights the lack of correlation between the two even further. Between 1981/82 and 1982/83 central government increased GREA youth service by over 50%. LEAs failed to match this, increasing actual expenditure by only 12.9%. This resulted in a situation in 1982/83 where 78 of the 96 English LEA's spent less than their GRE youth service assessment by a gross total of over £35 million, which represents almost 30% of the money which government assessed needed to be spent on youth service that year (1984, p. 3).

D. I. Smith has found that between 1979/80 and 1982/83 the Youth Service in England experienced a real expenditure reduction of 6.3 per cent. When ILEA is omitted from the calculation the reduction was 9 per cent. Also, when the effect of changing population sizes are taken into account it would appear that the amount spent by the Youth Service for each young person aged 14–20 was £22.31 1979–80 and £20.26 in 1982–3 – a reduction of 9.2 per cent. The reduction when ILEA is excluded is 12.3 per cent (1985, tables 2 and 4). 'The variations in provision seem to reflect variations in commitment to the Service rather than variations in the numbers or needs of young people' (ibid., p. 1). A point already noted by the Review Group and, indeed, by Albemarle some twenty years earlier. In 1982–3 Cornwall was spending on its Youth Service the equivalent of £5 per head of the 14–20 year old population, St Helens £11, Cheshire £11, Buckinghamshire £20, Liverpool £30, Newham £37 and ILEA £83 (1985, table 4). Similar patterns are documented for Wales (HMSO, 1984).

The picture is less clear in Scotland. There, 'Youth Service' expenditure forms part of the Community Education budget and it is difficult to make accurate comparisons between authorities because of the different accounting conventions used. Indeed within any one authority the construction of budgets is such that actual expenditure upon what might be called youth work is not easy to isolate. Horobin (1980), in his survey of community education statistics for Scotland, analyses the returns that are available and concludes that they have to be approached with extreme caution. More recently King (1986) has detailed the relationship between voluntary and statutory provision within Scottish youth work, but here again much of the material about resources is at the level of policy, without any quantification, and her summary of the proportion of the regions' community education budgets that goes on youth work show a wide variation and, in the case of some regions, is impossible to quantify.

In Northern Ireland, where youth work is administered through the Education and Library Boards, a uniform series of figures is available. These show that there has been a marked increase in real expenditure upon youth work since the early 1970s. Actual expenditure oscillated between £8 million and £9 million in the years 1978–9 to 1984–5 (DOE (NI), 1986). Such differences are only in part explicable by a cutback in the building programme at the end of the 1970s as there are considerable movements in recurrent expenditure. The Youth Committee for Northern Ireland argues that levels of provision have fallen and that some sectors appear to have suffered more than others – full-time workers in voluntary clubs seemed to be worst affected, while school-based youth tutors reported least ill-effects from the shortage of resources (1985, p. 27). Cutbacks have been made in expenditure upon plant and there was a 'drastic reduction on part-time paid leadership which placed increased pressure on (full-time workers) in maintaining an acceptable programme of activities whilst keeping clubs operating to accustomed hours of opening' (1985, p. 27). In addition, there would appear to be the same pattern of variation in expenditure between different geographical areas. A Report to the Northern Ireland Assembly noted that 'there is some inconsistency between Boards in their application of funds to the Youth Service' (HMSO, 1984, p. 21).

Two initial conclusions can be drawn from our analysis of the data concerning expenditure upon the Youth Service. First, in England and Wales, on the Government's own figures relating to their estimate of need, there was prior to 1984–5 a considerable shortfall in expenditure on youth work. In England, Wales and Northern Ireland, things were deteriorating in real terms. Second, variations between authorities in England, Wales and Northern Ireland cannot be explained on the basis of need. Authorities with broadly similar socio-economic profiles and voluntary organisational infrastructures appear to have significantly different expenditure levels. In terms of large scale comparative analysis, possibly the only significant variable concerning the different levels of expenditure is the political complexion of the respective council, with Labour authorities consistently spending at a higher level than Conservative, Alliance or indeed hung councils.

Any judgement relating to the overall level of resourcing for the type of activities and opportunities that youth work enables young people to undertake, would also have to include a number of other headings under which expenditure occurs. Here four areas of expenditure require particular consideration:

1. Budgets associated with formal educational institutions. Of specific interest here is expenditure through community education initiatives and the amount granted to student unions in further and higher education.
2. Intermediate treatment. During the period 1977–8 to 1984–5 total IT expenditure reported by local authorities in England and Wales increased in real terms by more than five hundred per cent (Morris, 1984, p. 4). Total local authority expenditure on IT in 1984–5 was just under £20 million. Direct government transfers to national agencies such as NACRO and the Save the Children Fund considerably increase the figure.
3. Leisure Services. Some youth work has been relocated within leisure services departments in a number of authorities. However, consideration also has to be given to expenditure upon play; sports and leisure centres and schemes such as Action Sport; and upon the provision of events like discos. Some of these may not only involve local authority funding, but also Sports Council grants.
4. MSC schemes. As Davies (1979; 1981) amongst others has demonstrated, key elements of the youth training schemes contain practices which youth workers have previously claimed as their own. However, there are immense difficulties in calculating the actual amount that might be spent on 'social education' within YTS as such expenditure is largely undifferentiated within scheme's accounts.

Any comprehensive view would have to examine the total services to young people and, at the time of writing, this has not been attempted in the UK. Thus given the range of funding sources already outlined and the scale of hidden transfers it is impossible to arrive at any satisfactory, let alone definitive, empirical conclusion concerning the overall level of expenditure upon youth work.

Cutbacks and restrictions

The impact of variable levels of funding and the effect of real decreases in expenditure have been highlighted partly as a result of the growing public profile allocated to H. M. Inspectorate. In one report, Cornwall, the lowest per capita spender upon youth work, was recommended to almost triple its expenditure (DES, 1986a, p. 17). The Inspectors reported that inadequate expenditure led to low staffing levels both full- and part-time; poor rates of pay for part-time workers; a lack of purpose-built centres; buildings in a very poor state of decoration and furnishing; and a relatively low level of grant aid to voluntary organisations.

The current pattern of cuts goes back beyond 1976. There was a halving of expenditure on capital projects which took place between 1970 and 1974. These have continued and in 1979 it was found that two-thirds of local authorities had no capital programme in this area whatsoever (D. I. Smith, 1979, p. 11). The Inspectors' review of the Youth Service in Wales comments:

No examination of expenditure can ignore the effect of cuts and illustrations of their impact upon the fabric of the service will be found in the report. Pruning of the service has been taking place in some LEAs since 1976 and, in that time, many planned developments have been reversed (HMI Wales, 1984, p. 15).

A further theme which appears in HMI reports is the misuse of resources. In the conclusions and recommendations section of just about all the published reports there is some reference to the improvements that could be made. These range from the provision of increased clerical and administrative support, changes in the deployment of workers, the lack of clearly articulated objectives and a policy framework and extent to which provision was tied to the requirements of school timetables (DES, 1983b; 1983c; 1983d; 1984a; 1986a).

This apparent under- and mis-resourcing is experienced in a number of ways at the front-line. Inevitably it means that young people will be offered more limited programmes and opportunities. In particular cutbacks tend to squeeze intensive work such as that with small groups and individuals and to press workers into activities that are revenue producing. Here we want to comment upon two outcomes – the impact on premises and equipment and upon part time paid staff.

It is rare to find a group meeting in purpose-built accommodation. Only in groups associated with boys' clubs does the figure rise much above 25 per cent (Thomas & Perry, 1975, p. 44). This can lead to a disproportionate amount of time being spent on fund-raising and upon the routine tasks of maintaining and patching up inadequate plant. Indeed one of the major diversions of time away from face-to-face work concerns maintenance, the administration of lettings and similar tasks (Holmes, 1981, p. 75; Stone, 1987).

A further problem with equipment has been highlighted by Leat *et al*. In their survey of a small number of voluntary youth organisations situated in four local authorities, they found that groups had been able to obtain grants for limited amounts of equipment rather more easily than for maintenance or staff or for particular events. However, having got the apparatus they were then faced with major problems concerning the lack of storage space and the inability to obtain the funds necessary to make use of it (1986, p. 167).

A second major feature of under-resourcing and the way in which cutbacks are executed is the impact it has upon part-time paid workers. As Callow comments, although the Youth Service relies very heavily on its part-time staff, part-timers themselves get a raw deal, experiencing 'job insecurity, lack of basic rights, and a jumble of pay rates with many people working for peanuts, are the realities of part-time youth work' (Callow, 1983, p. 19). Part-time workers lack rights to sick pay (except in ILEA), maternity pay or leave, holiday pay or pensions. With centres closed for up to 14 weeks of the year, not receiving holiday pay constitutes a serious loss of earnings. Similarly, when centres close for redecoration and the like, part-timers are generally laid-off without remuneration (ibid., p. 18). In addition, some authorities expect paid part-time workers to undertake a number of additional hours on a voluntary basis, although this may not be admitted formally.

There is now considerable evidence that the part-time element of Youth Service budgets is markedly prone to pruning at times when finances are squeezed. For instance, when central government controls and restraints on public expenditure were introduced in 1979, this resulted in the first real overall cut in Youth Service provision for a decade. In 1980–1 real expenditure on the Youth Service in England dropped by 3.7 per cent (D. I. Smith, ibid, p. 5). In Wales, not strictly comparable figures show a cut in real terms of around 4.4 per cent for the same financial year (HMI Wales, 1984b, tables 10 & 11). In half of the Welsh authorities there was no apparent change in the number of part-time hours allocated, but in the remaining authorities cuts were substantially in excess of the 4.4 per cent in all but one case. One authority made a 60 per cent cut (ibid., table 33). The combination of poor employment practices, wildly different pay rates, lack of benefits and the vulnerability of those short-term contracts makes for the exploitation of part-time paid workers and can create major problems at unit level. It may also have major ramifications in personal terms. The income from part-time youth work has come to play an important part in many household budgets and is one route by which a number of women have been able to re-enter the labour market. It is perhaps significant that in one local authority which recently reviewed the nature of its part-time paid youth work labour force, that women made up some 44 per cent of the labour force. In addition, 40 per cent of workers were found to be teachers and 25 per cent were otherwise unemployed. An increasing trend is for people to consolidate sessional work. Often this entails employment in a number of youth work units. In this way sessional workers can end up working 'full-time hours'. Some 14 per cent of the workers in the authority quoted above worked in more than one unit. However, in terms of the number of sessions they undertook, this 14 per cent of workers accounted for nearly 50 per cent of paid sessions within the particular Service. To counter this a number of authorities place a limit on the hours undertaken by individual, sessional youth workers.

Aside from the impact that cutbacks and restrictions may have had upon different financial categories of expenditure, it is also important to examine the types of work and organisation that local authorities and other grant-making or funding bodies have traditionally been prepared to support. At one level we see the operation of 'Grantmanship', which is described by Brenton as:

an art cultivated by any voluntary body which seeks to survive [which] consists essentially of blending an image of innovatoriness and creativity with the assurance of apolitical respectability and safeness into a basic framework of a trust's known preferences and predilections (1985, p. 68).

This phenomenon does not, of course, only apply to funding applications directed towards charitable trusts. A number of those interviewed gave examples of what they felt to be the difficulties in obtaining funding for the 'bread and butter' aspects of the work. It is possible to get grants for discrete and concrete items such as sports equipment but it is not, as we have seen, always easy to get the resources, for example, to make use of such equipment, to provide secretarial back-up for projects, and to pay for premises. 'Apolitical respectability and safeness' is often built into funding criteria. Here groups such as the Woodcraft Folk, with their emphasis upon enabling young people to appreciate the value of cooperation, justice and peace and their perceived connection with the Left, have clearly received less than their fair share of grant aid. For a short period during the late 1970s the DES small grant towards their headquarters costs was actually cut-off because of accusations of 'political bias' – a charge rarely laid at the door of more conservative but equally political organisations such as the Scouts. Indeed, the outcry that greeted the GLC's threat to restrict funding to the Scouts following allegations of militarism and discrimination against homosexuals, black young people and young women is an indication of the different way in which conservative and left youth work organisations are generally perceived (Scene, 1983).

The implications of mixed funding

Funding for youth work comes from a wide variety of sources. In the balance sheets and reports we analysed, income for front-line organisations was derived from eight broad areas:

1. Young people (and their households) in payment for goods and services;
2. Traditional fund-raising activities such as jumble sales, spon-

sored events, flag days and appeals to charities, trusts, commerce and industry;

3. Rent or payment for the use of the unit's facilities and equipment. The hire of premises for things like receptions, dances, playgrounds and adult education classes is a major source of finance for some organisations. There may also be other sales and royalties from trading activities directed at the general public.

4. Local education authority grants. These were the main source of income in 36 per cent of the boys' clubs associated with NABC, 33 per cent of the youth clubs associated with NAYC and around 3 per cent of the Girl Guide Troops surveyed by Thomas & Perry (1974, p. 46). From our analysis it would appear that the intervening years have done little to alter these figures.

5. Other local authority sources. These include social service departments – in particularly monies that flow through Intermediate Treatment budgets; leisure and recreation departments, some of whom have taken over responsibility for youth services, but who in any case may provide resources for play-schemes, holiday and other provisions; and parish and town councils in the form of special grants.

6. Direct support from central government departments and agencies. Here the Cadet Forces are reliant on military sponsorship and some youth organisations have sought resources under MSC schemes such as the Community Programme and VPP.

7. Various forms of specialised and short-term forms of funding in association with local authorities or national organisations. This would include monies such as Urban Aid and Section 11 money.

8. Resourcing and direct provision by Police, through such things as community policing budgets.

The success of fund raising activities is highly variable. Many areas of youth work are seen by sponsors and workers as having little appeal to those making both corporate and individual donations. Aside from questions concerning the relative attractiveness of different areas of youth work for potential funding, there is a broader question about the ability of traditional fund raising to keep pace with inflation and with the growth in real costs. Posnett's

survey shows some significant shifts in the relative importance
of the different funding sources within the voluntary welfare
field. In the period studied, 1975–6 to 1980–1, traditional fund
raising and donations decreased by 40 per cent in real terms. At
the beginning of the period they amounted to some 28 per cent of
voluntary organisation's income. By the end this had fallen to just
over 12 per cent. Rents and investment income had experienced a
similar relative decline equivalent to a decrease in real income of
23 per cent. Whilst grants from statutory bodies increased by 50
per cent in real terms, as a proportion of income they remained
fairly constant. Fees and charges increased by 167 per cent in real
terms, representing a near doubling of their relative contribution
to the income of voluntary organisations. The overall real increase
in income to the voluntary welfare organisations studied was 38
per cent.

The substantial increase in the scale of the contribution charges
to the finances of welfare organisations needs setting in the context
of debates about the purposes of charges. Parker (1976) suggests
at least five different purposes can be seen behind the implementation of consumer charges in social services. To:

1. reduce the cost to taxpayers of providing a constant supply of
   service by raising new or additional revenue;
2. reduce the cost to taxpayers by reducing demand from consumers and lowering the level of supply;
3. shift priorities from one consumer group to another;
4. to prevent waste or abuse by customers that might arise from
   the provision of a 'free' service; and
5. to act as 'symbols' or 'ideological marker flags'.

The symbolic importance of charges within youth work has
already been discussed and there is a great deal of evidence in
annual reports and such like, concerning charging for the use of
equipment in order to counter abuse. However, there is little to
suggest that the relative significance of these has grown. In addition, whilst there may be a shift of priorities away from young
people, this may not be particularly expressed in the pricing of
youth work services, especially when the situation is compared
with charging within provision for the elderly. The use of charges
in order to restrict demand for services within youth work may be

significant in some specific areas of provision, but on the whole it is our judgement that the managers of front-line units want a higher, rather than lower, level of consumer demand. Inevitably we are drawn to the explanations which, in the present context, emphasise the need for revenue generation. Crucially, any cost reduction is usually perceived as accruing to the front-line organisation rather than to the taxpayer.

We have not been able to analyse accounts over time in any substantial way, but it is our impression that youth work may not follow all the trends that Posnett identifies. For instance, it would appear from our research that lettings have grown as a source of income in front-line units. There is mounting pressure both to make efficient use of plant and to make it pay. Many youth work premises are used for private functions, particularly at weekends. In the daytime it is common to find playgroups, adult education classes, groups for the elderly and other community groups meeting in centres and clubs. What is significant is that these groups are often now expected to pay an 'economic' rent or make an appropriate contribution. In this way those youth work organisations with buildings export or re-export their financial problems. The knock-on effect is often to place strains upon the finances of other community groups. A further development is the letting of halls in the evenings to private concerns and enterprises offering services to young people. Here one of the largest users is the martial arts. All this has major implications for the work of the leader or worker responsible for the plant, but crucially it also leads to a more limited access to facilities for the young people who are members of the club or unit.

Many other statutory sources of funding have come to assume importance. Sadler (1981) found a wide range of statutory monies flowing into front-line units. These include payments from the following central government departments: DES (through developmental and experimental grants to headquarters organisations); Department of the Environment both through Planning Policy Division 1, and the Urban Programme; DHSS; the Home Office through legislation such as Section 11 of the 1966 Local Government Act and via the Voluntary Services Unit. Quasi-governmental bodies giving statutory money included the Commission for New Towns; the Commission for Racial Equality; the Commonwealth Youth Exchange; the Countryside Commission; the

Equal Opportunities Commission; the Regional Arts Associations; the Sports Council; and, of course, the MSC. Monies had also been obtained from the European Social Fund.

It is difficult, if not impossible, to get accurate figures concerning the dispersement of monies to specifically youth work purposes through these sources. Aside from MSC monies and the various Urban Programme schemes which are channelled through local authorities, the bulk of central government money dispersed goes to national organisations. However, it was apparent that the little money that did flow via this route into front-line units went to club, project and detached work, rather than into uniformed organisations, although some special projects such as tree planting were dominated by the uniformed groups. The only local uniformed organisations receiving a substantial proportion of their income from central government were the cadet groups through the Ministry of Defence.

The most prominent central government resourcer of youth work was the MSC. Again it is difficult to obtain accurate figures, but when central government grants to voluntary organisations as a whole are considered, it can be seen that the MSC dispersed £138.8 million in 1982–3. This figure represents a massive 55 per cent of the total central grants given in that year (Leat *et al.*, 1986, p. 20). Indeed, the scale of MSC funding can easily alter the shape of an organisation. As Scott comments, the YMCA 'Training for Life' (TFL) programme (a MSC-funded YTS scheme) is ironically labelled an arm of the YMCA (1986, p. 99). Yet TFL staff number 50 per cent more than the YMCA mainstream staff of 300.

Compared with MSC funding, the Urban Programme is only of limited significance. The total money granted to voluntary organisations in general under the programme comprises less than 10 per cent of that dispensed by the MSC. The Programme provides grants, normally of 75 per cent towards local authority expenditure on their own projects and those of voluntary and other bodies that they choose to support. The other 25 per cent has to be found by the local authority. Where these monies are used to support youth work there appears to be a tendency towards keeping them in pieces of work that are directly controlled by the authority. Thus in one of the authorities we examined, which had a strong tradition of voluntary management, the Urban Programme-funded practitioners were the only workers directly managed by the Youth Office.

One further source of statutory funding is local authorities acting under Section 137 of the 1972 Local Government Act. This enables them to spend up to the value of a 2p rate each year for any purpose which they judge to be to the benefit of their area (except where this runs counter to other statutory provisions). As discussed elsewhere in the book, the lines of demarcation between some of the leisure and play provision provided by district councils and the work funded through the local education authority can be blurred. In our survey, we encountered instances of local groups receiving substantial resourcing simultaneously from both their district and their county councils.

A number of consequences flow from this apparent growth in the significance of resourcing for youth work not derived from education budgets. Here we want to note four tendencies to which this has contributed:

• a growth in the administrative function of full-time youth workers;
• a skewing in activities towards that work which can be readily funded and an increased susceptibility to moral panics;
• a pattern of labour substitution and deskilling; and
• the resourcing of work with black young people and 'work with girls' from outside mainstream and continuing funding.

Any involvement with MSC forms of resourcing involves substantial paperwork and attendance at meetings. The additional staffing that results requires management and work, the latter often at times and in areas where the unit has not traditionally operated. Some of the full-time workers we interviewed found themselves devoting up to half their working hours in the maintenance and supervision of MSC staff and projects. Further, any form of short-term or special funding or resourcing requires a case being made and reports submitted on their progress and results. Frequently such money has to be kept in special accounts and a specific record of expenditure in that area noted. Inevitably there is a growth in the administrative function of the unit. This can place a heavy burden on the central full-time worker.

Workers in conversation, particularly in self-consciously voluntary organisations, stressed the extent to which they have to undertake those forms of work for which they can get funding. The high degree of discretion held in front-line units means that local authorities and those funding the work have sought to find means of influencing their programme. Some resources have been offered for specific forms of work, some units threatened with a cut-off of resources if they do not follow certain policy guidelines. Resources have a tendency to become available in youth work on a 'flavour of the month' basis. Moral panics about drugs and alcohol misuse, or the lack of 'discipline', or unemployment, or about 'black youth', have often found a ready audience in a Youth Service hungry for funds. Schemes are dreamt up to tackle the 'problem' and monies sought often without regard what the essential purpose of the unit's work is or what the nature of the particular moral panic constitutes. An unfortunate consequence is a substantial history of misdirected and questionable work and a vicious circle of failure. Unrealistic aims are set in order to get funding, workers then struggle to fulfil those aims and the consequent inability to turn rhetoric into concrete results leads to personal frustration and questions by funders and managers regarding competence.

Thirdly, the widespread adoption of MSC schemes has contributed to a pattern of labour substitution and deskilling. A number of authorities, at different times, have made the allocation of part-time paid sessions dependent on whether the unit has CP workers attached or has applied for them (Scott, 1986, p. 95). Beyond a certain level they will not allocate sessions to clubs not participating in a CP scheme. In addition, many units have used CP workers to compensate for earlier cutbacks in staffing. For example, the Youth Committee for Northern Ireland has said that temporary employment schemes have been a major means by which cutbacks in the funding of part-time workers have been 'remedied' (1985, p. 27). Such workers with one-year contracts and with limited opportunities for training are being substituted not only for part-time youth workers but also for full-time workers. Indeed as Pond (1986) has argued, the growth of CP, which doubled in size in 1985–6, 'could actually destroy real long-term jobs as well as traditional volunteering'. Many of the workers we interviewed, who worked in areas of high unemployment, described how it was becoming increasingly difficult to get voluntary help. This they attributed both to the impact of unemployment and to the expectation created by CP schemes, that such work is paid. Quite aside from any social or political questions concerning such a shift, workers reported a significant impact upon the work as, on the whole, voluntary workers tended to give longer service than did those employed under MSC schemes.

Fourthly, there is considerable evidence that work with young women and a great deal of provision for black young people is funded from these temporary sources. For instance, N. Smith in a survey of 43 local authorities found that none employed statutory workers with a full-time brief to work with girls and no responding education authorities gave grant aid for the salaries of workers with a similar brief (1984, pp. 38–9). Fourteen of the authorities grant aided the salaries of full-time workers with a brief to develop work with boys and young men. Monies to fund full-time workers with girls was forthcoming from other sources such as trusts and central government grants but only on a limited scale. The financing of such work from marginal or short-term funding sources not only creates uncertainty but also labels the work as being outside the 'mainstream' and leaves some questions about its legitimacy in terms of youth work policy beyond the realm of the immediate unit.

A political economy of youth work

The fact that the bulk of resources for youth work are generated at the front-line, and the importance, in policy terms, of the decisions made within local units, means that we have to look beyond established explanations if we are to understand the relationship between the deeper workings of the economy and youth practice. In what remains of this chapter we want to sketch in some lines of analysis which could lead to a more adequate political economy.

If we consider formal education then there are those, such as Bowles & Gintis, who argue that major aspects of the structure of schooling can best be understood in terms of the 'systematic needs for producing reserve armies of skilled labour, legitimating the technocratic-meritocratic perspective, reinforcing the fragmentation of groups of workers into stratified status groups, and accustoming youth to the social relationships of dominance and subordinacy in the economic system' (1976, p. 56). Further they suggest that the social relationships of education 'replicate the hierarchical division of labour' (ibid., p. 131). This is an analysis which can yield some insights into the relationships within youth work (Bunt & Gargrave, 1980, p. 110). Certainly much early work placed an emphasis on discipline and order (Blanch, 1979). Springhall argues that elements of it offered considerably more and that the early uniformed youth movements helped 'smooth the way for upper-working class and lower-middle class assimilation into the urban industrial order of British society (1977, p. 121). During this period it was also feared that the involvement of young women in the labour market and their consequent spending power would tempt them away from their allotted roles of wife and mother. A number of youth work organisations therefore directed their attentions to young women (Dyhouse, 1981, p. 105). However Springhall, amongst others, has further argued that in the second quarter of the twentieth century, with the extension of secondary schooling and with mass communications reinforcing popular commitment to national norms and values, alternative forms of affirming social and political responsibility became more readily available (ibid., p. 124). Thus youth work could not be seen as a central element of an explicit policy to prepare young people for the requirements of the productive process. However, whilst youth work's place in welfare policy may be marginal, the nature of the processes within front-line units may well make a significant contribution to the preparation of young people for the social relationships of production and, perhaps more importantly, to the relationships of consumption.

That Bowles & Gintis over-emphasise domination and severely underplay human agency has often been commented upon (see Karabel & Halsey, 1977), but what is a further disappointment for us here is that they do not provide an analysis of the mechanisms of power and domination. The way in which formal educational institutions may have come to replicate the hierarchical division of labour or the process by which the systematic needs to the productive system are perceived and acted upon within education are not explored in any depth. This is the very area that any satisfactory political economy must address. Nor do they fully explore the various contradictions and forms of resistance that occur within schooling. Having pointed us in the direction of a relationship between the demands of the economy and the structure and functioning of educational institutions, their analysis does not enable us to explore with any sophistication the nature of relationships within youth work.

By placing an emphasis on social reproduction, Bowles & Gintis failed to examine the way in which culture acts as 'a mediating force within the complex interplay of reproduction and resistance' (Giroux, 1983, p. 86). Here the work of Bernstein (1977) and Bourdieu and his colleagues (1977a; 1977b) has come to assume some importance in the sociology of education. Bourdieu rejects the view that schools are simply replications of society in favour of a belief that they are relatively autonomous institutions only indirectly influenced by more powerful economic and political institutions:

> Rather than being directly linked to the power of the economic elite, schools are seen as part of a larger universe of symbolic institutions that, rather than impose domicility and oppression, reproduce existing power relations subtly via the production and distribution of a dominant culture that tacitly confirms what it means to be educated (Giroux, 1983, p. 87).

Thus the school embodies the dominant culture and only those young people who have the appropriate 'cultural capital' can make full and effective use of it. Those who have economic capital have a greater chance of possessing cultural capital. In youth work this is, perhaps, illustrated by the class basis and orientation of the uniformed organisations. However, whilst the idea of cultural reproduction is highly suggestive for our purposes here it does, in the form presented by Bourdieu, have certain problems. Insufficient attention is paid to the impact of the economic system on working class people and how such material conditions affect their experience of formal education. In addition, whilst schools may be relatively autonomous, the notion of culture that Bourdieu uses is one-way. Subordinate cultures are seen as reflections of the dominant culture rather than having some integrity of their own. Again, little thought is given to the possibility of resistance and reflexivity (Giroux, 1983, p. 163).

Resistance is something that has featured in much of the work done on British working-class subcultures. The attempt to integrate ethnography with Marxist social theory has provided some analytical advance. For instance, Willis (1977) has demonstrated schools are sites where culture and ideology are produced, rather than being places simply where they are imposed. The culture and ideology produced are filled with contradiction and, like the work-place, the process is itself based on contestation and struggle.

In this we have followed the broad lines of argument suggested by Giroux. We appear to have the beginnings of a useful analysis, one which connects with the Friday night world of youth work. Instead of viewing the youth organisation as simply a place for the social control of young people, we can see that all those involved in such institutions, be they young people, sponsors or workers, make a contribution to the cultures, ideologies and practices which become expressed within the club, project or unit. We need only take one example here – the payment of subs. Within clubs and projects, the task of eliciting membership dues or door money is often a thankless one. Where the unit has a clear culture and ideology, one that is subscribed to by members and staff alike, then this is likely to be less of a problem. Elsewhere subs can become a symbol of resistance. For managers and sponsors the reasons for their existence are self evident – 'you get nothing for nothing'. For some young people they provide a ready means to test boundaries and to celebrate their transcendence. The workers may view them as a necessary evil. The outcome of this process, at any particular moment, is likely to be a series of accommodations between conflicting ideologies and cultures. In this sense the tensions and drama that can surround the payment of subs or entry money provide a ready starting point for understanding the dy-namics of youth work. However, the actual mechanisms that connect the deeper workings of the economy with the day-to-day practice of youth work remain hazy.

Salter and Tapper have attempted to explore these mechanisms in the context of education and they argue that whilst schooling is constrained by the needs of capital, these needs are only influential if they are expressed in effective political terms. At this point the tensions of capital will be revealed. The state bureaucratic appara-tus 'has assumed the task of helping capital to define what its needs may be, of reconciling the tension inherent in the definition of those needs, and demonstrating in more precise terms the ways in which schooling must change if those needs are to be met' (1981, p. 31). They argue that central state bureaucracies are increasingly dominating other educational power centres (ibid., pp. 40–5). A point underlined by governmental discussions concerning the fu-ture of the rate support grant and the expressed desire for in-creased central direction within education (HMSO, 1986).

When this is translated into the realm of youth work we can see similar patterns in operation, the rise of the MSC, the strengthening of the Inspectorate and the development of NACYS. But, for the bulk of youth provision, the role of the central state in directly setting policy remains limited. Voluntary organisations and frontline units still have a high degree of discretion. However the fact that they require funding does allow the state to influence their policy. Davies has argued that the apparent fragmentation of youth services in the UK masks 'the common aspirations and orientations of the state policies which underpin those administratively separate services. For not only do these common aspirations and orientations exist, but when placed together they form into a 'youth policy' of surprising coherence' (1981, p. 3).

The scale of such coherence is open to debate, but it does lead us to explore the contribution of ideology. All groups and societies generate sets of ideas about themselves. There will be dominant and subordinate ideologies, with the former securing the coherence of the dominant class. The way in which people are affected depends, to some extent on their class position and, of course, on factors such as gender, ethnicity and geographical location, and the sense they make of these. People's perceptions of the situation will vary within classes. In developed capitalist systems there may not be a well defined dominant ideology and different elements or fractions of the ruling class may interpret or oppose aspects of it in different ways. (Abercrombie *et al.*, 1980). We have to recognise how key groups perceptions may have differed one from another and become manifested in some of the debates about the nature and direction of the youth organisations and how their position may have led to a somewhat different interpretation of the needs of capital. In this way some of the different emphases of say Scouting and club work can be understood (Smith, 1988).

Such ideologies and cultures do not float free. For example, culture may be seen as being constituted by the relations between different classes and groups and bounded by structural forces and material conditions and informed by a range of experiences. These are partly mediated by the power exercised by a dominant class (Giroux, 1983, p. 163). Inevitably the subordinate ideologies will carry in them elements of the dominant one and here one key theme is the way the current mode of production is presented as eternal.

The advance of capitalist production develops a working class which by education, tradition, habit, looks upon the conditions of that mode of production as self-evident laws of nature . . . The dull compulsion of economic relations completes the subjection of the labourer to the capitalist (Marx, 1974, p. 689).

In this view both capitalists and workers are seen as being pressed by economic forces and within the capitalist system such forces have their own autonomy and dynamic. Whilst it may be possible to modify the play of market forces, it is not possible to take them over. All youth work units are subject to the 'dull compulsion of economic relations'. The common-sense imperatives of balancing budgets, of keeping the building going and staff employed and of charging for services all contribute to and reflect a dynamic and a particular view of the world. Such imperatives, combined with a consciousness of being 'in the market', offer us a route to an adequate political economy.

There is a sense in which the front-line youth work unit operates as a firm and various insights into its operation can be gained from viewing it in this way. To stay in business it has to be responsive to the demands of its actual and potential customers and to take full account of the money market and its bankers (Ingram, 1987). It also has to know the competition and develop a product which can maintain the necessary market share. Thus front-line youth work units respond to the deeper workings of the economy because key actors within them see themselves as being part of, and committed to, that economy and because the material circumstances in which they operate make for the need to be aware of, and to connect with, such workings. Failure to do so may extract a severe penalty. As Roberts has noted, 'the histories of youth work and education are graveyards of impractical objectives. Leisure services have proved barren territory for "missionaries" hoping to rescue and redirect young people's lives. . . . The commercial sector has never found leadership a profitable formula' (1983, p. 178).

Since Eggleston's 1974 study, there has been no substantial investigation of the relations in the front-line youth work unit. The way in which the perceptions and actions of sponsors, managers, full-time workers, part-time workers and different groups of young people interact and the nature of the power relationships require analysis. Only then can we come to any firm conclusions concerning the way in which the relation between youth work practice and the system of production operates.

At this moment we know relatively little about the economics of youth work. What we can see is the impact of having a variety of resource providers; the results of individual units, national organisations and local authorities making resource decisions without a clear picture of what those resources are; the effects of the exploitation of part-time workers; and the detrimental effect that under-resourcing has upon the provision offered. A recognition of the importance of the front-line unit has led us to focus upon the way in which workers, sponsors and young people can exist within their own cultures, with their own ideologies. To go any further, we need to explore the way these interact and carry the requirements and contradictions of capitalism into the relations of youth work.

4

Local Authorities and Youth Work: the Consequences of Declining Local Autonomy

KEITH SHAW with TONY JEFFS and MARK SMITH

The last chapter examined the relationship between the Youth Service and the DES and further chapters explore the links with other central government agencies. Yet for many youth workers central government seems to be somewhat distant, if not irrelevant. It is the local authority 'down the road' which appears to shape so much of their daily work and determine their professional future. For almost all youth workers are, as we saw in Chapter 3, to some degree or another, dependent upon resources allocated by a local authority. This chapter will examine the changing environment of central–local relations, and how the declining autonomy of local government affects the context within which youth workers operate.

Local authorities and the Youth Service

The direct involvement of local authorities in youth work can be traced back to the 1918 Education Act which invested local education authorities with the power to spend money on facilities for physical training, organised games, holiday camps and for the social training of young persons in the evening which in essence meant that they could, if they so desired, make grants available to youth clubs and groups. This was strengthened in 1921 in the Board of Education Circular 86, which gave LEAs the powers to set up their own 'Juvenile Organising Committees' where local voluntary organisations had not already done so. Little tangible grew out of this legislation, for few LEAs used such committees to channel grants to juvenile organisations. During the inter-war years via other legislation, including Housing Acts, Special Areas legislation and the 1937 Physical Training and Recreation Act, funds were transferred to voluntary youth work agencies (Jeffs, 1979, pp. 10–22).

The Second World War represented a genuine watershed regarding the involvement of local authorities in youth work. Local authorities began, on a mass scale, to grant aid voluntary organisations, appoint staff, and where gaps in provision existed, establish their own units. The 1944 Education Act, recognising the reality of local authority involvement in Sections 41 to 43, created a legislative framework which integrated the Youth Service within the national educational structure. This formalised many of the practices that had developed on an ad hoc basis during the preceding four years of the war. Out of that period has grown the contemporary pattern of local authority administrative involvement. The structure of youth officers, youth committees, and the local mixing of voluntary and statutory provision ensures there is no single model of local authority youth work provision. Legislation is such that it leaves local authorities with considerable discretion as to levels of funding, the administrative structure and pattern and style of delivery.

If there is a predominant location for local authority youth work, it is provision through the auspices of the local education authority. Usually this means that the Youth Service is administered through the Education Committee which delegates many of its powers to a sub-committee which may deal solely with youth and community work but more usually will have a broader remit embracing in addition such areas as adult, further and community education and careers. Below the level of chief officers and their assistants, the structural 'norm' is of a principal youth officer with a coterie of officers divided either according to spatial criteria or through the designation of special areas of activity such as training. In many authorities these spatial and specialist responsibilities may be combined in a profusion of seemingly incomprehensible permutations that have grown out of individual interest or bureaucratic convenience. Below this level the allocation of staff is largely idiosyncratic, as we have already seen.

Trying to explain the structure of the Youth Service to someone who has not encountered it before is made more difficult by the growing intervention of other local authority departments within this sphere of activity. Especially since the 1969 Children's and Young Person's Act, the local authority personal social service departments have engaged themselves in the area of youth work, establishing and funding intermediate treatment groups for offenders and potential offenders which now amount to an alternative national youth service. Further, these departments both directly and indirectly fund, in many areas, community centres, Family Service Units and projects that engage in forms of work which can be readily seen as youth work. As if this was not confusing enough, we have to add to this cocktail of local authority involvement, youth work carried out under the auspices of recreation, leisure, libraries and museums, and play departments. The scale of this involvement in the case of recreation and leisure has been such, in a number of localities, that this department has become the dominant partner or provider. Notably in Avon and Birmingham responsibility for the Youth Service has been relocated within recreation and leisure departments. Finally it has to be pointed out that the local authority structure not only leads to their existing within one authority anything between two and four departments engaging in youth work with young people aged between 14 and 21, but there can also exist a parallel service funded and controlled by second tier authorities. Thus, for example, a number of district councils in non-metropolitan areas, such as Leicester, sustain a 'youth service' with full- and part-time staff operating in traditional youth centres as well as recreation centres; independently provide training programmes; and fund voluntary youth work provision. Their legal authority for this is derived for their responsibility for leisure services. It is hardly surprising that a division of services that 'appeared neat and sensible in theory . . . in practice has been the source of endless disputes between county and district councils, each jealous of their functions and prestige' (Elcock, 1982, p. 35).

The structure we have outlined only applies to England and Wales. In Scotland responsibility for education lies with the

regional councils and there what would have been called the
Youth Service is located within community education. However,
there still exists parallel and alternative provision via personal
social services and leisure departments in district councils. The
situation is administratively different in Northern Ireland where
direct rule from Westminster has virtually disenfranchised the
population in terms of control over local services. However we do
find the same basic mixture of duties, powers and requirements
alongside traditions and practice. The directly appointed Education and Library Boards (of which there are five) and Health and
Social Service Boards (of which there are four) possess responsibility for the functions normally executed by education and personal social service departments in England and Wales. Not only is
the position confused by the Board areas not being coterminous
owing to the different number of each, but there exist district
councils who possess discretionary budgets for leisure and youth
related activities. A number of these operate leisure centres which
cater for young people and some also employ community workers
with a clear remit for working with young people.

In the largely autonomous Channel Islands and the Isle of Man
totally different administrative arrangements apply.

The administrative structure through which local authority provision is channelled and controlled is complex and an ever-shifting
terrain. It is often difficult for workers and students to come to
terms with and it frequently leads to confusion concerning local
authority youth policies. It is important to be able to understand
the administrative minutiae and nuances that set one authority and
department apart from another. However, in focusing upon these
care should be taken not to lose sight of the context in which
administrative structures are located.

Local government in Britain: the context

Although one may be forgiven for overlooking the fact amidst
present debates on the 'decline of local democracy', Britain is, and
always has been, a unitary state. As Cockburn notes, 'there are no
ancient rights of grassroots self-government in Britain' (1977,
p. 46). Local government is thus very much the creation of the
centre: the structure, functions, expenditures, and even the very

existence of local authorities are crucially determined by Act of Parliament.

Confusion about the constitutional status of local government in Britain stems from the dichotomy between its formal constitutional subordination to the centre, and the autonomy that local government has actually achieved in specific historical periods. 'British history shows how an unchanged constitution can accommodate great variations in the relative authority of central and local government' (Foster *et al.*, 1980, p. 21).

The growth of the modern local government system after 1835 is closely linked with the early phase of capitalism. Thus the development of adequate law and order provision to protect private property; the creation of local monopolies in relation to public utilities such as gas, electricity, water and trams, where such services were important to local industry; and the creation of a 'healthy' workforces via health, poor relief, and sanitation measures, can all be seen as functions of local government which were beneficial to the embryonic capitalist order. The development of such services were often largely supervised by the practical 'men of industry' themselves for much of the nineteenth century. It was local notables drawn from the emerging bourgeoisie that provided leadership in the Victorian city and town.

The dominant business interests who tended to control the local authorities, also held powerful sway over local voluntary organisations. Early youth work was dependent for its establishment and survival in many areas upon the largesse of this class. A problem that this presented was that the areas where industry was less prosperous or ownership more distant from the community, tended to both lack the administrative and voluntary support of such classes and access to the charitable support they might bestow (Thane, 1982). These inequalities continued right into the twentieth century. Indeed, government funding in the 1930s via assistance to Special Areas was designed, in part, to overcome this problem. Those localities with the highest unemployment, declining industries, an absentee-bourgeoisie and the lowest rate income were also those which had markedly less voluntary provision. This form of inequality could not, of course, be simply solved by a transfer in political power via an extension of the franchise.

The liberalisation of the franchise, the growth of trade unionism and the formation of a political arm of the labour movement meant that groups began to colonise local government by the early twentieth century who had a different conception of the potential for local action. These new groupings saw local government as an important weapon in the articulation of pressure for the alleviation of the conditions experienced by the working class.

The increased penetration of local government by representatives of the working class was not unrelated to a gradual disengagement of business representatives. The latter was partly a reflection of the increasing national and international nature of production which made the control of local government less important to big business. Also this shift was aided by the growing migration of the middle classes to the suburban and rural hinterlands of the cities and large towns; a move which created a distance between workplace and residence. During the early years of this process, the migration did not necessarily entail severance, for the 1918 Representation of the People Act allowed the holders of business premises to vote in both their business and their residential constituency. The 1928 Act even allowed their wives to do so on the same basis. These privileges were removed by the 1948 Act (Punnet, 1968, pp. 38–40). However, recent years have witnessed the re-emergence within the Business community of the demand for 'no taxation without representation'. This call is supported by sections of the Conservative Party, who wish to see business re-enfranchised via the restoration of an 'extra' business vote (Newton & Karran, 1985, p. 106).

For some writers the distancing of business representatives constitutes a 'problem' for local government in a capitalist society. It exposes local government to colonisation by non-capitalist classes who can then challenge the 'supportive' role of the state in capital accumulation; advocate municipalisation and put social need above private profit; defend fair wages for local authority employees; or use local government as a 'politicising' agency to counter the hegemonic control of capitalist ideology (Corrigan, 1979).

So while this 'relative autonomy' of local government needs to be viewed with an overall context of central control, its importance should not be overlooked. Indeed, Saunders (1980) has called local government the 'Achilles Heel' of the capitalist state, as its 'pluralist' mode of decision-making allows it to be more vulnerable than the 'corporatist' centre to working-class pressures for change.

Certainly it has been in terms of local campaigns that community work has been most successful. The smallness of the constituency and the low turnout of electors have often encouraged a feeling of vulnerability amongst councillors. This feeling is readily exploited by some community workers and youth workers both in the interests of securing resources for those they work with and for themselves. A number of youth workers and community workers have entered 'full-time' local politics.

The nationalisation of local government

The traditional view of the functioning of local government has, often *a priori*, pointed to the crucial importance of local political influence in the formation of policy. Dunleavy has neatly summar-ised this approach, stressing that:

> these studies almost invariable suggest that local elections and public opinion exert an important influence on local policy-makers; that elected local representatives are collectively and continuously involved in the process of policy-making; and that the deliberations of those representatives and the policies which result are distinctly local or specifically related to the issues under consideration and to the particular 'needs' of the area administered by the authority (Dunleavy, 1980, p. 135).

In response to this, it can be argued that local initiatives are becoming more influenced by non-local factors: that local policy-making is being nationalised, and that local authorities have dim-inishing influence over local decision-making. In this respect several points deserve consideration. Firstly, in a general sense, we can note that local authorities have less influence because during the last 50 years they have experienced the gradual loss of hitherto local functions to public corporations, regional authorities and central departments. Thus the loss of such responsibilities as poor relief, gas, electricity, health and water has been partly masked by an increase in total spending. It is the two services of education and housing plus more recently the personal social services, that have swallowed up this increased budget. For example education and housing accounted for a quarter of all local expendi-ture in 1900, around 35 per cent between the wars, half the total in the mid-1950s and 60 per cent by the mid-1970s. However, by 1983 this had dropped to 52 per cent of total local spending.

Indeed, local control of education is increasingly under threat from the centre. A dual concern with rationalising the use of resources and introducing a more vocational element into education forced the Thatcher administration (via the MSC and DES) into detailed interventions within the education service. The creation of City Technical Colleges; the restructuring of the curriculum; the recasting of the examination system; the changing role of parents in school government; the imposition of guidelines on sex education and political indoctrination; and the rapid centralisation of decisions on teachers pay and conditions of service (including pressures to accept a 'no-strike' agreement) are features of the nationalisation of education in Britain. As one senior DES official reportedly argued, 'we are seeking to restructure education. To do so we need control. There is a need, especially in the 16–19 area for a centrally formulated approach to education' (quoted in Ranson *et al.*, 1986).

Secondly, attention has also been drawn to the development of a 'national local government system', which Dunleavy describes as a 'complex web of inter- and supra-authority relations which can exert a strong influence on the policies pursued in particular localities (1980, p. 105). Thus the role of local authority associations (Issac-Henry, 1984), national party organisations (Gyford & James, 1983), public service unions (Walsh, 1981), MPs with local authority backgrounds (Burch & Moran, 1985), and academics writing in the field of local government can all be seen as contributing to the political linkage between centre and locality and to the values adopted by authorities in particular localities. Recent studies have attested to the importance of local authority associations (such as the AMA, ACC, ADC) in representing a local view to the centre. Dearlove has also illustrated the leading role played by academics in the corporate revolution in local management in the 1960s and 1970s (1979, p. 287).

Finally, it is important to pinpoint the growing role played in policy determination by professions, operating more in line with nationally defined notions of 'best practice' – practices which tend to predominate for long periods of time and which are adopted by a range of authorities with little variation between them. This has certainly been the case in youth work. The wholesale replication of

Withywood-style youth centres during the 1960s (Jeffs, 1979); the spread of school-based youth work; the development of work targeted at girls and young women; are all examples of the distillation of 'good practice'. However the mechanisms by which this occurred has varied widely. Dunleavy (1981) monitors the complex way in which this uniformity of practice can surface in his study of decision making with regard to the building of high-rise housing. He notes in particular within that context the key role of an architectural 'ideology' in which professional fashions of modern housing predominated. Not dissimilar professional fads and fashions have cut a swathe through youth work policy. Similarly, recent studies of local authority economic initiatives have highlighted how the growing involvement of professional groups such as RTPI has produced a standardised view on how to stimulate economic development; a view reinforced by other national agencies such as central departments, private management consultants and international corporations (Shaw, 1986).

Clearly there has not been 'nationalisation' within youth work of the scale Dunleavy encountered. The diversification of control through different departments, nationally and locally, and the still significant presence of a voluntary sector and large unpaid workforce constrain the ability to construct a unified youth work policy. Davies (1986a; 1986b) argues that the central state has shown a clear determination to adopt a more interventionist approach to the formation of youth policy and the shaping of practice. Indeed he suggests that 'British youth policies have been run through with some important common threads which in some conditions have been woven together quite tightly to produce a recognisable and distinctive youth strategy' (1986a). This weaving together has been restricted to a limited range of areas. Unlike a number of policy areas, such as housing, there has not been an unambiguous attempt to remove youth work functions from the local authorities. So although it is possible to interpret from the actions of the MSC a desire to manipulate policy at the local level this has to be set against the rearguard actions of the DES and educationalists, not least youth workers, to frustrate and fudge such incursions as threaten their relative autonomy. The MSC has paid the piper but found it incredibly difficult to call the tune.

An expansion of central state control significantly beyond the present scale in youth work is inhibited by the absence of funding and an administrative framework capable of monitoring and in-

specting practice. Such a framework would necessitate a restructuring of the whole departmental division of responsibilities at
both a national and a local level and the harmonisation of often
conflicting ideologies. Some have, naively, argued that such continuity and single-mindedness of purpose could be achieved by the
creation of a Ministry of Youth or Youth Affairs (Ewen, 1972).
This idea has a certain aura of timelessness about it, an attraction
based upon a belief that coordination can be achieved simply by an
amalgamation of disparate activities and functions under one
umbrella organisation. As the experience of the Minister for the
Disabled, who has a much smaller constituency and remit than a
Minister of Youth could expect, has shown, such artificial cre-
ations which fly in the face of the established administrative
structure are doomed to marginality. They neither control the
budgets nor have access to the key areas of decision-making.
Beyond this, the notion of the 'client-based' ministry simply fails
to dovetail with the dominant managerial and intellectual traditions which compartmentalise social policy by 'service area'.

The re-organisation of local government

If we consider the nature of local government reform during the
1960s and 1970s, in terms both of 'external' re-organisation (achieved
in 1974) and of 'internal' re-organisation following the Maud
Report (HMSO, 1967) and the Bains Report (HMSO, 1972), we
can note certain consequences of these dual processes, which have
a bearing on both the functioning of local government and/or its
political control.

Whilst details of the long process of reform which culminated
with the 1972 Local Government Act are covered in great depth
elsewhere (Wood, 1976), some important by-products can be
noted here. Firstly, one of the basic effects of the new system of
local government eshrined in the Act was to transfer 6.7 million
people (some 16 per cent of the population outside London) from
potentially Labour controlled county boroughs to mainly Tory
controlled shire counties. The new system saw 58 per cent of the
population of England and Wales living in areas of 'safe' Conservative control; the 'safe' Labour total was only around 20 per
cent. Such a change not only had political implications for working-
class control of local government, but it also had distributional

implications: the transfer of key functions (such as education and social welfare services) from high-spending urban authorities, usually Labour controlled, to low spending, quasi-rural and solidly Tory authorities (Dunleavy, 1980, pp. 89–90).

Secondly, the creation of larger authorities in the Act had, according to Dearlove (1979) the rationale of re-asserting a measure of control by business over the decisions of local government. Thus, larger and more powerful units of local administration would tackle the problem of 'declining councillor calibre' created by the withdrawal of business representatives from the council chamber. Service as a councillor was to be made more financially viable and more relevant to business interests. Moreover, the redrawing of boundaries to include the suburban hinterlands further enhanced business participation in local affairs. As Aims of Industry noted about the old boundaries: 'Given the present pattern of local authority boundaries and social structures in England, industrialists, directors and executives rarely live in local authorities where industry is situated, and are even more rarely represented on these authorities' (quoted in HMSO, 1969, p. 6). With larger local authority areas, this separation was reduced.

Along with changes to the structure and function of local authorities, came developments in the way in which decisions were made, both in terms of organisational structures and policy-making processes. While the resulting emphasis on corporate management and planning is discussed fully elsewhere (Stewart, 1974), it is important to note that the search for increased co-ordination, integration, and more rational planning of an authorities resources culminated in the creation of a crisp hierarchical structure based on the Council Leader, Chief Executive, Policy and Resource Committee, and Management Board (Rhodes 1979). This move had some problematic consequences. Firstly, the search for more 'rationality' in decision-making highlighted the problem of the decision-maker in defining exactly what a local 'need' entailed and who was to define this. Also, since a key concern within the rational model was to evaluate the best potential policy for implementation, it raised the issue of how monetary values, that is to say cost effectiveness could be injected into aesthetic and social programmes. And conversely, it showed that areas such as youth work would be detrimentally affected as a result.

Secondly, internal reform has also led to the exclusion of rank
and file councillors from decision-making. Cockburn (1977) has
pointed out how such management reforms had been transferred
from business corporations, where the centralisation of control in
the hands of a small board of directors and a chief executive may
be sound business sense, but whose utilisation in the public domain has negative consequences both for democratic accountability and for the quality of service provision. Corporate management
has been viewed both as contributing to the growth of a central
'policy elite' of key councillors and officers, and also as involving
the re-structuring of the local authority decision-making and
budgeting process. Thus concerns for efficiency and value for
money become paramount, and financial retrenchment is easier to
rationalise and implement (CSE State Group, 1979).

What emerges then, well before the age of monetarism and
privatisation, are changes in the nature of local government which
have crucially affected its functions, political composition and role
as a service-delivery agency committed to meeting local needs.

Moreover, since 1979, Conservative Administrations have
pushed through a concerted programme of privatisation. This has
been underpinned by an ideological view of state provision as an
inefficient, ineffective, and generally demeaning means of providing services to the public or of running the affairs of large industrial
concerns. Moreover, conventional wisdom has it that an active
state inevitably 'crowds out' and stifles private initiative, which is
an integral part of an entrepreneurial culture, and which contributes to individual enterprise and innovation. Obviously, local
government as a major provider of public services has been particularly drawn into the privatisation debate. We can note several
areas where the desire to inject private initiative into hitherto
publicly run services, have developed at the local level:

- contracting out services. Here the local authority, often under
  pressures from the centre, puts part of their work out to
  contract to private firms. Activities 'contracted out' include
  school meals, cleaning, parks maintenance, refuse collection,
  road maintenance, street cleaning and meals on wheels (Critical
  Social Policy, 1983);
- alternative or parallel private provision. Increasingly the private

sector is providing services directly to the public. Examples here include nursing homes and sheltered schemes for the elderly, the mentally ill and the disabled (Lawrence, 1983).

- the development of services provided by voluntary bodies. Some services have been increasingly placed in the hands of such bodies. There are a number of reasons for this including government policy, for example, towards council house building and housing associations; the ability of such bodies to tap other sources of finance; and employment considerations. Being a funder rather than a direct employer can have particular advantages to certain local authorities in terms of overheads and the 'handling' of industrial relations. Whilst the statutory/ voluntary relationship contains a number of contradictory trends within youth work (see Chapters 3 and 2), a number of organisations have been major beneficiaries of this trend, especially in the area of intermediate treatment.

Finally, these developments need to be seen against a background of the increasing influence of the business community at the local level. Not only are local authorities now forced to hold consultations with local business over the setting of the non-domestic rate, but areas such as planning, industrial development and tourism have witnessed an increasing role for organisations such as Chambers of Commerce in recent years. One example of this is the growth of enterprise trusts and agencies in the field of small firm development.

The context for youth work, then, is one of an increasingly 'rational' definition of needs, with the local input being eroded by financial, political and professional concerns emanating from the centre. This is linked to a tremendous squeeze upon the local provision of services, both from the central government cutbacks, and from efforts to contract out services to the private sector. Finally modern local government is under pressure to tailor its services, and open up its decision-making procedures more and more, to the business community. One can note certain possible developments for youth work within this overall context.

First, in a period where local, and particular community, interpretations of an authority's 'needs' are under increasing central pressure. The impact of professional notions and standards, particularly within the local bureaucracy, can be viewed as being crucial in the analysis and assessment of the youth work 'needs' of a locality. In this respect the role of the Inspectorate and CETYCW, in reinforcing and prosletysing particular interpretations of 'good practice', requires careful analysis (see Chapters 3 and 11).

Second, as a marginal service, in terms of expenditure, youth work can expect to be peripheral to debates relating to the budgets of the major spending departments of education, housing and personal social services.

Third, it is possible that 'statutory' youth work will come under increasing pressure from those who want to see the voluntary sector taking on more work and from the further developments within the MSC. However such moves pose major questions of accountability and control, particularly in the case of the latter. Indeed the way in which some voluntary and 'community' youth organisations have used public money has been a matter of concern to a number of officers (personal conversations with the authors). In some authorities this has resulted in changes in grant regulations and a concern to place resources into projects and units that are more easily controlled.

Fourth, if the trend towards centralisation continues, then it is likely that there will be mounting pressure brought to bear regarding variations in welfare and other expenditure between authorities. This will apply to both low spenders on youth work such as Cornwall and high spenders such as ILEA. Specifying how much of the Rate Support Grant given to local authorities can be spent upon different services according to some national criteria would bring about both a standardisation of welfare provision and a diminution in the degree of discretion that locally elected bodies have over the services for which they are responsible. It is to this which we will now turn.

The erosion of local financial autonomy

The last decade has witnessed a growing curtailment of local authorities' ability to raise and spend resources as they think fit. Indeed, more than any other issue, it is the shifting financial relationship between the centre and locality that is at the root of the bitter conflict that has characterised the last few years. At the outset we need to note the complexity of the finance debate which makes full comprehension difficult for the specialist, let alone the layperson. The purpose of this short section is to provide a simplified account of developments in recent years, and to locate them within the overall picture of declining autonomy.

A useful starting point for this discussion is the growth and decline of local authority spending in relation to GDP. In 1900 local authority spending consumed some 5 per cent of GDP, by 1950 this amounted to 9 per cent, in 1970 it was 15 per cent, and by 1976 local spending constituted 15.4 per cent of GDP. This amounted to nearly a third of all public expenditure. Local government had become 'big business'.

More particularly, the major increases in local spending tended to occur between the mid-1950s and the mid-1970s (Bridge, 1984). During the heyday of social democracy, local spending grew under the combined influence of central governments committed to the expansion of public services, and local authorities anxious to placate increased demands for such services emanating from social and demographic changes (Newton & Karran, 1984).

With local spending on the increase and authorities becoming more innovative in their use of resources, the relationship between central and local government was increasingly portrayed as a partnership. It was seen as a relationship of co-equals in which the expanding, innovative and vibrant local sector was to play a crucial role (Dunleavy & Rhodes, 1986).

Alongside the expansion of local spending went an increase in the amount of local income derived from central grants, and a concomitant reduction in the amount derived from local sources such as rates, rents and charges. As has been noted:

> Grants have grown steeply and steadily during the course of the last hundred years. In the 1900s they formed barely more than 10 per cent of grant and rate income. By the end of the First World War they were up to 25 per cent; by the end of the Second World War they were over 50 per cent. They reached their peak in the late 1970s when they contributed £2 for every £1 raised through the rates (Newton & Karran, 1984, pp. 73–4).

This change indicated not only that British local government has very limited means of raising its own resources, but that if central government is to impose new duties or insists on national minimum standards, then cash must be provided. However, the increased percentage of local spending financed from the centre not only reflected the growth of local functions, often at the centre's behest, but also reflected the structure of the grant system itself. Under the pre-1980 system, the indicator of 'need' was calculated on the basis of what the local authorities assessed was their requirement. This was then related to the local authorities' previous year's pattern of expenditure. It was, in terms of logic, a circular argument as grants were distributed according to needs, needs were revealed by expenditure and expenditure determined grants. Thus whilst grant distribution was locally determined, it was viewed as systematically encouraging high spending since under the system big spenders would receive big grants (Goldsmith & Newton, 1984).

Overall, up until the mid-1970s local authorities enjoyed considerable autonomy in raising and spending resources. However by 1977 the events had already occurred that were to lay the foundations for the bitter arguments over spending levels that were to characterise the 1980s. In the famous words of Labour's Environment Secretary, Anthony Crosland, in 1975, 'For the time being at least, the party's over'.

This remark to an assembly of local authority representatives highlighted the government's concern that local spending could not continue to spiral upwards during a period of intensifying economic crisis. The acceptance of an IMF loan in 1976 following the sharp rise in oil prices and the effect this and other factors had upon exchange rates and the balance of payments, led directly to cuts in public expenditure. Local spending, which amounted to almost a third of all public expenditure, was obviously a key target. The selection of local authorities as a target had the support of the Treasury which had long regarded local spending as something of an 'Achilles Heel' and in need of more central control (Goldsmith, 1985). Labour undertook to cut both current and capital spending by local authorities by a mixture of persuasion and coercion. The major instrument utilised was that of 'cash limits' designed to cut the volume of spending by setting the level of grant support without adjusting to inflation. Through this mechanism the volume of grant support fell by 15 per cent between 1975–6 and 1979–80. This was matched in the area of capital spending. Here rising interest rates had made borrowing considerably more expensive. By 1979 local spending accounted for 12.4

per cent of GDP (as opposed to 15.4 per cent in 1976); it absorbed 28 per cent of all public expenditure as opposed to 32 per cent in 1976; while in the years between 1975–6 and 1978–9 the highest overspend was 1.8 per cent in the final year.

The election of a Conservative government in 1979 did involve an element of continuity in the attempt to restrict local spending in total. However, the challenge to the scope and very functions of local administration itself, and the accompanying changes in the basis of local–central negotiations and bargaining, did mark the onset of a new era. The Conservative approach since 1979 combines a mixture of old style Toryism and modern libertarian thinking, and views local government as 'wasteful, profligate, irresponsible, unaccountable, luxurious and out of control' (Newton & Karran, 1984, p. 116).

Along with organised labour, local authorities have been singled out by the New Right as the major offenders on the modern 'road to serfdom'. Four issues can be mentioned in this respect. Firstly, the desire to cut local spending is tied to the government's monetarist view that inflation is the central problem, and money supply the key variable to control. Thus the Public Sector Borrowing Requirement (PSBR), to which local authorities contribute, must be reduced to lower the rate of inflation.

Secondly, following the argument of Bacon & Eltis (1976), modern Tories stress how the role of local government as employer, spender and an agency of taxation, 'crowds out' the private sector, starving it of both human and capital resources. Such an argument, of course, is based upon the dubious premise that public spending is intrinsically unproductive and local government a major waste of resources; in contrast private spending is seen as intrinsically productive.

Thirdly, the increasing burden on non-domestic ratepayers, particularly local manufacturers, is viewed as making a significant contribution to closure and job loss. It is also seen as a hurdle to entrepreneurial activity amongst the British workforce.

Lastly, local authorities are viewed as threatening personal freedom and engendering unhealthy dependency, whilst discouraging the development of self-help, self-reliance and individual liberty. The concomitant desire to 'roll back the state' has, at the local level, involved such measures as the selling-off of council housing, the 'contracting out' of particular services, the reduction of the scale of direct labour organisations and the increased use of the private sector in areas such as the social services.

This view of local government has underpinned the vast changes that have taken place since 1979 in the relationship between central and local government and posed a serious challenge to the autonomy of the latter. The 1980 Local Government Planning and Land Act marked a fundamental shift in the way in which local spending was to be financed. Firstly, the previous 'needs' assessment in the Block Grant was replaced by GREAs (Grant Related Expenditure Assessments). This judgement of an individual authority's 'need to spend' was to be calculated via a complex formula by Department of Environment officials. This transfer of responsibility from the local authority to central government raised the criticism that non-elected officials in Whitehall were now deemed to be better placed to assess the needs of an authority than its councillors and officers. Moreover, such assessments are far from being scientific indicators of need. Indeed the initial factors used to assess needs such as miles of roads, numbers of school children, and numbers of houses in poor condition, largely ignored the number of people unemployed. Authorities with high unemployment rates and the associated increased demand for certain services were not adequately remunerated under the GREA system. As Greenwood notes, 'The GREA have a spurious appearance of accuracy when in fact they are based upon an element of subjective assessment' (1982, p. 261).

Secondly, as a consequence of the 1980 Act, authorities who overshot their 'thresholds', that is to say, who spent in excess of 10 per cent of their GREA figure, would have their grant reduced. The greater their overspending, the more local authorities would have to fall back on their rate income. However, the cuts in spending that the government hoped would materialise from the legislation, were a long time in coming. In 1981–2 local authorities overspent by 8.7 per cent, with many Labour councils (elected in 1981) showing little inclination to reduce spending. Meanwhile, several Tory authorities, now aware they were now spending well under their GREA figure, increased their expenditure in order to take account of the amount that the government deemed they needed. This led in 1982 to the Local Government Finance Act, which aimed to close the loopholes of previous legislation. Through this Act the Secretary of State for the Environment acquired the power to hold back parts of a local authority grant which were deemed to constitute overspending. Clause 12 of the Act, in addition, enabled the government to withdraw grant during the financial year. This was achieved by the application of the 'multiplier', whereby the specific authority's grant entitlement would be multiplied by a figure of less than one. In addition, local authorities were prevented from making good any loss of grant by levying of a supplementary rate during the course of a financial year.

The introduction of these measures after 1982 did begin to make a dent in local expenditure totals. By 1983–4 the overspend was down to 3.3 per cent. However, the government continued to argue that expenditure levels were excessive, and, in particular, that rate increases were a considerable burden on citizens and the business community. So in 1984 additional legislation was introduced to allow the Secretary of State to 'cap' the rates (fix the rate level) for overspending authorities. All but one of the 18 councils listed for rate-capping in 1984–5 and the 10 re-selected in 1985–6 (plus 2 newcouncils) were Labour controlled.

By 1986 the situation had reached a point where central government had 'complete control over expenditure and rate levels in individual authorities' (Goldsmith, 1985, p. 150). This reflects a sharp break with the 'indirect' attempts to affect grant level and distribution prior to 1980; the politics of local finance in the 1980s is one of direct intervention to control spending and taxation. Concern with the latter is seen in the Green Paper, *Paying for Local Government* (HMSO, 1986). This advocates the centralisation of the non-domestic rate and the replacement of domestic rates by a flat-rate tax on all adults. These proposals, adopted by the conservatives in their 1987 Election Manifesto and already implemented in Scotland, not only severs the link between the services business benefits from locally and the contribution they make towards them; but also involves the widening of the tax net to include people currently exempt from rate charges and income tax, and who lack any independent source of income (Hughes, 1986). Further the mechanism for levying this charge via the voting register will offer a disincentive for 'non-household' young people to register or be registered. As such this mechanism threatens to disenfranchise large numbers of those with low incomes and un-waged young people.

In conclusion

This chapter has highlighted the decline in the autonomy of local authorities and the concurrent pressures for privatisation. When this is set alongside the front-line nature of youth work provision and the extent to which youth groups are self-resourcing and associational in structure, it can be seen that the room for manoeuvre of local authorities is limited. Crucially, however, local authorities do retain a degree of discretion in the deployment of the full-time and part-time labour force and have sought to increase their control in this area. Yet it is important to note how the tensions in this situation may be manifested in the development of policy.

Firstly, the pressure for privatisation may result in a growing amount of youth provision being 'contracted out' or 'left' to commercial concerns. Here we are not simply talking about services such as cleaning and catering but of whole areas of direct provision. Central to this is the growing profile of 'leisure' in many of the debates about youth work. Roberts has argued that the 'growth of leisure' favours greater diversity of public and commercial provisions and that this means a more limited role for all specialised agencies (1983, p. 179). In the commercial sector we have seen the development of 'theme pubs', specialised sporting clubs, night clubs, domestic based activities such as computing and video, and machine halls – all aimed at young people. In many respects they offer very similar activities and services to those offered within, say, youth clubs and centres. However, they do so often with a much higher degree of technical sophistication; an atmosphere and ethos which attempts to have the users feel adult; a pricing structure which covers costs and makes profits; and a view of the world unencumbered with notions of 'improvement'. Their attraction to young people is obvious and could become increasingly so to local authorities keen to divest themselves of responsibility for substantial pieces of decaying plant and for aspects of a service which commercial interests have been able to provide at no 'cost' to the public purse. Any lingering concern about improvement or young people's safety could be handled through licencing systems, financial inducements and, perhaps, the attachment of youth workers to commercial provision. Indeed, in the case of the latter, it has been a concern with profitability which has sometimes fired a demand for youth work intervention, as for example, in the case of the deployment of detached workers in some shopping precincts. Whilst it might be that 'privatisation' would recommend itself more to Conservative administrations, there are still substantial attractions to those tied to the idea of municipal provision, particularly in a situation where there are other powerful demands for resources such as housing, care of, and provision for, the elderly, and education.

Secondly, we need to consider the impact of debates around the notions of welfare pluralism and community care. The desire to locate many welfare services in the community, whether on grounds of cost, or concern to de-institutionalise services or some idea of citizen participation, has grown in recent years. For example Hadley & Hatch (1981) have argued that state welfare services tend to be over-centralised and bureaucratised and would benefit from a policy of more localised decision making and involvement by local people. The 'patch system' in social work (Hadley & McGrath, 1980) and neighbourhood policies of a number of Labour councils (Seabrook, 1984) have been examples of this. Voluntary organisations, with their associational structure, have not been slow to make a case for themselves in this respect. In youth work, where the bulk of provision is made through the medium of voluntary and community organisations, there have been calls for further 'voluntarisation' (NAYC, 1981, p. 46). Within IT there has been a substantial provisioning of voluntary organisations in order to undertake work. Just how attractive this option is, in the context of the debates about local government outlined here, is a matter for some conjecture. In a number of local authorities attention has been focused upon developing funding and review arrangements which give voluntary organisations a more appropriate degree of accountability to their local authority funders. This may involve more rigourous inspections, the submission of more detailed reports and the inclusion of local authority representatives on governing bodies. It is possible that work could be increasingly contracted out in the manner described in respect of commercial organisations. However, this runs counter to much of the current tide of concern relating to the enhancement of line-management and the attempts to centralise the control of significant areas of youth work (see Chapter 2).

Lastly, we need to consider the impact of declining local authority autonomy upon those local authorities whose administrations would appear be sympathetic to radical ideas and approaches. As we have already seen, the notion that it is possible to develop a radical utopia within a particular area of welfare is, on past evidence, doomed to failure. In many respects the same fate awaits those who attempt such a project based on some administrative area. Such authorities are constrained by central government financially, legally, and administratively as well as bounded by 'nationalised' notions of 'good practice'. In youth work they have to engage with long-established traditions of work and with powerful voluntary organisations. Crucially, delivery of the service is through front-line units who retain a large degree of discretion. At the same time youth workers, like any others, have to deal with the imperatives of the capitalist system. Inevitably freedom of manouevre will be heavily constrained. Whilst, on the whole, Labour authorities are higher spenders on youth work and have often been host to more radical initiatives, the tide pulls ever more strongly towards centralisation and national uniformity. As in so many other areas of welfare, for local authority youth work the key dynamic is provided by a central state that feels threatened and uncomfortable with devolved power and local autonomy.

5

Youth Work and Schooling

TONY JEFFS and MARK SMITH

Much early youth work was established to offer a partial compensation for inadequate or non-existent schooling. As a consequence not only did many of the pioneering clubs boast such facilities as libraries and reading rooms, but it was also not unknown for them to engage in what now might be designated remedial education. In addition youth clubs, groups and uniformed organisations sought to offer a diet of games, sports, cultural activities and hobbies that were to a large extent woefully absent from the Board Schools. These activities were viewed as valuable in themselves and, it was believed, they would also constitute an inducement capable of drawing young people to agencies that sought to convert them, rescue them and mould them. An approach well encapsulated within the following comment of Baden-Powell, but which could equally have been voiced by a representative of almost any mass youth movement of the period, 'We . . . are credited with supplying for the boy who has not had the same chance as one brought up in a Public School an equivalent character training, especially in the directions of responsibility and discipline' (1918). Inevitably the relationship between the schools and youth work agencies that underpinned that assessment and modus operandi has altered during the intervening period. In particular reforms within the school system have had a continuous and continuing impact on youth agencies, statutory and voluntary alike.

The changing relationship between schools and the Youth Service

For the purposes of this chapter three changes and reforms need to be examined at the onset. The first is the introduction within the state school system of a progressively more liberal and expansive curriculum. Over time this has meant that the youth 'club is no longer the only place where young people can express their creativity' (Matthews, 1975, p. 69). Indeed it has partially been in order to accommodate the new elements of the curricula and teaching styles that schools have had to undergo a physical restructuring. The mass school building programme of the post-war period has meant that, although grim relics of the earlier Victorian and Edwardian eras linger, the majority of secondary schools have acquired sports facilities, specialist art and drama rooms and the like. Such facilities almost invariably eclipse those encountered within even the best equipped youth centres and clubs. To an extent these curricular changes have also led to activities once viewed by young people as recreational becoming re-designated as compulsory 'subjects' within the timetable and therefore to be avoided outside of school hours. For as one study has found 'pupils from all ability ranges tended to reject the types of activities promoted by the school in their own free time' (Hendry, 1986, p. 40). The re-structuring of the school curriculum has also meant that for those young people with an interest in a particular sport or pastime it has become exceptional for them to perceive the Youth Service as the medium through which that commitment can or may be expressed. Indeed those young people commited to such activities, often as a consequence of guidance from the school, now seek out sports clubs and or the growing number of sports centres, or specialist groups and adult education provision, much of which may be linked to schools. Thus the Youth Service has only marginally, if at all, been the beneficiary of the rising levels of participation in sports and other leisure activities amongst young people during the course of the last two decades. Indeed in so far as that growth has shifted the focus from the traditional male-orientated youth club sports such as football, towards participation in those 'indoor sports, encouraged by the sports centres' (Roberts, 1983, p. 29), it has further eroded the 'pulling power' of the Youth Service. At the same time it has in part strengthened, albeit instrumentally, affiliation to the school as the sports and recreational facilities located within that institution become used by a growing number of young people outside of traditional school hours. Indeed the evidence suggests that the linking of sports and community facilities to school premises has encouraged heightened levels of participation in sports amongst young people in their late teens (Sports Council, 1977) – a group that overwhelmingly reject the fare on offer from the Youth Service.

Secondly, the relationship between schools, schooling and the Youth Service has further been reconstructed by the lengthening of the period of compulsory school attendance and the burgeoning rates of voluntary staying on in pursuit of qualifications. Inevitably as a consequence of these two shifts the proportion of young people affiliated to the Youth Service who are attending school has escalated. In line with this the *raison d'être* for the Service has had to be re-phrased in order to justify an autonomous existence. In particular it has been forced to re-assess its primary function. The earlier emphasis upon the remedial and 'child-saving' has been increasingly jettisoned and supplanted. By the post-war period a proclaimed contribution towards ensuring a smooth transition from school to employment had emerged. However that fiction has in turn been blown by the emergence of mass youth unemployment and to a lesser extent by the substantive rise in the numbers entering full-time post-school education. As noted in Chapter 2 the appearance of large-scale youth unemployment has in particular stimulated the expansion of MSC-linked schemes which have clearly usurped the transitional role coveted by the Youth Service. Inevitably this has meant that the Service has become uncomfortably trapped between the millstones of full-time educational institutions and the MSC. Survival has therefore increasingly depended upon the provision of a leisure service for those too young, too unsophisticated, too poor or too isolated to secure an alternative. As a growing number of HMI Reports on the Youth Service have indicated, it may well now as a consequence be catering for a clientele of which in the region of 90 per cent are in full-time, overwhelmingly school-located, education: 'The most striking point from the large number of visits made is that by far the highest proportion of those attending youth clubs and other youth units is under 14 years old, with many of those in the village clubs aged under 12' (DES, 1986a, p. 4; see also DES, 1986b; Welsh Office, 1986a; Welsh Office, 1986b). With a clientele possessing such a profile the rationale for a predominately free-standing and autonomous Youth Service has inevitably become ever more difficult to sustain. Certainly it cannot now seriously claim to provide comparable services and facilities to those offered by the school or college for, in the elitist terminology of the Albemarle Report (HMSO, 1960), those 'whose intellectual equipment has not been sufficient to keep them under the comfortable umbrella of full-time education' (p. 36). Yet this was the paramount justification for the retention and expansion of an 'independent' service. Equally in tatters is the subsequent expectation of the Fairbairn-Milson Report (DES, 1969) that the first priority must be to cater for the needs of those 'young people who have left school and whose social environment is inadequate' (p. 2). For not only does it have diminishing levels of contact with those young people but it also has never possessed the personnel, expertise or resources to cater for their needs at even the most rudimentary level.

Finally, account must be taken of the growth of 'pastoral care' and counselling services within the secondary school sector. To a marked extent this has flowed from the introduction of comprehensive schools which are obliged to cater for a disparate body of young people who are as a consequence less likely to be drawn from homogeneous communities and ethnic backgrounds; and all of whom will be located somewhere along a far more protracted continuum of ability. The Grammar, Secondary Modern and Special schools felt secure in allowing the problems of pupils and the needs for counselling to be met, except in extremis, by form teachers. Such a hit-and-miss and largely informal approach could not, as Judge (1984) notes, survive intact in the more complex generally larger comprehensives that tended to become the norm. Although Dawson (1981) may be exaggerating when he claims that the development of pastoral care is the distinctive contribution and achievement of the comprehensive system, nevertheless there has occured a concomitant advance. Inevitably, within a substantially de-centralised system the mechanisms for the delivery of pastoral support vary enormously from school to school as do the levels of commitment on the part of staff and the resources allotted. Yet once again the school has the ability to offer its students, and to an extent its ex-students, a range and quality of support and counselling that can rarely be matched by a Youth Service overwhelmingly staffed by part-time workers. To begin with, the institution operates for many more hours in the year and also theoretically has the wherewithal and status to mobilise resources more effectively where required. Of course the self-evident flaw in this model is that the school itself may well be the problem for many young people and the pastoral system can as a consequence be compromised and restricted as to the support and help it can offer. A weakness with this critique is that it is so often constructed upon a one-dimensional analysis of the internal workings of the school, failing to take account of the extent to which personality and more importantly ideology come to create divisions and conflict within schools (see for example Fletcher *et al.*, 1985; Gordon, 1986). Inevitably school students comprehend the existence of these groupings and the eddies, flows and undercurrents of staff relations; learning the survival skill of expoiting these to their own advantage, where and when required. Further, when cognisance is taken of the relatively low status of the Youth Service and the distance of the non-school based sector from the source of the problem it can be seen that that sector of the Service is rarely able to intervene effectively in this setting on behalf of a client. Indeed the cases where that occurs are exceedingly rare given the communality of the client group. As a consequence it can be argued that if such interventions are required it is more likely that they will be forthcoming from those youth workers who are school-based and therefore possess a ready entré to the institution and the inside knowledge to negotiate the pathways to the source of the conflict. Clearly the assumed weakness that a presence within the school compromises the professional integrity of the youth work cannot be dismissed, but in the absence of hard evidence neither should it be considered a self-evident reality.

Teachers in youth work

In terms of personnel there has been a continuous thread linking the Youth Service to the school sector as a consequence of shared staffing. The Youth Service has historically been dependent upon teachers as a significant provider of both full- and part-time labour. As Poster (1977) notes in this respect in Cambridgeshire during the early 1950s schoolteachers were:

> often the mainstay of the voluntary organisations and the county clubs, but this was the natural consequence of their concern for

young people, not a part of their professional expertise. . . . I can recall running a Youth Drama Group and taking young people from 14 to 19 on trips abroad, while other colleagues on the staff were running village youth clubs, Young Farmers Clubs, sports teams and similar activities . . . certainly if they had not taken responsibility for youth work, nobody else would have done so. Professional youth workers were so thin on the ground that I cannot in all honesty remember having met one in the six years I taught in a village college (p. 7).

Teachers, as a consequence of their status as the qualified 'experts' in working with young people and as the possessors of above average leisure time inevitably come to play a key role in the Service. That historic position of being to an extent the first amongst equals, when set alongside the mass of untrained, unqualified and unpaid volunteers, has never totally been eroded. The spread of car ownership and the escalating stratification of the housing market do mean that fewer and fewer teachers live within the catchment areas of the schools in which they work, especially where those schools are located within predominately working-class neighbourhoods. As a consequence teachers tend now to play a much less prominent role within the communities served by their school. They certainly figure much less prominently on the management committees and similar bodies of statutory and voluntary units. Even in rural communities they rarely play a disproportionate role or come to be looked upon as a potential catalyst for community development (Comber, 1981; Forsythe, 1983). The 'privatised mobility' described by Williams (1983) has largely destroyed those interlocking networks affectionately recalled by Poster. It should not therefore be assumed that the paid youth worker has driven out the volunteer. Indeed to a large extent it is apparent that payment has been required to compensate for the disappearance of that sort of commitment amongst teachers. The fading of a teacher presence in one arena should not be axiomatically taken as an indication that they have eschewed 'voluntary' work. Certainly Monks (1968) found that 60 per cent of teachers were involved in extra-curricular activities. Since that research was carried out industrial action has undoubtedly disrupted and curtailed many established patterns of extra-curricular activity on the part of teachers. Irrespective of the impact of conflict with employers, a trend of far greater import has been, we suspect, the re-locating of that commitment from the external, informal and largely voluntary arena to the setting of the school itself. Much of the pressure for this re-location has accompanied the development of community schools. Formalised at the administrative level in the personage of community teachers, tutors and flexible time-tables yet crucially dependent also upon an assumed voluntary contribution on the part of teachers to school-linked clubs, projects and educational programmes (see for example accounts in Rennie, 1985; also Allen *et al.*, 1987).

The linkage between youth work and the teaching profession was embodied at a more formalised level within the McNair Report (HMSO, 1944). This was the first official attempt to address the question of the structure and content of the training and qualification of full-time youth workers. It sought to build upon the key role played by teachers within the Service. In particular, it and a number of subsequent official and semi-official documents argued for inter-changeability between the professions of youth worker and teacher, stressing that without parity in terms of qualifications, youth workers would inevitably come to occupy a subordinate professional status to that of teachers. This was a view that was clearly shared by the Albemarle Committee (HMSO, 1960). This perceived important advantages in the large-scale recruitment of teachers to the Youth Service, not least because it promised a means of securing a constant through-put of personnel. Staff would be able to move into youth work and then return to school-teaching taking with them the skills and experience gathered during that relatively brief sorjourn. These attributes would make them attractive to employers and would in particular equip them to work with the older and less 'academically inclined' pupils and students both in schools and the then planned County Colleges.

Thus it was envisaged that, for the majority, full-time youth work would be a brief career, with a teaching qualification providing the passport out. Not only would this hopefully secure a youthful front-line workforce but it would also theoretically ensure that the career ladder of the Youth Service itself would be left uncluttered for the more mature entrants from industry and part-time voluntary youth work. It was overwhelmingly the latter who would possess the less negotiable youth and community certificate.

For this group the potential route out of face-to-face work, with its unsociable hours and isolation, was to be the beckoning Youth Officer posts. Of course such plans could hardly be expected to come neatly to fruition. Not least because many teachers chose to climb the Youth Service hierarchy rather than return to teaching or in some instances enter it for the first time. Not least because they often found that their degrees and three-year Certificates gave them a clear advantage over colleagues from the non-graduate one or two-year Youth and Community Certificate courses. As comprehensivisation led to the amalgamation of the Secondary Modern with Grammar Schools which had overwhelmingly been staffed by graduates; as the plans for County Colleges were torn up; and as teacher glut gradually superceded famine; so a return or initial entry into school teaching became both more problematic and less attractive for teachers in the Youth Service. This decline in intra-professional mobility has however been tempered by the expansion in school-based youth provision. Certainly Ritchie (1984) found evidence that qualified teachers employed in this setting were far more likely to move into teaching posts than those in the 'mainstream Youth Service'. This is perhaps not suprising as those who sought to retain links with schools would self-evidently be attracted to such posts and equally a school posting promised opportunities for lateral career movements.

Further it should be recognised that a significantly high proportion, 40 per cent according to the Ritchie survey, of teachers who entered the Youth Service between 1969 and 1979 remained. Therefore although the teacher presence within the Service may to some degree have shifted its location it has not overall seriously diminished with the passing of the post-Albemarle years. Indeed, according to Kuper (1985), of the full-time Youth Service staff in post during 1983 43 per cent were qualified teachers compared to only 27 per cent who had received specialist training. This represented an increase of in excess of 50 per cent in the presence of the former in little over a decade. Finally, it should not be overlooked that for employers and the government the widespread use of teachers has and still offers another advantage: namely, enabling them to side-step the necessity of creating and funding the requisite number of Initial Training places. Particularly for employers that remains an attractive option.

In the decades since Albemarle the continuing absence of serious investment in the Initial Training of youth and community workers and the linked failure to legislate a mandatory grant for students has meant the Service either by oversight or by design has been and will continue to remain dependent upon attracting significant numbers of teachers to fill its posts. Although the automatic right of teachers to secure recognition as qualified youth and community workers with the DES has been revoked, and the B. Ed. courses which offer a youth work module have been phased out, this will of course not lead either to professional closure or to the construction of a ringed-fence securing the Youth Service against further teacher incursion. Firstly because, as we argue elsewhere (Jeffs & Smith, 1987a), the Certificate in Youth and Community work lacks credibility with many employers when set besides the degrees and postgraduate qualifications of teachers and the CQSWs of social workers. Secondly, and not unrelated to a lack of faith in the efficacy of the designated qualification, those who wish or need to employ teachers can and will simply change their criterion for appointment by the re-designation of posts. Indeed, attempts to achieve closure may well encourage the very trends it is designed to contain through the encouragement of school-based posts.

It would be misleading to concentrate on the full-time youth work role played by those qualified as teachers to the exclusion of the numerically much more substantive contribution they make via the medium of part-time voluntary and paid work. This cross-over has always sustained an important link between the Youth Service and the school sector. The extent of employment has fluctuated over time, not least as a consequence of changes in the age structure of the teaching profession. Under the impact of falling school rolls and consequent reductions in the size of the teaching force, linked to substantive cutbacks in the outflow of teachers from the training agencies, the average age of the profession has risen. As consequence of the greying of the teaching profession the numbers involved in voluntary youth work appear to have declined alongside the volume employed in free-standing units and centres. However other factors need to be taken into account, in particular the extent to which the volume of teacher involvement has traditionally responded sharply to movements in the purchasing power of teacher salaries. More recently it has declined in a number of areas as a consequence of the, often unilateral, policy decisions of Youth Officers to employ on a part-time basis, where possible, those unable to secure full-time work. One North-East LEA has as a consequence of such a policy reduced the proportion of their part-time sessions allotted to teachers over a five-year period from 60 per cent to below 40 per cent. However the impact of all these factors must be set alongside the vogue for locating youth work within school premises. This appears to have encouraged in many localities an escalation in terms of the involvement of both teachers and ancillary staff such as caretaking, catering and maintenance staff. Further, in some instances, the use of school premises has undoubtedly led to headteachers exerting pressure on staff to undertake youth work. This is principally, one suspects, as a means of monitoring the use of the facilities and the behaviour of the pupils, whilst ensuring that the interests of the school are represented by someone 'accountable' to the school hierarchy. Young staff are especially vulnerable to the argument put by a head to a teacher, interviewed by one of the authors, that 'running the youth club will help get you a scale post'.

Although clearly substantial, the scale of teacher involvement is difficult to gauge with any accuracy. Kendra (1985) in an examination of Basic Training courses for part-time youth workers found the proportion of teachers varied within the ten LEAs between 25 per cent and 7.3 per cent. In contrast, Jeffs (1976) in a much more limited survey of a Basic Training Course in one LEA found the proportion to be 37 per cent. Interestingly, this study was carried out in an LEA with a well-established tradition of school-based youth work largely located within community schools. Thus it may be tentatively argued that such provision can generate heightened teacher involvement. In contrast, where positive discrimination policies are given a high priority then the proportion of teachers may sharply decline. Fisher & Day (1983) in their report of a training project for Afro-Caribbean part-time youth and community workers showed a complete absence of teachers in the cohort. The limited evidence would thus tend to indicate substantive variations in the numbers of teachers involved between and even within localities.

Irrespective of the motives, teacher involvement has always ensured that there resides within the profession a considerable reservoir of experience of youth work. This coupled with the

number of teachers who are trained and qualified full-time youth
workers makes it almost predictable that Venables (1971) found
little in the way of attitudinal conflict and a great deal of mutual
respect between the two professional groupings. However this
should not be assumed to be a permanent feature, least of all
within Community Schools. Certainly one research project encountered in that setting 'numerous examples . . . of problems
which have occurred as a result of the two professional groups
working in isolation from one another' (Aberdeen University,
undated, p. 2). Whilst Nisbet *et al*, (1980) argued in the light of
their research that teachers and community education workers
possess differing perspectives and 'conflicting ideologies' (p. 111).
In similar vein Welton (1985) reports that schools recorded higher
levels of contact with youth workers than any other welfare professionals, apart from school nurses, but he noted disproportionately
higher levels of dissatisfaction with their levels of performance.
Perhaps not surprisingly, then, a number of reports and published
accounts of school-based youth work stress the existence of serious
conflict between young people and other users, youth and community workers and other staff, and a general lack of sensitivity on
the part of the 'school' staff towards youth work (Kirby, 1985;
Dunlop, 1985; Whitehead, 1985; Fletcher, 1984). However these
accounts do not amount to an all-embracing condemnation of
school-based youth work or community school youth provision;
not least because they can be juxtaposed to accounts of successful
provision and integration (Webley, 1971; Linnel, 1983; Dybeck,
1981; Thompson, 1983; Whitehead, 1985). The overriding impression that perhaps can be gained from a reading of both sets of
literature is that success or failure for school-based work can
disproportionately be attributable to two factors. Firstly, the design and structure of the premises, with certain forms of layout
leading to intolerable tension between different user groups or
professionals. Secondly the personalities involved and in particular
the attitude of the headteacher towards youth work (Stone, 1987).
This is of course an unsatisfactory situation and one that can be
especially fraught for the youth workers involved, both full- and
part-time. But this is a reflection of the current distribution of
power and responsibility within the school system, a distribution
that locates within the office of the headteacher a totally disproportionate ability to shape the ethos of a given school. That so

much hinges upon the personality, attitude, ideology and disposition of one person, who is barely accountable to anyone, is perhaps simultaneously the Achilles Heel of school-based youth work and an obstacle to the further development of community schools. However, on balance, given the history of conflict within other settings which has surrounded the management of youth projects and units, school-based youth work does not seem overly accident-prone. Indeed in many cases the quality of provision and the levels of contact have been improved by closer line-management from the on-site Principal or Head. Equally, just as the presence of 'adults' has liberalised the atmosphere permeating community schools, so the impact of school-based youth work and youth workers should not be underestimated. Such achievements should not be lightly dismissed nor ignored and given the relatively short history of integrated provision need to built upon, rather than discarded.

School premises and youth work

The use of school buildings as a venue for youth work has long been a necessity. Indeed, so essential is access to school premises in many localities that the closure of a school can lead to the disappearance of youth provision owing to the absence of a suitable alternative (Bell, 1982). The levels of usage have certainly increased in recent years. The most recent national survey shows that 29 per cent of primary schools and 55 per cent of secondary schools are regularly used by the Youth Service as a venue (DES, 1985c). This compares with an earlier survey which gave figures of 22 per cent for primary schools and 46 per cent for secondary (DES, 1982c). The proliferation in the employment of school premises in part reflects the pressure upon LEAs to maximise the utilisation of the resources at their disposal and to raise income and reduce expenditure under other budgets. In addition it represents a by-product of the fall in school rolls which endows many schools with the 'space' to open up their facilities. Nevertheless the trend also bespeaks a sharp but unspoken reversal in policy. The free-standing, autonomous youth centres with their full-time leaders were in many ways the jewel in the Albemarle crown. They and the expansion of Initial Training were the tangible legacies of that Report and virtually the exclusive focus for the investment it justified. Certainly prior to Albemarle:

> most clubs had met in school halls and buildings owned largely by religious bodies. Few had premises over which leaders and members had direct control or exclusive use. . . . From 1960 onwards the Youth Service was to become not just a building-based service, but one located in new buildings, requiring large premises with full-time staff (Parkinson, 1987, p. 16).

The failure of these 'Albemarle Centres' to live up to expectations has led a drift back to the school, but on new terms. The free-standing centres have become increasingly marginalised, expensive to maintain and unpopular with young people. Also, many were inevitably built in the localities where young people were concentrated in 1960. Subsequent demographic movements have all too often left them stranded in districts with declining or ageing populations. As a consequence the bulk of purpose-built youth facilities opened since the initial post-Albemarle era has been in the shape of youth wings attached to secondary schools and in some cases FE colleges and middle and primary schools. By 1985, 16 per cent of secondary schools possessed youth wings which in addition to functioning as youth centres were also frequently employed during the day as a school or community resource (DES, 1985c).

The case for school based youth work

The case for the greater integration of youth work within the school system has to an extent gone by the board, not least within youth work literature. This body of writing has almost overwhelmingly been hostile to the expansion of school-based youth work. Yet in the light of this opposition it would be mistaken to view this re-location as predominantly the by-product of penny-pinching on the part of LEAs. For such developments have flowed also from the advocacy of writers such as Mays (1965) who have maintained that:

> It is only by centring family social services and youth welfare and leisure activities on the school that we can hope to avoid the

obvious error of trying to deal with individuals in isolation, or with single families in a piecemeal fashion (p. 75).

This approach is of course an echo of that espoused by Henry Morris (1924) and which led directly to the creation of the Cambridgeshire Village Colleges, the forerunners of the contemporary community schools and colleges. Certainly it also underpinned the contribution of Fairbairn to the YSDC report, *Youth and Community Work in the 1970s* (HMSO, 1969). This document added considerable momentum to the expansion of both school-based youth provision and community schools. The multiplication of school-based provision must therefore be seen as representing in many areas a positive policy choice rather than merely a pragmatic response to declining resources. As a consequence it is important not to let the case for school-based work go by default.

Firstly, it is argued that the location of youth work within schools has given young people access to resources that are over-whelmingly superior to those encountered in purpose-built youth centres. The sports halls, theatres, libraries, specialist rooms for the arts and crafts and the access to smaller rooms and lounges have also offered the curriculum of youth work much-needed breadth. They have provided a rare opportunity to expand beyond the narrow confines imposed by the paucity of space and equipment found within the majority of youth centres. Further, as Hall (1983) argues in the context of anti-racist work, though it is self-evidently a case that could be applied to other often-neglected aspects of youth work, the purpose-built community school enjoys an almost unique potential:

> to provide a variety of forums, conferences, debates and courses to help white society increase its sensitivity, awareness and understanding of the issues and to develop practical ways of defeating racism in whatever form it takes (p. 77).

This access to the specialist facilities and staff clearly has the capacity to enable the youth work curriculum more effectively to shed much of the current male orientation and cultural chauvinism that taints and constrains it.

Secondly, advocates of school-based youth work argue that it has gone some way towards eroding much of the traditional and damaging distance that has existed between the Youth Service and mainstream education provision, and between individual youth workers and teachers – a divide that becomes less defensible as the communality of the clientele grows. Unification can be beneficial to all parties, not least for teaching staff who may 'thrive in the youth centre environment' which can open up 'considerable areas for experiment, essentially for teachers with an informal approach, skilled in relating topics to the personal needs and experience of young people' (Webley, 1971, pp. 145–6). Thus the presence of youth workers and the provision of a youth programme may, advocates have maintained, lead to improved pedagogy, greater relevance within the curriculum and perhaps most importantly a more harmonious atmosphere within the school and between the school and the community. What Kidd calls 'the playback towards the school' which also leads to a 'changed attitude of the community towards the school, its staff and its youth centre' (Kidd, 1972, p. 19).

Thirdly, for youth workers integration within the school can generate the removal of much longstanding ambiguity over management roles and function. Once youth workers become members of the school staff they are less likely to be trapped in a void between management committees, local authority officers, clients and other agencies. Instead they acquire an unambiguous location within a clearly defined management structure. The Secondary Headteachers' Association has suggested that such integration will offer youth workers the 'strength, security and career structure . . . that is to the mutual benefit of those involved' (1979, p. 177). Linked to this is the argument that as a by-product of integration the youth worker and youth provision may be protected to a much greater extent from the vagaries of local authority decision-making, particularly with regard to resource allocation. In a climate where cuts are the order of the day, size does offer an element of safety; one that youth workers would be unwise to dismiss in a peremptory fashion.

Fourthly, the integration of youth work within the school provides a unique opportunity for the youth worker to make contact with both actual and potential clientele. Through the school doors will pass the majority, if not virtually all, of the young people living in a given catchment area. The youth worker as a consequence is blessed with an unparalleled opportunity to meet those young people, to unearth their needs and wants and where feasible to respond in a positive fashion. In particular, via the school setting, it becomes possible to make contact with those young people who would, for whatever reason, feel reluctant to enter the 'average' neighbourhood youth club. As Shillito (1986) highlights, unemployed young women and especially young black women do not relate to such provision and attempts to make contact with them via detached work are difficult and highly labour-intensive. It is especially in relation to such long-neglected client groups as these that links can be forged in the school setting and for whom the facilities of the purpose-built community school may be far more suited than those of the traditional male-orientated unit. Certainly in the case of young women, in the 16–19 and the 20–9 age ranges, the participation rates for school-based leisure classes and activities is already higher than involvement with the Youth Service and interestingly in most categories, apart from outdoor sports, equals or exceeds that for males (OPCS, 1986).

Finally, school-based youth work may not only break down barriers between youth work and the school but, possibly of equal importance, it may erode other divisions. For it is not only youth work that has been increasingly re-located within the school but also adult, non-vocational and further education. These, as well as the growing use of school facilities for leisure pursuits, mean that the age boundaries previously embodied within the school can be blurred through the opening up of 'social and recreational facilities . . . shared by all age groups' (Jones, 1972, p. 16). As already noted, this is close to the vision long promulgated by advocates of the Community School from Henry Morris onwards. These have sought to create 'a concept which . . . subsumes the role of school, adult education centre, recreation centre and youth club' (Poster, 1982, p. 14; see also Fairbairn, 1969; 1978; 1980). The evidence that this has occurred on any scale has been questioned, in particular by Wallis & Mee (1983), who in the aftermath of their research concluded that 'in the context of the wide range of claims made for community schools they represent a fairly limited achievement' (p. 39). Yet whether or not community schools are living up to the expectations of their advocates seems almost an irrelevance to educational planners who have in area after area opted to introduce them. Community schools are flourishing to the extent that whereas little over a decade ago they were found only within the confines of a restricted number of oft-referenced LEAs, they can now be found within a clear majority. Expansion of community education means that more rather than less youth work will be situated within the schools and that a higher proportion of statutory resources and staff will inevitably be located within school premises and structures.

Opposition to school-based provision

Scott in a not untypical comment sums up much of the perceived Youth Service wisdom concerning school-based youth work provision when she writes that it 'has many critics, most of whom feel – with some justification – that young people are inhibited by clubs so closely associated with the rigid rules and less flexible outlook of school life' (1987, p. 16; see also for a more thorough-going critique Davies, 1969; 1986b; Booton, 1980), We do know that amongst specialist trained youth and community workers a great deal of opposition and even resentment exists towards teachers who enter youth work on a full-time basis (Holmes, 1981). However, concerning the criticisms raised by Scott little research actually exists to sustain them. Questions should be raised as to the merits of school-based youth work and provision but opponents are ill-advised to use the assumptions paraded by Scott's argument as a corner-stone for their critique. Young people who reject school, for whatever reason, are not surprisingly prominent amongst those most likely to turn away from school-based youth provision (Holland, 1976). Similarly, those who are amongst the 'low achievers' according to the predominately academic criteria of the school are also noticeable only by their marginal presence (Whiteside, 1984; Tann et al., 1983). Findings such as these are unlikely to amaze anyone who enjoys a passing acquaintance with the Youth Service. However, what is worthy of comment is that identical criticisms to these have traditionally been levelled at the Youth Service itself. Research into patterns of affiliation to virtually all forms of youth provision show the same profile as those encountered within the school-based sector and highlight the same absentees (Jephcott, 1967; Bone, 1972; Scarlett, 1975; Hendry et al., 1981). It is even impossible to point the finger at school-based work and accuse it, with any confidence, of disproportionately catering for those either in full-time education or below the statutory leaving age. For as one recent report shows, the percentage of those affiliated to school youth wings who are in full-time education is slightly below the rate earlier research has shown to exist within the Youth Service overall (Welsh Office, 1986a). Likewise the diet and content of the fare offered young people within the school-based unit bears more than a passing resemblance to that served up elsewhere by other youth work agencies. As Whitehead notes on the basis of her research, 'there seems to be very little difference in these clubs and the ones you would expect to find outside schools' (1985, p. 4). Further, it cannot be overlooked that much of the criticism levelled at school-based provision is founded upon an accusation that what prevails are 'fairly stereotyped youth work responses . . . such as discos, five-a-sides and an ear-damaging background noise' (Hall *et al.*, 1984, p. 16). This view was reiterated in an HMI Report on school youth wings which found that 'the social dimension of youth work forms the basis of provision in every wing' (Welsh Office, 1986, p. 11). What needs to be stressed is that this is in essence the mirror image of criticism that has been directed by the Inspectorate at almost every Youth Service unit or locality that they have surveyed. The weakness of the school-based sector lies not in its uniqueness of approach but in its failure to create on any scale a new and imaginative style of work, and in its inability to break away from the tired but tried and tested formulas. Young people appear to recognise this congruence, perceiving little difference in the style and approach of teachers and youth workers or between the ambience of the two settings (Scarlett, 1975).

As Corrigan (1979) implies, once you dig beneath the rhetoric it is the similarities that come to the fore rather imagined contrasts,

> like the school itself, like the education system as a whole, like the Duke of Edinburgh Award Scheme, like the Scouts, like the Youth Service and like school based leisure, Youth Clubs describe themselves as non-authoritarian (p. 98).

As a consequence it is a nonesense to claim, as one writer has done, that the expansion in school-based provision has 'actually jeopardised the concept of the "open" youth club, and with it the Youth Service philosophy of social education' (Booton, 1982,

p. 83). Firstly, because the threat to the traditional youth club comes not from the 'schooled youth work' but from the overwhelming indifference of the young people, the designated clientele, themselves. The traditional club was already in terminal decline long before youth wings and their like entered the arena in any profusion. And it should not be overlooked that the accretion of the school-based sector was in part an attempt both to provide a resource where often none existed previously and or to overcome the manifest short-comings of what was available. Secondly it is impossible to envisage how it has or can threaten the 'Youth Service philosophy of social education'. This will-o'-the-wisp has like the Holy Grail been much sought after, endlessly discussed but never credibly sighted. The reality is that the Youth Service has no philosophy of social education to either threaten or defend. Indeed as has already been argued the school-based centre, through its links with the schools and their physical and staffing resources, may well have saved from the verge of extinction elements of activity-based youth work that are now rarely encountered elsewhere.

Increasingly it is becoming less plausible to conjure up a case against school-based provision per se and much of what passes for criticism of it represents little more than a romantic attachment to a lost golden age of centre-based youth work. A great deal of this when examined without the aid of the rose-coloured spectacles can be seen as being of a lamentable standard and scant merit. Given that school-based provision is not only an inescapable reality but is gaining in prominence, what needs be stressed at this juncture is that school-based provision must be seen as a component, possibly in the future the preeminent one, within a pluralist statutory response. The Wolverhampton survey indicated with a degree of precision, previously not encountered in this area of social policy, what the 16–19 client group in that locality wanted in terms of services. They sought more skills training, more advice and counselling services, provision which remained open later and did not operate according to the school calendar, that lays on more educational courses and a wider diet of activities (Willis, 1985, p. 196). To live up to that mandate would entail a generic restructuring of those elements of the Youth Service that are worth preserving and closer operational integration with those other agencies, statutory and voluntary, that have the capacity to make a

realistic contribution. Integral to any coherent attempt to construct at a local level along these lines a responsive youth policy
must inevitably entail the expansion of access to the resources of the
school and FE sectors – a process that will strengthen their role
rather than erode it. Paradoxically, a failure to undertake that sort
of initiative will also further feed the expansion of school-based
provision as it becomes both the logical and unavoidable location
for the bulk of leisure and non-vocational education for young
people in the absence of substantive investment in alternative
facilities.

Whatever policy option is taken up, it appears that the Youth
Service has no alternative but to negotiate an effective *modus
operandi* for working with and alongside the school system both in
the interests of its clients and for the sake of its own survival in
many localities. At the same time schools will have to question
their own performance and structures. Not least because they will,
in a harsh climate, need in the future more than ever before to gain
the willing affiliation of their students and the long-term support of
ex-students and the wider community. To a degree, that will entail
learning from the traditions of youth work in order to create:

> a school for young grown-ups in fact, where the discipline and
> sanctions applicable to younger age groups have no place and
> where the informal approaches and techniques of student-
> centred learning are much more germane and akin to those
> applied in youth work (Fairbairn, 1971, p. 15).

Implicit in any attempt to secure that ethos and commitment will
be the provision of educational and leisure services for young
people. If it is to procure that affiliation, what the school provides
young people must, unlike that of the overwhelming bulk of
existing and past offerings, succeed in catering for a much less
homogeneous group of young people, by custom and practice
mainly male. Further, it must ensure that any future relationship
of young people with the Service does not of itself confirm the
marginality and immaturity of the young person. The all-age,
all-purpose community school with integrated youth provision
may not be the answer but it must be an improvement on the bulk
of what is currently on offer to young people. Self-evidently it
would have to be supplemented by other forms of provision but,

without it as a cornerstone, it is difficult to envisage any other educational foci. Certainly not one possessing the capacity to counter-balance the leisure orientation of the bulk of non-school provision perched on one end of the seesaw with the re-active and predominately casework responses of the statutory and voluntary sector welfare agencies seated on the other.

6
The DES and Youth Work

DUNCAN SCOTT with NEIL RITCHIE

There is little doubt that the Youth Service does not sit entirely comfortably inside the DES . . . it moves into the welfaring and policing as well as the educational traditions . . . and its very informality and structure on the ground make it not the easiest bedfellow with a machine that is generally about formality . . . schools, colleges, universities (Youth Work HMI*).

The basic terrain upon which DES intervention (financial and political, organisational and individual) takes place is not easy to summarise. Grant Related Expenditure Assessments (GREAs), the direct funding of some training, course endorsement via CETYCW, course assessment via HMIs and the provision of information and other services through the auspices of NYB are perhaps some of the key elements. In addition there is also grant aid to individual agencies such as the British Youth Council, to the headquarters of national voluntary organisations and the provision of funds for certain experimental and developmental projects.

In and out of all these organisations move the fourteen youth work HMIs, sometimes with other HMIs, making informal visits as well as more formal observations and inspections. More occasionally there are 'reports' on the whole of the Youth Service (HMSO, 1982) or on specific agencies (Cockerill, 1983).

This chapter focuses on two aspects: the work of the Youth

*All quotations of this kind were obtained by Duncan Scott in interviews and/or personal correspondence between February and May 1985. Anonymity was not always requested, but has been adopted for consistency in presentation.

Service-related HMIs; and the 'field' of DES–Youth Service inter-action. As a consequence of concentrating upon these, a number of other areas, such as inter-departmental relations, have only a limited coverage in this chapter, although further discussion can be found elsewhere in Chapter 2 and in Scott (1986).

The work of Youth Service-related HMIs

At the time of writing there were 458 HMIs in England (DES, 1985a). Within these, the small group of Youth Service specialists consists of 13, plus a staff inspector. In view of the assertion that HMIs are expected to be 'informed' about a wide range of social issues, their overall social composition and continuing recruitment patterns give cause for alarm. About one in six of all HMIs is female and this is a declining percentage (Rogers, 1983, p. 9). A white, male view can only be a partially informed one.

Formal details of the work of HMIs are available in the Secretary of State's response (DES, 1983a) to the Rayner report (HMSO, 1983b). Much of the material is familiar enough: ' . . . assesses standards and trends . . . identifies and makes known more widely good practice . . . advice and assistance . . . through its day-to-day contacts, its contributions to training and its publications' (DES, 1983a, p. 2). Moreover all of this is deemed' informed and independent' (ibid.).

Two themes underpin such activity. The first relates to ' . . . the overall thrust . . . [is] towards achieving an education system more actively concerned with the standards of its products and more cost conscious' (ibid; p. 1). A second theme is connected with external relationships and here 'Priority will be given to those organisations, like the National Advisory Body for Local Authority Higher Education and Manpower Services Commission . . . who are most actively involved in the development and implementation of the government's current policies' (ibid., p. 11).

The central work of youth-related HMIs who spend up to a third of their time on other areas of education is coordinated by the Youth Service Staff Inspector via 'Committee C43 Youth Work and Community Organisations'. Here a rolling programme of inspections and less formal visits is proposed, monitored and discussed. Any proposals from C43 go to a Chief Inspector whose recently re-organised task areas now include youth work and YTS.

A high proportion of HMI work is written down in memos and internal documents. Until very recently most of this was invisible to the wider public. Now, the results of formal inspections are being published. In the absence of insight into the internal material, assessment must begin from publications. Ritchie has recently examined these (Ritchie, 1986) and the following section presents a summary of his findings.

Four full inspections of youth work were traced – Bedfordshire (DES, 1983d), Lambeth (DES, 1982a), Wales (HMI (Wales), 1984) and Sheffield (DES, 1984a), as well as two examples of relevance from larger reports – Walsall (DES, 1983c) and Sutton (DES, 1983b). From such a range, there is a good deal of material which is simply descriptive and which gives little or no indication that this policy or that practice was particularly good or bad. Background detail includes information about the economic geography of a region, alongside information about the youth population or a potted history of the Youth Service in this or that part of the world. Even the dedicated sleuth would find it difficult to work out the size and shape of the wood when confronted by so many trees. The problem is compounded by lack of consensus. Some issues warrant a mention in Wales but not in Lambeth, or in Sheffield but not in Bedfordshire. Nonetheless there are enough clues to at least hazard some guesses about what some of the HMI criteria for good youth work might be.

These criteria are organised under four broad headings;

1. the organisational or political framework: 'partnership'
2. the use of appropriate funds and staffing: 'resources'
3. the focus on particular categories: 'special needs'
4. the employment of relevant practice: 'the youth work curriculum'.

Partnership

A statutory voluntary partnership of some kind is seen to be important for coordination of services, although no mention is made of the role of commercial or independent provision of leisure-time facilities and activities for the young. A similar 'emptiness' concerns the political location of the Youth Service in relation to other local authority and non-statutory services and the fabric of local representative democracy.

In Bedfordshire, the County Youth Officer was in the throes of trying to establish a Council of Voluntary Youth Services, which the HMIs hoped would encourage more systematic cooperation at area and unit level. In Lambeth, this kind of structure does not seem to work too effectively. There is an area youth committee with representatives of the statutory and voluntary Youth Service partners but this has not prevented 'a lack of coordination in this provision and, indeed, a seeming lack of knowledge among the various providers and workers which results in replication of effort' (DES, 1982). One suggestion for remedying this is the creation of another tier of statutory voluntary partnership in the shape of neighbourhood support groups or house committees which could promote clubs as a focus for neighbourhood work and a community resource.

Use of resources

There is a concern throughout that the use of resources should be maximised and that provision should take account of young people's leisure patterns and not administrative convenience. For example, clubs should be open in school holidays in Bedfordshire's case, where the policy is to base youth provision in school sites. There are some critical comments about the extent to which schools' administrative conveniences prevail over youth clubs' concerns and their conflicting aims and policies. As indicated in an earlier section of this chapter, a clarification of the local patterns of resource allocation and use is not seen as relevant.

Special needs

The HMI Reports commonly earmark some particular groups of young people for special attention. Many of them refer to such groups as having special needs for which special responses are required. This is not to deny that special attention or concern is justified, but it does feed the growing unease about the tradition of focusing separately on the needs of girls or the unemployed, or those 'felt to be Socially Disadvantaged', to borrow a phrase from the Welsh Report. This tends to suggest that girls or black youth, or working-class youngsters from the inner city are problem groups, whereas the white male, heterosexual, middle classes are not. HMIs are by no means unusual in adopting this approach, but in using it they are in danger of reinforcing some notions that they appear to want to challenge, judging by the comments they go on to make about provision for these groups.

The overall flavour of HMI comments is of tentativeness: should there be separate provision for racial minorities or young women? What to do about racism and sexism? How to clarify the Youth Service role in developing responses to YTS? Some of this hesitancy may be derived from the intractable nature of the problems and an acute awareness by HMIs that local Youth Service resources are inadequate. What comes across is the need for better management and coordination despite the problem of inadequate resource allocation. A commendable realism perhaps but one that puts excessive faith in good professional practice.

The youth work curriculum

For all that HMIs are critical of the kinds of practice that they commonly see, nonetheless they still perceive a need for a programme of activities. Faced by an apparently unending round of bad, depressing or just uninspiring practice it is not easy to work out quite what a good programme would look like. Fortunately the Welsh Report provides such a picture. The five aspects of youth work it identified as fundamental elements of provision are: the social dimension, activities, community involvement, extending horizons and participation.

A social area, usually centred on a coffee bar or informally arranged seating area where a range of games and amusements are based, is seen as a key way of fostering good relationships between members and between members and staff. Attention is drawn to clubs where loud music stops conversation, or where members sit around passively watching TV, and other kinds of purposeless, desultory activity. Essentially it is the group work element of youth work which the social area may facilitate including counselling or discussion which the Report seeks to encourage.

Activities are divided into physical recreation, domestic arts and personal care, creative arts and allied subjects and performing arts. Physical recreation includes the casual, recreational games like pool or darts, as well as those which are intensively coached or played competitively in organised competitions. Domestic arts and personal care appear in club programmes under a number of guises – including cookery and needlecraft and design for living. Those are somewhat neglected in Wales, although one or two voluntary organisations cater effectively for their members in this kind of activity.

Community involvement, extending horizons and participation are shorthand references to an even more diffuse range of activities; from setting up PHAB (Physically Handicapped and Able Bodied) clubs to reclaiming wasteland, and from exchange visits overseas to innovative management structures at the level of individual clubs. We do not have the space to develop references to these areas of work. Nevertheless we remain a little uneasy that the mere existence of such activities may be regarded as an antidote to uninspiring youth work.

The good youth club programme would include elements of all these kinds of activities. Juggling these categories enables a worker to respond effectively to the needs of young people. One feature of the youth work curriculum which is mentioned often enough to indicate some consensus amongst inspectors is the Duke of Edinburgh's Award Scheme. Either HMIs do see this as a key component of effective youth work, or their superior's do, and they were all instructed to check its availability.

Inspecting the Inspectors

On 1 April 1985 the Government announced plans to assess civil servants including HMIs for special performance bonuses. A spokesman for the HMIs said that because most of them work alone in the field such a scheme would be unworkable (Norton-Taylor, 1985). Subsequently, after a secret ballot of HMIs, their Association confirmed its opposition on intellectual and practical grounds. They were opposed to the lack of openness of the proposed assessment procedures and considered the plans a threat to their independence (Norton-Taylor, 1985a). What was not offered was a different system of inspection – guarding the alleged 'independence' was a predictable frontline position. Possibilities for collaborative evaluation and self-evaluation – all known to HMIs and the DES – were presumably seen as different from 'Inspection'. All of this is familiar enough – the 'threat' of evaluation and inspection applies to all sorts and conditions of people.

But because HMIs, like many professional groups, wish to protect their status we have few insights into the day-to-day uncertainties of their work. Even a careful academic study of LEA inspectors reluctantly concluded that "because . . . much of the information . . . is of a sensitive kind (politically and personally) . . . I have written very little about the substance of the study" (Walker, 1981, p. 30).

Some of the following criticism of HMI reporting have to be assessed in the light of such political and personal sensitivities. A major question, discussed in the final section, concerns the options open to the 14 HMIs. Are they really all that indepedent if their remarks are so constrained? Can they envisage alternative models of evaluation and inspection? What would the costs and benefits of these models look like? Finally, the most elusive set of questions is derived from the possibility that a consensus does not exist and that youth work objectives may vary according to context, issue and even individual HMIs. Consider, for example, the contrast between youth workers' relationships with the police in Sheffield and Wales. Detached workers in Sheffield act as advocates and mediators on behalf of young people with the police, a role which HMIs recognise to be important, particularly since the young people they work with share a universal suspicion of the police. In Wales this kind of role does not appear to be appropriate. Is the different in emphasis attributable only to the differences between the young people of Sheffield and of Wales?

Inconsistencies of this kind suggest that HMIs have not yet developed any overall framework with which to understand and assess youth work practice. It may be that this is difficult or even impossible to achieve. In which case HMIs could do worse than 'surrender' a little of their independence and share their concerns with others interested in the complexities of evaluation and assessment. The scarcity of comments on the practice of youth work, coupled with the strong consensus on only two fronts, namely (a) the need for aims, objectives and strategy for translating these into practice; and (b) the need for illuminated nameboards and more secretarial staff, would suggest that, like the Youth Service itself, the framework for the interpretation, and subsequent translation into practice, of the higher ideals of social education is at best patchy. Within such a diverse field as youth work the role, actual and potential, of HMI Reports needs some clarification. Is it to acknowledge, describe, and help interpret the diversity of this practice? Or does the emphasis on good management as a solution to the Youth Service's dilemmas signify a further move towards 'professionalism'?

If the reports are to be used to promote debate within the Service as a whole, then the Inspector's assumptions and starting points will need to be spelled out. Currently there seems to be some doubt about whether they are even used as a basis for dialogue with those who are inspected. ILEA's angry responses to the Lambeth Inspection questioned both the facts that the Report presents and the tone of trial by innuendo in which it was couched. Clearly some work has still to be done if HMI Reports are to realise their constructive and creative potential. Practitioners at a number of levels do have positive perspectives about youth-related HMIs, but there seems to be little clarity about how more collective strategies of evaluation and discussion can break out of the informal visit or the formal committee. We conclude this section with samples of such perspectives:

My contact with HMIs has been mainly through being on such things as Advisory Committees . . . and various conferences. . . . I have never been sure of their role except that where DES money is involved I have assumed they are monitoring the usefulness and possibly the general competence of that particular project. In general I have found them very pleasant and not very different from anybody else in these situations except that when they speak, they appear to have given more thought to what they are saying. To me they usually come across as objective and rather wise. However there are one or two exceptions and I won't name them.

(Senior Youth Officer).

The visit consisted of a two- to three-hour chat with the two full-time youth workers and then a visit to two of the estate clubs . . . they appeared interested and asked pertinent and helpful questions. They did not offer any overt judgement or criticism. My memory is that one of the two HMIs took part in the face-painting activity that was going on! However we never heard anything further from them again. We understood that a report was going to be written which we just assumed we would see . . . we reckoned we couldn't have been breaking too many policies around 'what is youth work', and that no news could be taken as good news . . . but I'm still not convinced that it was completely unconnected to the youth office/project 'battling' – certainly, the people in the estate clubs thought it was strange and a bit 'off' that there was nothing more concrete resulting out of the visit.

(Neighbourhood Youth and Community Worker).

The field of DES–Youth Service interaction

In order to understand the roles of the DES in relation to the Youth Service it is necessary to outline.

1. the administrative and political location of the DES within central government departments
2. the mechanisms of Grant Related Expenditure Assessments and block grants, and the extent to which LEAs follow the economic guidelines from central government
3. the mechanisms of DES grant aid to national voluntary youth organisations.

The DES, with 2435 employees (DES, 1985a), is a minute central ministry because the administration of education is largely a local matter. One consistent theme in commentaries about the DES in relation to the Youth Service is, therefore, that we expect too much of it. An HMI observed that the DES 'never really wanted the Youth Service in 1939 and has continued to demonstrate a very limited commitment ever since' (personal interview).

Within the DES, the Youth Service Section is located in one of the Further and Higher Education branches. The section is headed by an Assistant Secretary who devotes two-thirds of his time to non-Youth Service issues. There is then a Principal Officer, and two or three Executive Officers. A HMI recently noted, 'They're constantly busier than their level of staffing permits' (personal interview). Such a perspective must be assessed against the extent to which clear patterns are discernible, and which policy initiatives are taken relatively quickly. In other words, where resources are limited the subsequent choice of priorities may be revealing of underlying intentions and tendencies.

Analyses of the DES have necessarily been more concerned with its policy and practice in relation to the mainstream work of schools and FE. They have concluded about the latter that the DES has lacked clear-cut priorities (Cantor & Roberts, 1979, p. 13). In recent years the MSC has 'captured' large areas of training because of its greater resource base (the much larger Department of Employment), the value orientations of the Conservative government, and the roles of individual ministers (see St John-Brooks, 1985). The role of the MSC in youth work territories is a massive one and underlines the precarious role of the DES.

Other central government departments also have a stake in different aspects of youth provision. The DHSS presides over IT by, for example, funding NYB to provide an information service on this area of work to the ranks of practitioners employed in local authority social service departments. Over the period 1977–8 to 1984–5 IT expenditure reported by local authorities has increased more than fivefold in real terms; an increase equivalent to an annual growth rate of 26 per cent per annum (Morris, 1984). This expenditure is a DHSS not a DES responsibility and contrasts with the conclusions of Smith that between 1979–80 and 1982–3 the Youth Service in England (excluding ILEA) experienced real expenditure reductions of 9 per cent (D. I. Smith, 1985, p. 1).

The Home Office is in on the act too. It has a branch called the Voluntary Services Unit which keeps various youth agencies and networks afloat by its grant aid, most notably the National Association of Young People's Counselling and Advisory Services and the National Working Party of Young Volunteer Organisers. Some of the territory could legitimately be claimed by the DES. Their own Review Group stated that information, advice and counselling services must be one of the mainstream forms of youth provision (HMSO, 1982). Yet NAYPCAS continues to live a hand-to-mouth existence because the DES seems reluctant to take over funding of the organisation.

The central regulatory mechanism used by the DES in its relationships with LEAs is an economic one. GREA indicates the amounts local authorities should spend on a particular service. However, it is unclear how GREA is calculated. The situation is further complicated in two ways. Firstly, local authorities receive block grants (or rate support grants as they used to be known) via calculations from the Department of the Environment; GREA and block grant have not always been coordinated. This has led some local authorities to be in danger of rate-capping for spending according to a GREA calculation which was higher than the block grant.

A second difficulty arises at local level. Since the Youth Service is not mandatory, since there are no minimum standards and since the DES has not provided strong central guidance, local 'interpretations' of GREA vary considerably. Hence, as described in Chapter 3, we have examples of adjacent LEAs regularly and systematically under- and over-spending in relation to GREA. Even if the basis of GREA is a mystery and/or plain wrong, it does allow comparisons to be made.

Clearly the LEAs, in the absence of DES guidance feel able to exercise discretion at the expense of the Youth Service. There are at least two components in this. In the first place, it is likely that other economic pressures on mainstream education spending have encouraged the use of Youth Service allocations for the more institutionally tangible and professionally defended school-based sector. This was denied by the responsible Minister 'There is no evidence that the Youth Service is being discriminated against by local authorities despite their difficulties' (*Hansard*, 11 July 1984). Yet the discretion clearly has a systematic rural–urban dynamic. There are grounds for believing that 'youth' as a high profile issue is at least perceived as more urban-related, and that professions, pressure groups and the like combine to reinforce this.

In addition to the somewhat loose economic controls of LEA's, the DES attempts to maintain a central information role via the records of full-time youth workers, and a confidential list (List 99) of those deemed 'unsuitable' for such work. The former is known as the 'Register' and is now maintained by CETYCW. It contains names of youth workers employed by local authorities and some (but not all) voluntary organisations. These include names of qualified and unqualified workers and CETYCW could only think of one potential use – it would reveal to an employer if someone had completed a probationary year. Other than this it is only an inaccurate guide to numbers of full-time workers in the Service. On List 99 are those people who have been deemed unsuitable for teaching, youth work or other posts in the Education Service because of serious misconduct. The Secretary of State has powers to bar or restrict the employment of youth workers and teachers guilty of such misconduct. The list is circulated on a confidential basis to local authorities and 'certain other bodies concerned with the employment of teachers'.

To co-ordinate these economic and administrative tasks the tiny DES secretariat continues to depend heavily on the work of two overlapping sets of individuals and agencies, the youth work HMIs and that mesh of intermediary agencies such as NCVYS, NYB and CETYCW, which links with both the LEAs and voluntary agencies. A recent 'insert' between the DES and the Youth Service is the National Advisory Council for the Youth Service (NACYS). NACYS was signalled in the Thompson Report, and formally confirmed on 11 July 1984. Walter James (ex chair of CETYCW) was announced as Chairman on 7 October 1985, and the membership confirmed on 11 December 1985. Only 5 days later Archie. Kirkwood MP put a written question to the responsible Minister regarding the nature and criteria for council membership. The Principal of the Youth Service Unit replied (17 December 1985) giving details concerning the organisational origin of those selected but avoided all reference to criteria used.

The original 23 council members (plus Walter James; two DES Assessors and a Welsh Office colleague) were clearly not organisationally representative. But there is an impressive spread from the Chairman of Rubery Owen Holdings, to a Director of Education, and on to a Black neighbourhood worker in Brent. There are 6 women, 4 Black people and 2 members of the British Youth Council. Otherwise the overall flavour is of middle to upper management of statutory and non-statutory youth-related agencies.

When the Advisory Council was first announced, the terms of reference seemed impressively catholic – the DES, the Welsh Office, local authorities and voluntary organisations would all be advised. At its first meeting a clear priority was identified as responding to requests for advice from Secretaries of State (NACYS, 1986a). The Junior Education Minister at the time, Bob Dunn, spoke to the inaugural meeting about what he called one or two areas of 'great topical interest'. His speech clearly indicated that he did not wish to 'pre-empt' discussion, yet this was interpreted, in the Youth press, as a call on the Council to 'identify and encourage the Youth Service's distinctive contributions in three particular areas of work' (Scene, 1986). According to the article these were unemployment, drugs, and law and order.

Several members of the Council (in personal communications to the main author) quickly identified the tension between the interests of the DES, the detailed papers (in particular NACYS, 1986b and 1986c) provided for their scrutiny, and their own processes of prioritisation.

As one member concluded, 'the full council is only to meet 3 or 4 times a year, much will depend on what the four sub-committees get up to. In any case a number of us will construct our own informal networks.'

Whatever the outcome of these formal and informal processes of negotiation it is probable that:

the normative assumptions on which such interaction is based [that] are the real source of power albeit unremarked and unopposed since they carry the power to determine selectively the way in which issues are discussed and the solutions proposed (Broadfoot, 1986, p. 61).

Within the NACYS papers and discussions, there are clearly a number of inter-related assumptions about young people and the Youth Service which have yet to be realised. In the space available it is only possible to identify what appear to be two potentially crucial assumptions.

In the first place, *Young People* are differentiated according to their employment status or 'at riskness' (re drugs and the law) by the DES and in relation to gender, race, disability, 'disjunctions in personal development', and 'cultural impoverishment' by the Youth Service Unit (NACYS, 1986b; 1986c.). Despite the fact that there is a long tradition, within the school system, of researchers and policy-makers identifying young people in relation to social class, this does not appear to be the case in the Youth Service. As a consequence these analytical perspectives related to a structuralist approach may be underdeveloped or ignored.

Secondly, the *Youth Service personnel* seem to be embedded within assumptions about management and hierarchy which reinforce traditional notions of professional and non-professional, expert and subordinate helper. In a section on human resources the central issues are defined as:

the personnel function in its wider sense, including selection, training, career development, ensuring support for the consultation with *junior staff* [our emphasis], creating clear and effective management structures and good information systems, may prove to be the main aspect of management on which the Council will wish to concentrate (NACYS, 1986c).

The fact is that most youth workers, that is to say those who actually work face-to-face with young people, are not professional careerists or personnel managers. They may need to be supported and developed by way of very different sets of assumptions. What is clear is that the NACYS is being well resourced by the YSU of the DES and is seen as an important shop-window and clearing-house for DES youth policy discussions in the late 1980s. In such a role it may be increasingly used as a legitimation for the work of HMI's, the LEAS and the voluntary agencies.

The remit for the HMI's is divided up between formal inspections, District and Divisional responsibilities and membership of committees. Examples could range from an inspection of a college or LEA, preparation of all or part of an annual report for a shire county and visits formal and informal to LEA and non-statutory youth-related provision across eight or nine local authorities. Definition of 'considerable contact' (was 'equivalent of five HMI days in a year' (HMI-personal interview). Not surprisingly, tactical use is made of AGMs and key meetings in order to gain access to the largest number of individuals and agencies.

For the hard-pressed HMI, access to local units is always difficult. Where linking intermediary agencies exist, e.g. regional Councils of Voluntary Youth Services (there are 47) or national voluntary youth organisations (64 are linked to NCVYS), these provide an appropriate entrée to the networks. The problem is a similar if less complex one *vis-à-vis* LEAs. Given such diversity, it is difficult to generalise. It may be that particular groupings of gatekeepers, HMIs and DES officials will develop, as with the parallel elites in national voluntary social service agencies, into 'a closed circle of social, political and economic connections where "the old school tie" plays a relatively powerful and privileged role both domestically in forming the agency's policies and externally in its relations with government bodies' (Brenton, 1985, p. 22).

It is not possible to provide hard evidence that 'closed circles' of influence exist at the interface between the DES and such bodies as national voluntary youth organisations (NVYO). One index of

Table 6.1 *DES funding to national voluntary youth organisations 1984–5*

	£
Training (NYB, CETYCW, Durham University, YMCA), and	1 000 000
Innovative work (much of this is coordinated by NCVYS)	
a) Developmental work	305 000
b) Experimental projects	135 000
c) Management innovation	75 000
NVYOs	2 500 000
Overall total	3 500 000

* The MSC Training Budget for 1984–5 was £1136 million. Of the 5069 employees in the Training Division, 3632 were described as in *Youth Training* (MSC, 1985a, 41).

'closure' might be the extent to which DES grant aid to NVYOs demonstrates a degree of continuity in relationship. If the same organisations consistently get the largest amounts of grant-aid this might suggest that they are both dependent on the DES, and significant instruments of youth-related policies. In the absence of the appropriate qualitative data, the following paragraphs offer to the reader some hints as to the plausibility of such a thesis.

An overall picture of direct DES funding of NVYOs is provided in Table 6.1. NCVYS is the co-ordinating and advisory agency for the NVYOs and receives 80 per cent of its annual income in excess of £100 000 from the DES. An NCVYS spokesman claimed that the only recent major point of contention with the DES was derived from the slowness of the department rather than matters of substance (personal interview). Somewhat similar points were made by a youth specialist HMI: 'my impression [of NCVYS Experimental projects] is that what has been turned down has not been significant for its content so much as the quality of its submission . . . the only example of conflict might be the processes around the NAYC's work with girls' (personal interview).

The bulk of DES grant-aid goes to NVYOs. Between June and October each year they must fill in a 7-page form with reference to 8 pages of guidance. The Staff Inspector (youth work) then advises the DES in liaison with the NVYO HQ Grants Review Committee. This advice remains confidential whilst the reviewing processes tend to surface as lists and amendments to the notes of guidance. Discussions of the latter could be of great interest, particularly where what is known as the 'complementary element' is discussed. This provides for the reviewing process to negotiate 20 per cent of any requested HQ grant via specific criteria: (a) current policies and priorities for the Youth Service; (b) the nature, efficiency in operation, and quality of the organisation's work; (c) the type of organisation and its effectiveness; (d) age range; (e) financial need; and (f) the possible need to make special provision to consolidate the results of development work (DES, 1984b, p. 3). These tiny sums are now to be further co-ordinated within a DES-based 'unit'. In the absence of public discussion within the Youth Service concerning the potential of such an institutional development, spectators may be forgiven for thinking this is a shuffle of names rather than structures.

It is not possible to obtain an oversight of the above mentioned procedures. Some might argue that only the agencies concerned should receive such details. Others might speculate that the professed absence of critical debate signifies that the processes exist within sets of taken-for-granted assumptions isolated from broader public debates. Regarding how they operate in practice we are left to speculate largely on the basis of a study published a decade ago (Thomas & Perry, 1975). If the same NVYOs receive the bulk of DES grant-aid from decade to decade would this suggest a high degree of 'closure'? There is no doubt that, overall, NVYO numbers in receipt of some money have expanded, from 23 in 1959 to 63 in 1984. A distinct impression is gained of a virtually 'quasi-statutory' grouping of agencies heavily dependent on DES funds which come to them because they employ staff rather than because of how this relates to young people.

In 1939, Circular 1486 mentioned 14 'Principal Voluntary Organisations'. Nearly half a century later, 7 of the 'Top 10' recipients are from this original list. Table 6.2 indicates how large NVYOs have continued to dominate; the top 10 receiving nearly two-thirds of the total allocated to the largest 50 agencies. Calculations as to the present 'worth' of 1973–4 expenditure patterns can be crudely measured against changes in the retail price index. Since the middle of the financial year 1973–4 to the equivalent period of 1984–5 there has been approximately a 200 per cent change. Multiplication of the earlier figures by three can therefore

Table 6.2   *DES funding to 'top 10' national voluntary youth organisations*

	1973–4[1]			1984–5[2]	
		£			£
1	NAYC	72 750	1	NAYC	265 100
2	NABC	62 100	2	NABC	159 600
3	YMCA	37 580	3	YMCA	134 550
4	YWCA	22 675	4	MAYC	74 800
5	SCOUTS	19 400	5	D of E	70 550
6	D of E	18 090	6	National Federation of Young Farmers	69 750
7	Girl Guides	18 040	7	YWCA	65 200
8	CSV	16 370	8	SCOUTS	47 100
9	URDD	14 285	9	GUIDES	44 400
10	MAYC	13 780	10	PHAB	36 500
50th	Anglican Young People's Association	275	50th	Union of Maccabi Associations	3750
Total	(Top 50)	476 285	Total	(Top 50)	1 558 400

Source: [1] Thomas and Perry (1975, pp. 68–9).
          [2] NCVYS (April 1985).

provide a rough guide as to whether they have kept in line with inflation.

Changes not revealed in the table include the appearance of two separate Muslim youth agencies. Other South Asian youth agencies and comparable Afro-Caribbean youth organisations either do not meet DES criteria or have gone for funding elsewhere. In particular, two government departments stand out as sponsors; the Home Office, then the Department of Environment, in the development of the Urban Programme, and the Department of Employment via the MSC in the development of YOP and YTS. HMIs and DES officials have been involved in local and national aspects of these developments, but their activities are even less visible than within the traditional Youth Service territories.

Pluralism and polarity – some issues in interpretation

The commonsense view of the Youth Service is that its complexity
defies generalisation; there will always be too many exceptions.
Nevertheless two related tendencies seem to have been significant
in interventions by the DES and HMIs. The first of these can
almost be termed an ideology about the very principles of youth
work practice, assessment, regulation, development and so on.
We can, for shorthand purposes, call this 'youth work professionalism'. By 'professionalism' we mean the assertion that there exists
a defined area of knowledge and skills about youth work which can
be obtained primarily via formally approved training programmes.
These are then capable of being assessed and certificated as
'passports' into practice for the new professional.

The chief proponents of this ideology are the HMIs and many of
the small number of full-time youth professionals who occupy key
points in LEA and voluntary youth organisations. In broad terms,
both these sets of actors have attempted over the last 25 years to
construct a profession of youth work relatively 'free' from or
'independent' of the political and economic constraints of their
respective occupational contexts. Of course their practice has
revealed how such freedom and independence is not possible.
Indeed, one of the strongest 'voices' reminding them of such a fact
has come from the coalface of practice, from the full-time, part-
time and voluntary youth workers.

Two themes have been evident from within the practices of
youth work. Both have raised question marks about the professional emphasis. The first of these has used the rise of the MSC
to show how an over-emphasis on the DES can distract attention,
at both national and local levels, from the fundamental political
and economic 'building bricks' of the Youth Service. Here we are
referring to such features as the initial allocations of resources and
the debates or 'non-decisions' about these (see Davies, 1981). A
second critique has argued that the professional concentration
concerning practice is useful but flawed. Whilst not rejecting the
frameworks of training, assessment and certification so carefully
built up over recent decades, there is some scepticism as to the
independent, omni-competent image of HMIs for both political
and pragmatic reasons.

This position does not see the present government tolerating a full independence among its HMIs, even though there have been some recent trenchant comments from them about the state of school buildings and equipment. One piece of evidence here is the recently announced MSC Inspectorate who, if the experience of the MSC is any guide, are likely to be even further removed from the checks and balances of representative democracy than their DES colleagues (MSC, 1985a). A further piece of evidence is that HMIs are informed by a realisation that the professional part of the Youth Service rests upon a massive majority of workers who could not, will not, and may not want to become professional. They are volunteers and part-timers whose resources need support and development in alternative ways (Bolger & Scott, 1984).

The second major tendency in contemporary interventions by the DES and HMIs is the advocacy of 'management' as the appropriate non-political response for the Youth Service of the 1980s. An HMI captured this by insisting that:

> you over-estimate what the DES is about . . . it's much more about the . . . broad level of resource . . . current DES thinking is 'what we need are frameworks', a different NYB a National Advisory Body, a Unit . . . nobody's saying 'what you do with this machine?' . . . there isn't the high level of policy debate about where the machine should point . . . it takes place at the level of something should be done about . . . (personal interview).

The implication is of structures without content, or rather a content where consensus or a healthy pluralism of ideas prevails. Only grudgingly does this perspective admit that 'in the last two or three years there has been a shift towards a tightening up . . . a greater specificity of spending . . . so we may be seeing a critical break with that 40 year tradition of distancing and devolution'. (ibid.)

Other commentators seemed less sanguine:

> There was a noticeable change of emphasis post-1979. My feeling has to be that HMIs were more influential because they were more listened to by previous administrations . . . the open confrontation [between the NYB Advisory Committee on the Enfranchisement project and the HMI] was not because the HMI disagreed . . . but because he was trying to protect NYB

from giving the DES a reason for stopping or cutting funding (Senior Youth Work Trainer in NVYO, in personal communication).

As another put it:

A general hunch I have is that there has been a hardening within the Inspectorate and that this occurred since 1979 . . . we have seen a more directive, interventionist role . . . in recent years the Training Agencies Group has moved to excluding the Inspectorate from parts of its meetings. A part of the old elitist old boy network was a gentleman's agreement that the Inspectorate were automatically invited to attend the whole of weekend meetings. There has been a realisation in recent years that this had become politically naive (Youth and Community Work Lecturer in personal communication).

Clearly the HMI is not universally perceived as a threat, an agent of management; he or she can be an ally. But, there is little evidence that individual HMIs are prepared or even able to forge consistent institutional alliances with fractions of the field who seek major change. They exist within a major political and practical dilemma – aware that their much-prized 'independence' is under pressure both from government and the field, yet unsure as a tiny fraction of HMIs as a whole how to proceed.

Broad agreement seems to exist that a major state response to the needs of young people is being translated in terms of 'resource management'. Thompson emphasised the importance of the experiences of different categories of young people and the importance of providing greater participative opportunities. Keith Joseph dismissed the notion of a youth crisis and quickly threw the 'blame' back onto the Youth Service for their under use of resources (House of Commons debate on Thompson, 11 July 1984).

Both tendencies, the professional and the managerial, contain major elements of interest and relevance to the worlds of youth policy and practice. But it is at least a matter of strong, perhaps conflicting debate as to whether they can be regarded in a vacuum, independent of the prevailing philosophies of government. Before Thompson's report received the responses of a Draft Circular in July 1984 (DES 1984c), the Under-Secretary's address in November 1984 (Brooke, 1984) and the full Circular (DES 1/5, 1985), critics were arguing that even the Report itself contained the germ of an attempt to 'depoliticise' youth and community work practice (Cartlidge, 1983, p. 13). Far from doing that, argued another reviewer, it would open the way for the 'polarisation' of youth work (D. I. Smith, 1983, p. 12). Interpretation is not just a matter of possessing a perspective and applying it. Much depends on where you are located. Cartlidge's training course is 100 per cent DES-funded, but less implicated in the mesh of relationships than, for example, NCVYS. So we read that the latter 'warmly welcome' a 'shot in the arm' in the form of Circular 1/85 (NCVYS, 1985). Surely it is not just a case of Cartlidge and Cattermole (Director of NCVYS) having different perspectives, but also of charting their respective political and organisational relationships with the DES?

One set of answers to this last question can be found in the more immediate responses to Thompson. Whilst the DES was taking two and a half years to reach Circular 1/85, CETYCW and the Cockerill Report on the fate of the NYB appeared in four months and eleven months respectively. It is not out opinion that these more rapid responses deserve blame simply for their early emergence, but presumably they do represent some ordering of priorities. It remains to be seen as to whether CETYCW can respond more creatively to the largely non-professional field. The restructuring (or neutering, dependent on your perspective) of NYB has attracted that familiar range of views which accompanied Thompson. At least some of the proposals relating to NYB such as a single source of funding, the stress on 'data' and the purge of 'political bias' seem consistent with government policies in other parts of non-statutory welfare (c.f. the Citizen's Advice Bureaux and the Community Projects Foundation). The Government, in seeking greater control, attempts to insert more professionals and managers. In some aspects reaction to this control can have the very opposite effect to that intended. That is to say, a sharpening of opposed positions rather than their rendering down in an apolitical consensus.

In the absence of the 'firm ground' of youth-related legislation, the intermediary individuals (HMIs) and agencies (NVYOs) which form central channels for DES intervention may need to make hard choices. Individually they are 'pleasant' people and agencies, but the structures within which they work provide them with even less room for independent manoeuvre than the small amount they once had. Youth and Community work is still full of exciting possibilities – innovations take root there often more quickly than in schools and social services departments. But, it will need more than face paint to disguise the increasingly unequal resource distributions within both the social worlds of young people and the various Youth Services with whom they interact.

7

Youth Workers, the MSC and the Youth Training Scheme

HOWARD WILLIAMSON

The Youth Service in England and Wales has traditionally been primarily concerned with working with young people during their leisure time. Youth workers have defined their central role as contributing to the personal development of young people through the provision of informal social education. Consequently the Youth Service has barely been considered to be an appropriate forum within which to address the issue of youth unemployment, clearly one of the major problems facing young people today. This problem has generated new and significant dilemmas for youth workers. The Youth Service has in fact long been involved in youth unemployment initiatives, contributing both to the policy debate about relevant employment and training measures and to the development of practical interventions such as drop-in centres and the sponsorship of schemes for unemployed young people. Today it is not simply a question of whether there is a role for youth workers in the initiatives that are currently being developed or even whether the role should be direct or indirect, marginal or central. The more fundamental question is how should youth workers relate to interventions designed, funded and controlled by the MSC whose concerns, despite the rhetoric, may be somewhat different from their own.

Whatever noises youth workers may make about developing 'alternatives', realism points to the fact that the MSC has a tight grip on the resources available to the young unemployed. The financial and political climate of recent years has enabled a well-resourced MSC not only to induce the under-resourced Youth Service to collaborate but also to dictate the terms of that collaboration. It has been estimated that around 2000 people were employed by the English and Welsh Youth Service to work in YTS in 1983; this compares with around 3500 full-time youth workers employed by local authorities (YODU, 1983b). Despite what to many are 'obvious' tensions inherent in such a relationship, the availability of MSC resources has proved irresistible within some quarters of the Youth Service.

Where does this leave the already 'marginal' and 'anonymous' Youth Service (Jeffs, 1979)? There is a strong feeling that the Youth Service does have a proper role to play in MSC initiatives. This is despite reservations at all levels of the Youth Service concerning, for example, fears about the dilution of professional status and justified concerns regarding the exploitation of young people on training schemes. Marsland argued in 1978 that 'the Youth Service must be incorporated more fully and coherently into the work of YOP' (Marsland, 1978a, p. 110) and continues to advocate a similar position with regard to YTS (Marsland, 1985). Others have noted that criticism from the sidelines will have limited impact; that YTS 'will not go away if you ignore it' (YODU, 1983a, p. 14); that 'burying heads in the sand would serve no-one's interests' (Hobbs *et al.*, 1983, p. 15); and consequently that the Youth Service 'has no choice but to get involved' (*ibid.*, p. 14).

Yet Youth Service collaboration with, or opposition to, the MSC at whatever level is imbued with numerous tensions and dilemmas. Formally there are contradictions surrounding questions about the public, political and professional credibility of the Youth Service *via à vis* its involvement with, or antipathy towards MSC provision. Informally youth workers face dilemmas concerning professional credibility and personal integrity. These dilemmas emerge from the contradictions between the compromising position which may be associated with perceived collaboration and the relative benefits which may accrue from participation in MSC programmes for the young people with whom they work.

Depictions of YTS

The permanent YTS replaced the temporary YOP in September 1983. Though it built upon former YOP provision it was a qualitatively different programme designed to offer comprehensive education and training to minimum-age school leavers and to constitute a permanent bridge to work. Unike YOP, it was not (theoretically at least) about youth unemployment. It was deemed to be about providing high quality training in order to meet the needs of the economy and of employers, whilst providing for young people 'what they themselves so actively seek – greater opportunities to equip themselves to make their way in the increasingly competitive world of the 1980s' (MSC, 1982, para. 1.3). It was described by the Secretary of State for Employment as 'the most far-reaching and ambitious set of proposals for industrial training ever put before Parliament' (Morrison, P., *Hansard*, 10 November 1983).

The claim that YTS provides young people with high quality training has been used to justify the establishment of a two-year programme which offers 'training for skills'. The emphasis upon training has moved provision still further away from any concept of positive discrimination to even more employer-led skill training. As a result, growing concern has been expressed about the adequacy of the programme for 'less able' school leavers and those in areas of high unemployment where there are too few employers to offer sufficient places. Research has continued to expose the inequitable nature of training provision and the discriminatory practices within it.

The two-year scheme, which started in April 1986, aims to cater for around 360 000 young people in 1986–7 and a similar number in 1987–8. It is intended to establish a comprehensive system of qualifications which all trainees can enter for and which genuinely reflect competence in the work place. This will demand close co-operation between employers (and others who provide YTS opportunities), validating bodies and training agencies. Before the start of the two-year scheme, following a quite inadequate period of consultation and discussion, numerous reservations were expressed and potential problems identified. The new, less generous, funding structure led to the withdrawal of some managing agents from the scheme. Anxieties have continued to be aired about the legal rights of trainees. The reduction in provision for trainees with special needs has evoked condemnation in certain quarters. Even the Confederation of British Industry, while maintaining that it will do everything within its power to make this scheme a success, has voiced concern about costs, bureaucracy and the framework.

It is the involvement of trade unions, community groups, employers, local authority departments, colleges and voluntary organisations in the planning, implementation and monitoring of YTS which has enabled the MSC to depict it as having widespread support and a democratic base (Finn, 1984a). Consequently it is portrayed as a scheme which somehow manages to reconcile simultaneously the interests of government, local authorities, employers, the labour movement and young people. Rarely have the fundamental conflicts and contradictions within these different sets of interests been exposed to any degree. For some of these groups – notably colleges, voluntary organisations and employers – YTS has provided a fresh and much-needed source of both labour and revenue. Despite a growing awareness of the threat of the MSC to their independence, criticisms have perhaps not surprisingly been muted. Yet, far from provision being developed on the basis of discussion and collaboration, it has largely been a case of she who pays the piper calls the tune'.

Attitudes towards and depictions of YTS have to a large extent polarised. Some see it as a 'gift horse' with immense potential once certain teething troubles have been ironed out, while those who oppose it are viewed as 'looking a gift horse in the mouth'. Others maintain it is a 'trojan horse' seeking to undermine the power of the labour movement and remoralise working-class youth as the pliant dough of the capitalist economy (Scofield *et al.*, 1983), while those who collaborate are seen to be 'lying down with the trojan horse'. For youth workers neither perspective is particularly helpful in terms of their attempt to consider a relationship either directly, or indirectly through young people, with YTS.

The background to and meaning of previous government training initiatives

The MSC, established in 1973, was originally conceived of as a centralised instrument in the management of the labour market designed to identify and respond to changing needs. It had no concern initially with unemployment. However, by establishing the Job Creation Programme in 1975, a precedent was set for the earmarking of considerable sums of government money for the purpose of tackling the 'problem' of the young unemployed. The Work Experience Programme (1976) and YOP (1978) continued the trend of focusing on the 'needs' of unemployed youth. The YTS (1983) has built upon these earlier employment and training initiatives, on existing social and educational provision for young people and theoretically upon the best experiences of earlier programmes. It has been argued that for YTS to be effective it must 'provide an experience that is somewhere between the informal approach of the youth club and the rigid demands of the production line or factory' (Hobbs *et al.*, 1983, p. 14) and therefore draw on the experience of YOP, the Unified Vocational Preparation (UVP), apprenticeships, youth work and FE provision.

It is crucial to emphasise though that government interventions in the realm of youth training and employment may provide quite different experiences and meanings for participants (Williamson, 1982). Even if these interventions are overtly about training and employment (which some may doubt) they in fact have the potential to perform other functions. These may relate not only to 'occupational' but also to financial, social and psychological issues (Jones *et al.*, 1983). They may have little to do with enhancing opportunities for some speculative highly skilled economy but may (and it is a big 'may') present new opportunities for young people to do desirable and desired work in occupational areas from which they have traditionally been excluded on the grounds of qualifications, age, gender or ethnic origin. Yet most evidence would suggest government training initiatives compound and re-affirm traditional structures of disadvantage and opportunity (Jones *et al.*, 1983; Rees, 1985; Troyna & Smith, 1983). However there remains a complex relationship between the power of the labour market (and indeed training schemes) to determine the destinies of young people and attempts by young people to exercise at least a modicum of choice (Roberts, 1968; Jones *et al.*, 1983).

Various benefits may arise from participation in government training measures. They do offer some marginal material benefits. They provide a new arena for social interaction and are psychologically worthwhile (Jones *et al.*, 1983; Stafford, 1982; Breakwell *et al.*, 1984) in comparison to what is often the only other 'choice' available, staying on the dole. The debilitating and demoralising effects of unemployment need to be continually spelt out. It is quite false to perceive the young unemployed as the source of some imminent spectacular resistance. The vast majority have internalised the ideology of unemployment, seeing it as somehow their own fault, the product of their lack of skills, lack of 'personality' or lack of effort. The consequence is a 'widespread feeling of apathy, non-involvement, depression and quiet despair' (YODU, 1981).

More than half of the young people leaving school in the 1980s will struggle to find jobs. In some parts of the country there are simply no jobs to strive for. Whatever the underlying motives for the establishment of YTS it absorbs a significant proportion of school leavers who would otherwise be unemployed. In Birmingham, where I am a part-time youth worker, around 17 000 young people are eligible to leave school each year. Some stay on and some go into FE while a fortunate minority find real jobs. The numbers taking each of these paths is integrally bound up with the real and perceived opportunities available in the local labour market. Between 10 000 and 12 000 do leave and the extent to which YTS and previously YOP has absorbed those who faced unemployment is graphically illustrated in Figure 7.1. Officially recorded youth unemployment is the difference between A and B. This relates only to those who register as unemployed at the Careers Office. The real figure is no doubt even greater.

I have not yet addressed the question of the differential quality of provision within MSC initiatives. My point is to stress that YTS, like other MSC schemes, cannot be assessed in blanket terms from just one perspective. It may be viewed as a 'trojan horse', constructed by the state for both the economic purpose of restructuring youth labour in the interests of capital and the political purpose of containing and resocialising surplus youth labour in the interests of control. From the more personal perspective of some young people it may be seen as a positive and valuable opportunity for gaining experience and acquiring skills relevant to the modern world. It may also be perceived by others such as youth workers or those in education as genuinely beneficial for young people, given the limited alternatives available to them. There are a lot of significant 'mays' but YTS, like its predecessors, needs to be

Figure 7.1 *Policy-off youth unemployment and young people on special measures, Birmingham 1980–6*

Source: Birmingham Careers Service Statistical Summaries, March 1980–February 1986

Policy-off youth unemployment (registered unemployed plus those on special measures) (A) ———
Numbers participating in special measures (B) ----------

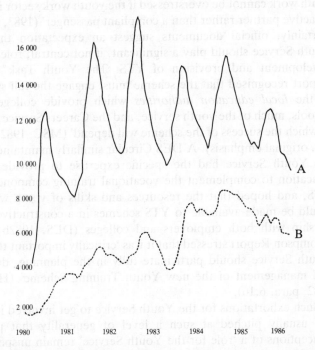

considered and evaluated not only according to its internal dimensions (cf. Mode A, B1, B2) but also on a number of different levels (cf. 'training', 'occupational', 'educational', 'psychological', 'social') and from a number of perspectives (cf. government, employers, trade unions, FE staff, youth workers, participating young people, young people who refuse).

Youth workers have to find some way of reconciling their own personal, professional and political perspectives on YTS with their understanding of young people's perceptions of the scheme. That is, of course, if reconciliation is required.

A role for the Youth Service?

Marsland has argued that 'in the Youth Service . . . we have *uniquely* a combination of commitment, values, understandings and skills such as unemployed young people need the help of urgently and imperatively' (1985, p. 3, original emphasis). More specifically in relation to YTS, Swain pointed out that 'the importance of drawing upon the distinctive experience and expertise of youth work cannot be overstressed if the youth work sector is to be an active partner rather than a compliant passenger' (1983, p. 11). Certainly, official documents suggest an expectation that the Youth Service should play a significant, if not central, role in the development and provision of YTS. The Youth Task Group Report recognised that the scheme 'must engage the full support of the *local education authorities* which provide colleges and schools, much of the youth service, and the Careers Service, on all of which the success of the scheme will depend' (MSC, 1982, para. 3.7, original emphasis). A DES Circular similarly maintained that the Youth Service had the specific expertise to provide social education to complement the vocational training components of YTS, and hoped that the resources and skills of youth workers would be made available to YTS schemes in a constructive partnership with both employers and colleges (DES, 1982b). The Thompson Report stressed that it was 'critically important that the Youth Service should participate fully in the planning, delivery and management of the new Youth Training Scheme' (HMSO, 1982, para. 6.16).

Such exhortations for the Youth Service to get involved in YTS are usually pitched at such a level of generality that precise conceptions of a 'role for the Youth Service' remain unspecified. The Youth Opportunities Development Unit (YODU) at NYB sought valiantly to define a relevant Youth Service contribution to YTS, drawing on practical examples to illustrate the diversity of roles which the Service is already playing within YTS. A survey by YODU suggested that Youth Service input into YTS fell within the following five areas of work:

1. programme planning and management
2. promotion, sponsorship and management of Youth Service YTS schemes

3. provision of 'off the job training', especially social and political education, and including residential experience
4. input into personal counselling and support services to trainees before, during and after their stay on the scheme
5. contribution to staff development and training programmes (YODU, 1983b).

Few connected with the Youth Service would argue in principle that these are suitable and necessary roles for youth workers within youth training measures. However, in practice there appears to be a degree of naiveté (though I am certainly not accusing YODU of this) about the degree of influence the Youth Service may have in terms of guiding the objectives and content of YTS in the face of the massive power and influence of the MSC. It is less an issue of the MSC requesting or accepting the expertise of youth workers than of the MSC demanding and *redefining* it. There has been a basic failure in some quarters to recognise that the development of employment and training provision for young people has been subject to the control of the MSC as 'managing director', not as 'partner'. There is furthermore a failure (or reluctance) to perceive elements of MSC ideology which clash head on with the theoretical basis of youth work and which, by implication, raise fundamental questions as to whether the Youth Service should be involved at all.

Some dilemmas for the Youth Service

Both at political and at ideological levels and in terms of practice there are persuasive arguments that to collaborate with the MSC is to collude in the betrayal of the interests of young people and, ultimately, to surrender any claim to a specific, independent role. There are fears that the Youth Service, along with FE and some voluntary organisations, is being bought out and appropriated by the MSC, so that its perspectives on relevant provision for young people are rendered impotent.

Politically and ideologically there are justifiable claims that the MSC has so far successfully exerted its economic strength to suppress alternative definitions of the 'youth problem'. This has enabled the MSC to serve the interests of employers and the 'market' under the guise of responding to the 'needs' of young people. Furthermore, using a similar ploy, the MSC has been able to set about the remoralisation of the young under the cover of 'compensating' for the failure of school to provide young people with the attributes and qualifications 'relevant' to the contemporary labour market (Atkinson *et al.*, 1982). There has been, some would argue, a massive vocational, personal, cultural, political and economic reconstruction of youth, turning attention inward on the 'deficiencies' of individual young people to conceal the wider political and economic crisis for which young people have become the scapegoat (Davies, 1981; Stronach, 1984). If this is an accurate portrayal of the real function of the MSC, no wonder youth workers may wish to have no part of it.

At a more practical level, youth workers are experiencing increasingly the concrete practices which are the product of a 'scapegoating' ideology. The MSC has become an adept 'coloniser', encroaching on the Youth Service and FE (Davies, 1981) and dealing competently and quietly with those who offer criticism or resistance. Its economic and administrative power is used to effect a policy of divide and rule; the resources it commands in stringent times are usually sufficient to secure conformity amongst those who make use of them. Furthermore, despite the assertion of the importance of a 'youth work' contribution to YTS, the Youth Service is not represented on the Area Manpower Boards which approve YTS schemes in local areas.

Youth workers who are involved in YTS find themselves expected to offer a regimented and 'relevant' social and life skills training rather than a critical, person-centred social education (Davies, 1979). They must not delve into political issues or issues which may cause embarrassment to the MSC. They find themselves colluding with the manifestly false but pervasive definition that it is the deficiencies of youth which demand attention. Moreover, they may find themselves accountable to individuals who are far less experienced in working with young people than they are. Finally, they will hardly fail to notice the contradictions between the constricting and controlling directives emanating from MSC bureaucracy and the language of 'adaptability', 'flexibility' and 'transferability' which 'are the watchwords of the new Scheme' (Swain, 1983, p. 11).

For those not working directly with YTS their awareness of

these issues combined with their knowledge of exploitative schemes, the cynicism about YTS which may exist amongst many young people with whom they work and their knowledge of the lack of opportunities for youth in the local labour market, presents them with a core dilemma regarding how they counsel young people about YTS. Such dilemmas are likely to become more acute as the MSC tightens its grip on post-school, and now in-school via TVEI youth 'opportunities'.

Davies has argued that 'with a youth crisis looking more and more like a metaphor for general economic, political and social upheaval, the need for more effective and more cost-effective responses has become very urgent indeed' (1982, p. 34). State responses have shifted from winning-by-consent to coercing compliance through compulsory training measures or increasingly punitive measures within the criminal justice system. It might be argued that the Youth Service itself has, in reality, never been very far from acting as an instrument for instilling conformity and exercising control, but its *methods* have never been so blatantly interventionist as those of the MSC and the courts.

With regard to YTS and earlier MSC training initiatives youth workers have struggled with or simply adopted one or other of the competing positions of pragmatism and expediency, or ideology and principle. The former position can be readily rationalised in terms of desperation or the desire to effect 'change from within'. The latter position can be justified on the grounds that the Youth Service should have no part in a process by which the state increasingly dictates the terms of young people's lives. Yet, even if such a critical stance on YTS is justifiable, do youth workers in fact have a real choice about whether or not to get involved? Engaging in opposition and resistance may have little effect and even prove suicidal. In the current economic and political climate there are fundamental issues of credibility which may constrain choice for youth workers as much as for YTS trainees.

Issues of credibility

The issues which affect the credibility of both youth workers and the Youth Service in terms of their relationship with MSC interventions are complex and often contradictory. The questions 'credibility with whom?' and 'credibility about what?' are central. Credibility issues connect with questions about finance and professional autonomy, which are, of course, closely related, and about public and political recognition, support and respect. Youth workers need to retain credibility with their political bosses, colleagues from other professions, the young people with whom they work and their families, and amongst themselves.

The credibility of the Youth Service is anyway at a low ebb. Its soft and all ill-defined methods do not fit comfortably within the law and order, value for money, hard-nosed, iron-fist policies favoured by the Thatcher Government. If it 'chooses' to work with MSC initiatives there is not only the risk of 'colonisation' by the MSC but also of increasing pressure to make compromises in its professional responsibilities and commitments. This is likely to undermine its claim to having the skills and expertise to make a distinct contribution and to raise public and political questions about its 'worth'. Yet only through collaboration with the MSC is the public and political credibility of the Youth Service likely to be sustained. For if the Youth Service refuses to collaborate in MSC initiatives which are claimed to be about 'meeting the needs' of (unemployed) young people, then the Youth Service will be seen as patently failing to discharge its explicit responsibilities and consequently its credibility will diminish. The Youth Service may argue that in refusing to collaborate it is in fact discharging its true responsibilities, that it wants no part in initiatives which it suspects do not meet the needs of young people. However, the counter-view is that there is a role for the Youth Service at various levels of YTS and that rejection of this 'new' role is both obstinate and somehow *unprofessional*, since it leaves everything to those with less skill and less knowledge about working with young people. All this, of course, is a somewhat simplistic representation of the 'Catch 22' facing the Youth Service. Nonetheless, the problem remains acute.

For youth workers these problems are perhaps even more imbued with conflict and contradiction. Acting as entrepreneurs in the realm of YTS may reap personal rewards. Political opposition to YTS may rule out their personal involvement but does not help them to think through how they 'connect' YTS with the young people with whom they work. Do they share their reservations and political concerns with them? Do they encourage young people to participate, in recognition of the absence of alternatives? Youth workers also face tensions to do with their professional and public credibility. To oppose and denigrate YTS may be seen by local young people and their parents as being 'out of touch', as failing to guide and counsel young people as they try to make sense of limited opportunities. In contrast, to encourage involvement in YTS may be seen by some parents and young people as exerting undue pressure to participate in 'cheap labour' schemes and thereby not acting professionally. Much hinges on differing conceptions of the 'professional' responsibilities of the youth worker.

Such tensions and dilemmas concerning credibility and 'what to do' are an inevitable product of the complexity of the issues which pertain both to YTS and other MSC provision as well as to the status of the Youth Service within the wider context of youth policy.

Youth workers and YTS

In some quarters there are strong demands for a boycott of YTS which could easily be understood as an attempt to defend 'a racist and sexist apprenticeship system and an elitist structure of education' (Finn, 1984, p. 4). If YTS is here to stay, a boycott would serve few interests. It is also crucial to recognise that there are both 'top down' and 'bottom up' perspectives, which may well be in conflict.

From the top down, there are very serious questions about the nature, purpose, content and quality of YTS and whether it is actually concerned with the needs of young people. But young people are involved. YTS is a significant route out of school for a large proportion of school leavers. The Youth Service must ensure that it does not adopt a pragmatic and expedient stance towards YTS but recognises its professional responsibilities to those young people who are involved. The Youth Service should project a willingness to get involved in YTS provided it does not prostitute its expertise, which would be a myopic survival strategy anyway. It needs to assert a role for genuine social education within YTS which does not impose a curriculum in the manner of much 'social and life skills training', which avoids a 'cultural deficit' model of youth (Atkinson *et al.*, 1982) and which is instead generated out of the real experiences, demands and concerns of young people themselves (Cohen, 1984). In this context Short cogently argues in relation to FE and and YTS:

> Not that we should or can ignore YTS, but we should expose the scheme for what it is and demand something better. Educators must do their best to get control for the three months to which they are entitled. They must struggled to develop a new style of education and a curriculum which is both useful and relevant to the bemused and battered generation of school leavers who will be there simply because they have nowhere else to go. . . . Educators must start to believe once again in education, and refuse to allow the MSC to set the agenda, redefine the language and control all the details of the curriculum (Short, 1983).

The argument is equally applicable to the Youth Service. It must attempt to challenge through collective professional action the 'abuses' within YTS and to resist on behalf of young people the straitjacket which is increasingly being thrust upon those who participate.

For youth workers the challenge on the ground is of a different order. 'Bottom up' perspectives on YTS suggest that there are strong personal, social and psychological as well as marginal but necessary material benefits accruing from participation, even if the claimed occupational benefits do not materialise. Unless youth workers and others can move beyond the rhetoric about 'alternatives' (such as co-operatives), YTS will remain for many young people the only realistic alternative to the dole. Indeed, its symbolic role in the transition from school to work is becoming increasingly important since joining YTS 'may now be the *only* way into work' (Willis, 1984, p. 224, original emphasis). The 'relevance' and 'usefulness' of what is provided on YTS, like the relevance and usefulness of much educational provision, may be questionable, but the symbolic importance of participation is not in doubt. YTS therefore becomes a crucial form of certification to demonstrate suitability for 'real work'. But there are significant differences in forms of provision within YTS. Only going on the 'right' YTS schemes provides valid 'certification' for real work; going on the 'wrong' scheme is a blind alley (Buswell, 1985). It is therefore necessary for youth workers to ensure that they are well informed about the structure, limitations and potential of local

MSC provision. In this way they may offer some 'neutral ground' upon which young people can weigh up the benefits and drawbacks of participation. In their direct interaction with young people youth workers have a minimum duty to explain the complex reality of YTS. Precisely how they do this is, as I have argued elsewhere, problematic (Williamson, 1983). I am not advocating that youth workers should actively encourage participation, but to discourage involvement or to deny any value in YTS would be a complete disservice to young people.

Whether or not youth workers become actively involved in YTS will depend upon both their own personal motivation and knowledge as well as higher organisational decisions. What remains important then is that they continue to 'defend a space' within which they can professionally represent the interests and concerns of young people. Those who remain 'detached' from MSC involvement may not only inform young people about YTS and similar measures but may actively engage with others in advocacy and criticism of specific schemes within the local structure of provision.

Conclusion

No doubt there are some youth workers who believe that collaboration with MSC initiatives is unproblematic, either because they remain convinced that YTS is relevant to the needs of young people or because they feel they have little choice. Others are likely to experience a constant struggle over precisely how they should relate to such measures. The diversity of arguments and positions which may be adopted concerning YTS makes this struggle a difficult and persistent one.

If youth workers are to reject for themselves active participation in YTS as it is currently formulated they must avoid rejecting it through the young people with whom they work, for whom involvement in YTS may be a relatively constructive and beneficial experience. Youth workers with personal, political and ideological hostility to the current structure and rationale need to build, first within the Youth Service and then with other equally concerned professional groups, a collective alliance to provide constructive criticism and a lobby for change. There is potential within YTS for all I have said. Never before have such vast state resources been

made available for young people and specifically for those from
the working class. However, youth workers have a professional
responsibility to young people and therefore they need to develop
a comprehensive practical knowledge of MSC provision. Only in
this way will youth workers avoid the invidious possibility of
themselves exploiting young people to fight the battles of the
Youth Service. The irony then is that they would be engaging in a
similar strategy to that attributed by some to the MSC itself: that
is, using young people as pawns in a wider political and ideological
game.

8

Finding a Way In: Youth Workers and Juvenile Justice

ROBERT ADAMS

Youth workers occupy a somewhat marginal position in terms of their formal responsibilities for working with young offenders. However, the reality of their job means that they often develop very close, informal relationships with young people. From this position they will appreciate the widespread nature of unrecorded, as opposed to officially known, offending amongst the young and the need for all workers to co-operate to minimise the penetration of young people into the juvenile justice system. These factors point to the need for all who work with young people in the community to acquire a sound working knowledge of juvenile justice. The attitude of many towards the propriety of youth work with delinquents has been somewhat ambivalent. This extends not only to commentators, academics and politicians but also to youth workers and is as old as youth work itself. Many lay people have not wanted to see their respectable youth facilities cluttered up with young tearaways but at the same time have hoped, even required, youth workers somehow, magically, to curb youthful crime. This conjuring trick has been expected to occur with a minimum of resources. The Britishness of the paradox is captured in the image of our massive youth crime problems being solved by great charismatic local figures in the proverbial tumbledown hut using two volunteers, the odd jumble sale and a football team. As we shall see, it has been as true in the last decade as it was in the

Edwardian era that this invisible mending of delinquency has been expected to be most effective when at its most amateur, built around the strengths of the voluntary youth organisations. Twenty years ago, Smith summarised the situation:

> It is a common view, of layman and expert alike, to expect the Youth Service to keep young people out of trouble: from the ordinary man in the street's attitude that youth clubs are there to keep young people off his streets to the more sophisticated view of the professional that it is cheaper to prevent crime in this way than to treat the criminal. . . . Even the Albemarle Committee, which came out against a problem-centred service, devoted fourteen paragraphs to an analysis of delinquency and decided that 'the crime problem is very much a youth problem, a problem of that age group with which the Youth Service is particularly concerned and towards which the public rightly expects it to make some contribution' (Smith, 1966, pp. 42–3).

Whilst it is not possible to examine in adequate depth the range and complexities of juvenile justice in the UK in one chapter, the dearth of available literature on how youth workers relate to the system makes this introduction to the subject even more necessary.

Responses to juvenile offending

It is not cynical to suggest that the police, social workers and probation officers only get involved in a small proportion of actual crime. One British Crime Survey (Home Office, 1983) concluded that official crime statistics represent only about 10 per cent of actual crime. Official statistics also indicate that for whatever reasons, recorded young offenders include about 6 boys for every girl. The peak age for known offenders is 15: the last year before leaving school, after which offending declines until in late middle age it is almost unknown save in certain special categories such as homeless drunkenness. The steepest decline in recorded rates of offending occurs when adulthood is reached. That is, a third of all officially labelled offenders are under 17 and nearly a half are under 21. Whilst recorded juvenile crime has risen about 30 per cent in the past 20 years, this is no faster than adult crime. The overwhelming majority of juvenile recorded offences are thefts and despite the impression given in the tabloid press serious violent offences, which peak in the mid-teens, represent less than half of one per cent of all juvenile crime.

In general, criminologists agree that for most young people offending is a temporary, transitional experience and, like the inclination to public recorded violence, it declines quickly, with one major exception. That exception is the relatively small propor-tion of all young offenders who become subjects of early treatment or punishment in the juvenile justice system. Private violence, like other aspects of violence against children and women, is no less permanently rooted in our society but maybe less likely to be recorded as such in official statistics (Freeman, 1979, p. 4). How-ever, to return to responses to crime as a rule, the earlier and the 'heavier', or more custodial, the intervention, the more likely the young person will go on to become a recidivist prisoner (Lipton *et al.*, 1975, p. 88).

The evaluation of available forms of disposal for convicted young offenders makes depressing reading. As far as custodial institutions are concerned, whether tougher or not (Home Office, 1984), they are remarkably consistent in their inability to reduce delinquency (Brody, 1966; Cornish & Clarke, 1975; Millham, 1975; Tutt, 1974). Within two years of discharge, over 80 per cent of trainees in borstals (now re-named youth custody centres fol-lowing the 1982 Criminal Justice Act), over 65 per cent in Deten-tion Centres and about three-quarters of offenders in Community Homes, re-offend. For any unlucky enough to proceed from residential care in a Community Home to further custody, the outlook is even more bleak. In short, sending juvenile offenders to custodial institutions is tantamount to giving them a further edu-cation in crime.

Neither can we assume that community-based supervision of young offenders will of itself prove effective in reducing or elim-inating their delinquent behaviour. Available research suggests that supervision in the community is no more likely to reduce the chances of further convictions than most other forms of disposal (Home Office, 1976).

The discouraging conclusion is that the most intervention pro-vides is reassurance to the agencies and public that 'something is being done'. Meanwhile, more rigorous studies either fail to demonstrate the effectiveness of particular measures, or conclude that further research is needed (Lipton *et al.*, 1975, pp. 627–8), or argue that the research, not the system itself, needs attention first (Farrington, 1978). More critical criminologists accept that the penal system is ineffective (Carlen, 1983, p. 203) while there is a general disinclination since the 1970s to initiate major new evaluative studies of the effectiveness of any parts of the system (Parker & Giller, 1981). At worst, institutional facilities are depressingly bad at reducing delinquency and good at actually increasing chances of reconviction. The most convincing policy is to try to minimise every young person's contact with the juvenile justice system and play for time in the knowledge that most youngsters simply grow out of offending, if they can be kept clear of judicial intervention (Schur, 1973).

Juvenile justice since 1970: England and Wales

Few subjects arouse such controversy as delinquency and in the post-war years few laws have produced as much feuding between professionals as the 1969 Children and Young Persons Act. Social democrats have seen the 1969 Act as the high water mark of their attempts to implement community oriented treatment of children and young people in trouble or at risk. However conservatives were soon to blame it for an alleged juvenile crime wave and radicals criticised it for encouraging potentially harmful intervention in young lives. Perhaps these conflicting views are unsurprising given that the Act was a compromise between those who saw young persons as sick, undersocialised individuals needing treatment and those who saw them as deliberate law breakers (Bottoms, 1974; Adams *et al.*, 1981, ch. 1).

The 1969 Act expressed rather than resolved a longstanding contradiction between justice and welfare orientations in our juvenile justice system. It aimed to abolish the distinction between young people defined as delinquent because they had come into conflict with the law and those otherwise felt to be in need. It set out to emphasise the importance of maintaining and supporting young people as far as possible in their own families and communities. Through the IT provisions in Sections 12 and 19 the intention was to transfer to local authorities responsibility for dealing with all but the most difficult. As measures like IT attached to supervision orders were phased in, detention centres for the under 17s, attendance centres, probation orders and the remand of children to Prison Department establishments under certificates of unruliness were to be phased out. Concern for a minority of young people who were felt to need secure accommodation led to Part Two of the 1969 Act requiring local authorities to develop a comprehensive system of residential community homes via Children's Regional Planning Committees, which were also to be responsible for setting up regional IT schemes.

The main provisions of the 1969 Act came into force on 1 January 1971, and IT schemes became operative from 1 April 1974. The only other major area of implementation was the age at which the Probation Service became responsible for supervision, which by 1974 had been raised to 13 years. The reasons for this delay are complex. The reorganisations of the Personal Social Services and local government delayed and disrupted development. Emerging Social Services Departments were burdened with new and onerous responsibilities in areas other than IT, such as the Chronically Sick and Disabled Act (1970) and certainly doubts were expressed as to whether social workers had the necessary skills to develop and manage IT schemes. However ideological conflicts about how problem young people should be dealt with lay behind many of the difficulties hindering the smooth implementation of the 1969 Act.

Growing criticism of the 1969 Act led to a review of its working by a House of Commons Expenditure Committee in 1975 (HMSO 1976) which prompted a White Paper in May 1976. This endorsed the principles of the 1969 Act and the extension of IT. However concern and criticism about the lack of effective means of dealing with 'problem' young people continued to increase.

As the 1970s progressed, it was possible to discern a clear trend in government thinking, one increasingly committed to offering IT to more serious offenders. The incoming Conservative Government of 1979 showed its commitment to IT by excluding it from public spending cuts and shortly afterwards officially countenanced it for delinquents with more serious criminal records (Brittan, 1979).

Certainly the 1982 Criminal Justice Act can be seen as a visible symptom of a shift towards a Thatcherite 'law and order' approach towards delinquency. However tempting this view is to ideologues of the Left, it does not tally with the fact that a strong 'law and order' lobby was influential long before 1974 (Society of Conservative Lawyers, 1974). Certainly we can see in the White Paper of May 1976 the onset of a policy shift continued by the 1982 Act.

The 1982 Act set out to strengthen the direct control of the courts over the freedom of local authority social work departments to deal with delinquents. It contained stricter criteria than had hitherto existed regarding the use of custodial sentences but there were fears that its extension of the powers of courts to give very short custodial sentences would tempt them to use, for example, detention centres more freely, particularly as tougher regimes were being progressively introduced. It is still too early to attempt to ascertain what is happening to non-custodial sentences in the wake of the 1982 Act. Interim indications at local level give little grounds for optimism that the Act has either contained the numbers of young offenders receiving inappropriate custodial sentences or has encouraged magistrates to make more confident use of supervision (Boyd, 1985). Perhaps this is partly because magistrates are able to impose more youth custody sentences in compensation for the increased restrictions on custodial sentences introduced in the 1982 legislation (ADSS, 1985, p. 25). At any rate Burney's (1985) study of twelve courts in South-East England has produced worrying evidence that magistrates are not heeding these guidelines which aim to maintain custody only as a last resort.

Juvenile justice in Scotland

Though the juvenile justice system in Scotland shared common roots with the English one in the 1908 Children's Act, by the time the Kilbrandon Committee reported (HMSO, 1964) Scotland was well on the way towards the more treatment-oriented approach adopted in the 1968 Social Work (Scotland) Act.

The Scottish system has been held up as the way forward by advocates of the welfare approach in England (ACC, 1984) and criticised by those supporting the introduction of due process based upon the principle of natural justice. Critics allege in particular that it emphasises a medically-oriented approach to the child and family at the expense of a recognition of wider social factors responsible for causing delinquency (Asquith, 1983). Uniquely, the Scottish system revolves around a children's panel composed of selected trained lay volunteers, to which the Procurator Fiscal rather than the police refers children for non-criminal disposal. Disposal may include supervision with or without a residential condition, or compulsory care to the age of 18 subject to continual review. More serious offences can be brought to a Sheriff's Court or even a High Court.

Recent concern in England and Wales about the need to deal with young people as far as possible outside the apparatus of the juvenile court has led to heightened interest in the Scottish system. A working party of the Association of County Councils (ACC, 1984) used a survey of juvenile justice in the UK as the starting point for its recommendation that a unified family court be established with civil rather than criminal jurisdiction over juveniles. This would have exclusive concern with care orders but would share powers to make supervision orders, including those linked with IT with the juvenile court (McCabe & Treitel, 1983). A more recent report from Social Services Directors argues also for the adoption in England and Wales of a non-judicial tribunal based on the Children's Hearings in Scotland (ADSS, 1985, p. 6). This report suggests at the same time that Scotland lacks intensive, possibly residential, IT provision along English lines (ibid., p. 24).

Juvenile justice in Northern Ireland

The more obvious differences between the juvenile justice systems of Northern Ireland and England illustrate contrasts in the social and political climate which are a feature of the constitutional and religious struggle in the former. A consequence of the longstanding problem of using the customary judicial arrangements to mete out justice to politically motivated offenders has been the use of solicitors and lawyers as paid professional magistrates.

The 1968 Children and Young Persons Act (NI) represented a truncated version of the 1969 Act in England. It stopped short of the kind of measures introduced in England and left the Probation Service responsible for preparing all social enquiry reports and for probation orders for 14–17 year olds. Younger children could still be put on supervision but in general the control of the court over the practice of social workers in much stronger than in England.

Of particular concern to youth workers in Northern Ireland has been a rapid growth of non-politically aligned community groups in the areas most disrupted by the troubles of recent years and ascribed by some to the failings of statutory social services (Kelly, 1979, p. 180). Further, a degree of 'local' critical comment (Caul, 1983) has followed the most significant policy initiative of the past decade, the Black Report (Home Office, 1979). Black proposed minimal intervention for juvenile offenders early in their criminal careers – cautions for first and second minor offenders – all subsequent offences going to a criminal court. Further, all truants and other children 'in need of care' (ibid, p. 56) would be processed through civil courts and separate institutions from offenders. Finally, prevention, co-ordinated by new District Child Care Teams, would emphasise family support and the importance of the school.

Doubts about the relative restrictiveness and practicability of the cautioning proposals have been voiced, not least by the police. The Northern Ireland Office itself has expressed concern about the practicability of a separation between civil and criminal courts. Also concern has been raised about the resourcing and staffing of school-based preventive teams (ADSS, 1985, p. 30).

In summary, it would appear that whilst Northern Ireland may have some way to go in reforming its juvenile justice system, in England and Wales there is no room for complacency given the extent to which the Scottish System shows up the limitations of juvenile justice further south. However, in Scotland there is evidence of the need to reconsider the balance between welfare and justice elements in decision-making concerning young offenders and to shift the emphasis towards the latter.

Problems and prospects for youth workers

In all the literature referred to so far there is scarcely a single reference to the role of youth workers in relation to juvenile justice. This may be indicative of a level of institutionalised myopia which predisposes commentators to neglect youth work practice. The activity-based ethos of IT provides an exciting opportunity for practitioners, yet in no area of youth work does history hang more like a millstone around their necks. In England

and Wales this is illustrated by the manner in which IT was introduced, in the particular image of youth work which pervaded official thinking. It was not surprising that in the 1970s many youth workers rejected the role assigned to them by IT, particularly the bland assumption of policy-makers that somehow sending a young offender on an IT order down to the local youth club to mix with a few 'normal' youngsters might magically transform a delinquent into a law-abiding young citizen. Possibly more important to their image was the way they were caught up in the ready formulation by many local authorities and agencies of IT as synonymous with outdoor pursuits. This was not confined to youth work, for many local authority Social Services Departments were devoting their underspent IT budgets to canoes, and camping and hiking equipment. In some areas it was not uncommon to find individual boys being sent on courses at Outward Bound Centres, paid for by IT funds. Other stories have acquired the status of modern myths: the grim-faced, exhausted social workers being dragged up Cader Idris by their delinquent caseload all day and being kept awake by them all night; the magistrate who complained about the uselessness of sentencing young offenders to nothing more than thirty days of continuous ping-pong.

In the early 1970s, many statutory and voluntary youth groups allowed themselves through consultation, often imperfect or hurried, to be registered by Children's Regional Planning Committee Schemes for IT with no detailed accompanying statements about what might be the how, what, why and when of their contribution (Adams, 1982). In the Yorkshire region, youth work clearly predominated over social work. Of 1038 registered facilities in the initial Scheme at its publication in July 1973, there were 326 civic and 288 voluntary youth clubs, 228 uniformed groups including 111 scout and 55 guide groups, 68 activity groups including 24 sports clubs, 55 educational facilities including 15 FE centres, and no less than 15 residential adventure and sea voyage facilities. Only 11 of the remaining facilities were identifiable as mainstream social work, being provided by community homes. There was not a single facility run by a field social worker in the entire scheme! (Adams, 1982).

At its worst the legacy of the 1970s may be of an image of youth work with delinquents which has embodied a number of linked assumptions: that boys were the problem, girls not being denied a place but for all practical purposes being invisible; that activity in groups, with an outdoor component, was the norm; that challenging activities would act as the catalyst modifying delinquent behaviour, through the development of individual initiative and leadership qualities in situations of stress (Adams, 1984). Many practitioners have rebelled against this view of youth work with delinquents, calling it anachronistic, sexist and politically and socially unacceptable, designed to promote individualistic, competitive and hierarchical values. It has as a result been necessary for many youth workers to reassess the contribution they can realistically make to work with delinquents.

In order for youth workers to make a credible input to the debate about responses to youth crime and policy provision they need to be able to offer approaches to practice which are both true to their own professional identity and marketable in the terms of other professions. In short, the ideology of youth work in juvenile justice has to be updated beyond its 1970s image. The dilemma is that many youth workers have hesitated to step outside the educational context and engage with social problems which may be viewed as the business of the Social Services Departments.

In an attempt to resolve this dilemma organisationally, NAYCEO proposed that the Youth Service should undertake IT as an agency service, for Social Services Depts, for it has:

> the expertise and experience in groupwork, activity work and social education. The Youth Service has experience, too, in youth counselling, in work with young blacks, young homelessness, young unemployed. It has developed methods of work which start with the needs which young people themselves have identified, through detached work, drop-in centres, night shelters (NYB, 1979).

However, that prescription has a certain blandness, a self-justificatory ring about it. What is missing is that rousing reveille from the early 1970s when community work still looked like a possible bedfellow with IT and before the white heat of radicalism had cooled into the resource-rationed aspiring professionalism of the 1980s. What is apparent is the very shortcoming Pinkerton identifies in the Black Report in Northern Ireland (Pinkerton, 1983), the tendency for prescriptions about juvenile justice policy to proceed from an implicit functionalist stance, a consensus picture of the community denying or seriously underplaying its internal divisions and emerging with a pragmatic, status-quo oriented set of policy statements, inevitably supporting the State as opposed to the individual. Pinkerton has also put his finger on the persistent tendency for debate about juvenile justice to exclude the involvement of the very groups so readily identified by the authorities as the enemy. To counter this he proposes a democratisation of juvenile justice, involving young people themselves. This has been discussed and even proposed in England and Wales (Bolger *et al.*, 1981) but hardly matches current government policy. Yet here surely, given the philosophy which the youth work field has been struggling to implement in recent years, is an aspect of involvement in juvenile justice which youth workers could take to themselves.

Dilemmas for youth workers emerge more sharply in the prevention versus intervention debate within juvenile justice. The division between preventive and delinquent sectors which has occurred in all parts of the UK to a greater or lesser degree poses a challenge to contemporary youth crime policy and practice. The question is whether prevention is better than cure. Put in these quasi-medical terms the answer might seem to be obvious. But in juvenile justice the stigmatising consequences of social agencies intervening early in the lives of juveniles who it is felt are 'at risk' are seen by some to outweigh the benefits of such intervention. For youth workers the problematic revolves around their 'preventive' role. It is not surprising that the self-contradictory character of the 1968 Act (NI) and the 1969 Act (England and Wales) poses dilemmas for practitioners. These two Acts are both Janus-faced. They illustrate a compromise between a justice approach towards already identified delinquents and a welfare approach towards preventive work with a much less clearly identified category of young people felt to be at risk. The problem lies in this last phrase 'felt to be at risk'. Attention has been drawn in recent years to the tendency of 'preventive' social work programmes in Britain and the USA to suck previously non-identified juveniles into what may become an ever-expanding net of intervention (Bakal, 1973; Lerman, 1975; Scull, 1977; Thorpe *et al.*, 1980). Specifically, there is some evidence to suggest that ironically, the deserving non-delinquent from a background of poverty is most likely to be

selected by social workers for IT, whilst the undeserving delinquent who stands most at risk of an impending custodial sentence,
is least likely to receive it (Thorpe, 1983, p. 85).

The juvenile justice system tends to produce dichotomies between the control of delinquents at its core and preventive work
with those at risk towards its margin. The structural marginality of
many youth workers in relation to the justice system processing
many of the young people they know so well provides the starting
point for a complex debate about if, when and how they should
intervene in the system. Whose side is the youth worker on? Is the
youth worker simply another social worker or police officer in
disguise? The youth worker operates in an ambiguous territory
between statutory imperatives and the informality of the street.
The preventive roles of police and youth workers illustrate just
such a paradox; indeed these roles may even converge in some
rare examples of inter-professional co-operation (McCabe &
Treitel, 1983, p. 12) which come to highlight the contrasts between
the ideologies of youth work and policing. Prevention, the buzz
word of the 1960s and 1970s, has now been outlived in the 1980s by
diversion. Diversion embraces the concept of prevention, stripped
of its unintended negative consequences. It covers all efforts made
to minimise the extent to which young people penetrate the
juvenile justice system or climb the tariff ladder of caution, conditional discharge, through to youth custody and prison. Diversion
aims to make minimal intervention the first resort and custody a
possibility only when all other non-custodial options have been
fully explored and positively rejected.

Diversion is an umbrella which increasing numbers of local
authorities are putting up to keep off a storm of calls for something
effective to be done to curb youth crime. Academic advocates of
diversion, led by the Centre for Youth, Crime and Community at
the University of Lancaster are wisely careful not to sell it as a
panacea. They package it as delinquency management. Diversion
may reduce crime but it will not cure an individual's delinquency.
They emphasise that whilst no known disposal will guarantee that
a particular offender will not re-offend, they stress that the use of
punitive, lengthy or custodial sentences can dramatically increase
the likelihood of further offending (Thorpe, 1980; Tutt, 1978).

A cynic might argue that diversion and delinquency management have taken off in the 1980s less in a spirit of corporate

idealism or a rational digestion of criminological truths than through simple cost-cutting expediency. Interestingly, some Conservative politicians have incorporated the arguments for diversion into their general philosophy concerning the curbing of juvenile crime through tougher sentences. The attraction of quick visible revenue savings if residential accommodation is reduced, resides alongside an abhorrence of too much state provision. In this respect there are parallels between what Mrs Thatcher's Government is encouraging local authorities to do about juvenile crime and the radical innovations in community-based youth programmes pioneered in the 1960s by the then Governor of California – Ronald Reagan!

There is no doubt that the management of delinquency is a step forward if it focuses attention on the entire system of juvenile justice and the need to monitor rigorously the activities and decision-making of its gatekeepers: police, social workers, probation officers, education welfare officers, teachers and associated workers. However the fact that it is attractive to both progressive criminologists and right-wing politicians is a clue to its inherent ambiguity. Just as in California in the 1960s many young people experienced more intensive control in the community than in custody, so we cannot assume in Britain that the technical progress of decarcerating delinquents guarantees that their experience of the alternatives to custody will be more positive than incarceration (Empey, 1983; Adams *et al.*, 1981, p. 22). This is not helped by the fact that decarceration may emphasise the negative character of institutions from which offenders are moved rather than the positive features of community alternatives.

Perhaps the fundamental truth is that we live in a society which has no great respect for young people in general and which responds punitively when young people step out of line by committing crimes. Britain's current incarceration rates are among the highest in Europe. So it would be naive to expect that mere technical improvements in the juvenile justice system would not contain within them the stimulus for their own undermining. Genuine progress may therefore only be by small degrees. Yet as one radical Scandinavian criminologist has argued somewhat bleakly, it may be possible that only by the total abolition of the residential system can we avoid its tendency to perpetuate itself and outflank even the best-intentioned reformers (Mathieson,

1974). Is sudden rather than gradual change then the only way forward in other parts of the juvenile justice system? Those who have struggled for years and feel they have made only slight progress may feel of this point trapped within our Darwinian inheritance which predisposes us to believe in the virtues of gradual improvement and the experience of the past decade. How can it be that we are still locking up so many young people despite the implementation of reforming legislation encouraging the opposite?

In concrete terms this points to the great difficulty we have in making changes in our very complex systems of juvenile justice at the local level, involving as they do networks of agencies and workers with no great experience of working together at any depth. Police, teachers, youth workers, probation officers, education welfare officers and social workers are likely to find that they are separated by historical, social and political factors, that they speak in different professional tongues and possess distinctive values and ideologies.

We seem to have reached a difficult conclusion whereby the promise of any real improvement in the situation of young offenders may not be realised simply through administrative reforms in the juvenile justice system. Unless that is, those reforms are accompanied by some genuine advances in the inter-professional activity of workers occupying frontier positions as gatekeepers of the system. What does this imply for youth workers?

Youth workers stand at the frontiers of juvenile justice. Like all frontier positions, theirs is crucial to the way young people are perceived and either excluded from or processed by that system. Youth workers need as a consequence to clarify the basis on which they decide either to intervene or not. It is not straightforward. It remains as important now as a decade ago for youth workers not to find themselves or their facilities becoming labelled as part of the treatment continuum. Yet they and their facilities have a role to play in preventing young people from being shunted into that very continuum. Somehow youth workers have to develop a working style which manages this dilemma.

Whether the task is to raise the cautioning rate or to improve the quality and effectiveness of social workers' court reports, the practical problem for youth workers is to work out in their locality tactics which will enable them to intervene in the juvenile justice system without becoming identified as annexed to it. The objective is (as far as is consistent with meeting individual development needs and, where appropriate, the protection of the community) to maintain the young person in the community, to act to avoid court appearances, convictions and custodial sentences. Often, youth workers possess the crucial information to transform a court report into a practical alternative to custody but how can they communicate it without becoming in the eyes of young people tarred with the same brush as social workers?

The dilemma for youth work practice surfaces more sharply in relation to schools. In many local authorities, supervision by social workers is seen as an appropriate first resort for teachers attempting to curb disruptive pupils. This is complicated by the insistence of many Social Services Departments that schools should cope with their own problems and by confusion about the respective roles of social workers and educational welfare workers or their equivalent (Thomas, 1986). However, this does not solve the problem for the youth workers who, by virtue of their very proximity to, and their more relaxed relationship with, young people can be caught between the more custodial and formalised role of the school teacher and the youth worker's appreciation of the experience of the pupil. So in the school the dual identity of teacher-youth tutor suffers all its implicit difficulties, uncomfortable at best and untenable at worst.

Youth workers face not only conflicting expectations and demands from others in a variety of settings but they are also not engaged in a unitary enterprise. It may seem as though centre-based youth work provides at least a clear-cut role but in many ways the youth centre provides a setting where the complexities and ambiguities of the job are exposed rather than resolved. After all, at least in the youth centre the struggles of the classroom may be temporarily set aside.

In the short run, no prizes await the worker who dares to break the harmony of silence of the closed politics of the school or the local community by daring to articulate a profane, or cacophonous demand for justice for young people. But in the medium term, perhaps the key to the problems of law and order among the young lies in negotiating for young people a real voice in influencing the conditions of their existence (Adams, 1981, pp. 315–6; Stein, 1983).

Perhaps, then, the ultimate heresy is to suggest that youth

workers and social workers together hold the key to opening a critical window on systems of juvenile justice which, for all their internal debates and rearrangements, still hold up the offender for scrutiny rather than the conditions which create crime. Certainly we have hardly begun to consider how we might hold accountable the institutional and social arrangements which confine and constrain many young people and dispose some to deviance (Garland & Young, 1983, pp. 34–5; Adams, 1981, pp. 318–9).

In all these matters there is no intrinsic reason why youth workers should acquiesce in the marginality of their situation *vis à vis* the traditionally accepted roles of other professionals involved in juvenile justice. For surely there is a case for viewing youth workers as potentially able to contribute to redressing the imbalance in a juvenile justice system. That system tilts all too readily towards the treatment and control of the individual offender and does not pay proper attention to the social conditions – poverty, poor housing, unemployment, inadequate leisure facilities – which contribute to crime.

9
Young People, Youth Workers and the Police

MARY MARKEN and DOUGLAS SMITH

Trouble between some sections of British youth and the police is nothing new. For generations a state of suspicion, tension, and sometimes overt conflict, has existed between mainly working-class young people and the forces of law and order (Pearson, 1984). If the period following 1945 has seemed relatively calm and placid, at least up to the 1980s, for those who cared to look the evidence was there that the underlying frictions and tensions still existed (NYB, 1978).

These accumulating tensions were expressed on the streets of many cities in the summer of 1981. Civil disturbances on a scale not seen for many years broke out as grievances and hostility finally surfaced. The protagonists in the street disorders were young people, both white and black, and the police. The main targets of young people's frustration and aggression, as many subsequent accounts have testified, were the ranks of police officers attempting to regain control of the streets (Benyon, 1984).

The years since 1981 have not witnessed a repeat of the scale of the overt conflict seen during that summer. But the problems are still there. There are still sporadic outbreaks of disorder and violence involving young people and the police, and there is a growing body of evidence pointing to continuing frictions and tensions surrounding the day to day routine policing of Britain's youth.

Two reports, published after 1981, show clearly the problems in the current relationship of young people with the police. The first of these was a survey of young people carried out as part of the review of the Youth Service (DES, 1983). Two thirds of the young people interviewed felt that the police wrongly suspected them of doing wrong. Half felt that the police dealt roughly with young people, and 20 per cent that the police had picked on them personally. The second survey, carried out by the Policy Studies Institute, was restricted to the Metropolitan Police area and found a dangerous lack of confidence in the police among substantial numbers of young people (D. J. Smith, 1983).

In Britain the relationship of young people with the police must be viewed in the context of the three main divisions which cut through and constitute the British social structure – the divisions of class, gender and race. On the basis of their own direct experiences the young people most likely to distrust the police, feel suspicious of them and enter into conflict with them are male, working-class and black. And young black people have been found to have significantly greater distrust and dislike of the police than their white counterparts.

In the DES survey 80 per cent of the black youths interviewed felt the police were suspicious of them and over half felt that that the police picked on them personally (DES, 1983). The PSI found a disastrous lack of confidence in the police among young people of West Indian origin. Among the findings which led them to this conclusion were the 62 per cent of young black people who thought the police often used threats; the 53 per cent who thought they used excessive force; and the 41 per cent who thought they fabricated records (D. J. Smith, 1983). These findings arise out of the young black person's experience of racism, a racism endemic in British society and magnified through the experience of policing.

If class, gender and race are the macro dimensions, then there is a need also to consider a host of micro or local factors which are highly influential in determining police–youth relations. Local areas, local issues, pockets of poor housing or high unemployment can all have a significant effect. Similarly, questions of territory arise and in some areas there can well be continuing struggles over who maintains a dominant presence and, in effect, who controls the streets. It follows, then, that the nature of relationships is highly variable, complex, and in many cases, quite volatile.

Overriding this variability though, is the widespread distrust and hostility found by the two surveys. If variability is a characteristic of the local level, the main characteristic at a broader level is that the tensions and conflicts between some major groups of young people and the police are approaching crisis proportions. It is a crisis which has no single or simple solution, which has its origins embedded deeply in the structure of British society and which is fuelled and intensified by the nature of current police practices. For notwithstanding the structural factors it seems clear that the attitudes of young people to the police arise partly out of their experiences with the police. Here two areas of police practice are especially significant.

The first is the area of stop and search, questioning and arrest. Drawing on the PSI reports, it can be seen that many young people believe that the police stop, question and search them at random without good reason. Indeed, the researchers themselves could find no reasonable grounds in one third of cases of stop and search. In greater detail for the London population generally there is a 16 per cent chance of being stopped in any one year. For young or black people the chances are in excess of 50 per cent. Of those who were young and black, 6 out of 10 had been stopped, and stopped regularly, on average about 5 times a year. (D. J. Smith, 1983, vol. I, pp. 89–102).

Clearly there is discrimination in operational police practices on the grounds of age and race. Yet as a method of combating crime stop and search is remarkably ineffective. In only 8 per cent of stops was any evidence of crime detected. The impact of this practice of stop and search lies not in the detection of crime, but in the feelings of victimisation and harassment which it generates.

The second area of police practice which has a significant impact on young people is what happens in the police station. The PSI report notes that 'it is not uncommon for officers to use bullying tactics in interrogation and to use threats, especially the threat of being kept in custody for a time' (D. J. Smith, 1983, vol. IV, p. 229). Correct procedures may be breached, with young people being questioned in isolation, not being given access to legal advice and feeling intimidated and threatened. The young person may make statements or confessions simply in order to leave the station. Regardless of the consequences for justice, these experiences add further to hostility and fear.

In recent years there has been extensive debate both in and outside the police force about overall approaches to policing policy. In general, concern about police–youth relations has led to two differing responses from the police. In looking at these it is important to note that they are not simply responses to 'the youth problem'. Simultaneously other threats to 'law and order' have been perceived as arising within opposition to nuclear weapons policy or in large-scale industrial conflicts such as the miners' strike of 1984–5. The policing of young people always takes place in this wider context.

The first type of response can largely be seen as oppositional or reactive. At one level, the police are now better equipped and better trained to deal with street disorder and popular opposition. Task forces, special patrol groups and other highly trained units are more in evidence as is the technology of physical control – shields, military style helmets and vehicles. At another level, this technology of control is buttressed by new and extended police powers contained within the Police and Criminal Evidence Act 1984.

The second type of police response is more ameliorative or pro-active with the emphasis upon community policing, community involvement and the bobby on the beat. The stated intention of this type of approach is the re-instatement of the traditional preventive role of the police, although some critics of the schemes see them more as ways of carrying out surveillance and control activities through intelligence gathering.

Within this second response are two aspects which connect directly to youth work – neither are new but they have received greater emphasis as policing methods have evolved. The increasing use of community constables is leading to more contact between youth workers and police officers and between the police and young people in youth work settings. In this case the police are acting as police officers, carrying out an identifiable police activity. The second aspect concerns the increasingly direct involvement by the police in youth work. This can range from off-duty officers working in their own time as voluntary youth workers through to the police providing and running their own forms of youth provision. In these cases the police are taking on a different role, as youth workers. The issue of the police in youth work roles, and the relationship of police force to youth service is both complex and contentious.

Clearly there is a wide range of competing perspectives, purposes and approaches to the police amongst Youth Service personnel, rooted ultimately in different world-views, but more specifically in different understandings of the relationship between youth worker and young person, with particular reference to the police. These lead to differing views on the nature of the issue and on which groups constitute the problem. At one end of the spectrum are those who see the problem originating in the attitudes and behaviour of the young people involved. For them the police are the victims. Óthers see the young people as the victims, with the problems emerging from the attitudes and actions of the police and the styles and systems of policing adopted.

Arising from these different perspectives are competing views on the purposes of youth work in this area. Some of those consulted in a recent NYB exercise, for example, expressed a concern with law and order and the instruction of young people in the duties of citizenship. They saw their first responsibility as being to society and the social order. Others felt that their first duty was to young people. Their concern was to safeguard the rights and interests of young people both individually and collectively.

Similar disagreements were apparent over the nature of the approaches to youth work interventions adopted by workers. These ranged from complete co-operation with the police to those who felt that supporting young people in their opposition to the police was the most effective contribution they could make. Within this range a number of workers adopted a position which stressed the 'neutrality' of the youth worker and the need to 'build bridges'. Although there are some common concerns there is no consensus and seemingly no possibility of arriving at one. The sharpness of these differences needs to be seen in relation to a number of other factors. For the understandings and actions of individual youth workers take place in the context of a relationship between the Youth Service and the police. A recent view of this was contained within *Police Liaison with the Education Service*, a report of an enquiry carried out by a team of HMIs. This notes:

About 20% of LEAs have police representation on Youth Advisory Committees and/or on the Management Committees of youth clubs. . . . In about 40% of the LEAs, the police run at least one youth club and, in most cases, this involves them in co-operation with youth workers and teachers. . . . The Duke of Edinburgh Award Scheme which involves boys and girls is an area in which there is extensive police involvement (DES, 1983a, pp. 4, 7).

This report was referred to in a talk given by Lawrence Byford, Chief Inspector of Constabulary, in an address to the Society of Education Officers. In this he stressed 'the need for co-operation between the Police, the Education Service and all sections of the community in dealing with the problems of young offenders' (Byford, 1984, p. 77). Such statements as these underline the consensus which seems to exist among policy-makers about co-operation between police and Youth Service. In practice responses vary between local authorities and are influenced by specific issues. This in turn connects to a second point, which concerns the translation of understanding into practice by practitioners. On this, it is important to note that the relationship between young people and the police is only one item, if at all, on the agenda of youth workers.

In determining the response to this issue it is clear that although youth workers may analyse the relationship between young people and police in a particular way, this analysis and the course of action that may be suggested by it is substantially outweighed by the constraints and by the circumstances in which workers find themselves. Practical responses to the police and young people necessitates a jump from being 'a youth worker' to acting as a participant in a more collective, political strategy. The resultant youth work practice is still very varied.

In 1983 a small-scale investigation into youth work practice in relation to policing and young people was carried out by the National Youth Bureau (NYB, 1983). This involved discussions with youth workers in different parts of the country followed by a day-long consultation in Leicester attended by about 40 workers, and uncovered many different types of youth work interventions. We can do little at this point than provide what amounts to a quick list of some examples.

First, workers were seeking to equip young people to deal with police encounters: using role plays, or ensuring that young people have a knowledge of legal rights and how to get access to legal advice. Others adopted a broader social education approach concerned with describing the roles of the police and the state.

Second, there is what might be called the relationship-building approach, which has involved the police being brought into youth clubs or young people visiting police stations, holding meetings, or having debates and discussions with the police.

A third area can be seen in youth workers helping to run help-on-arrest schemes or help-on-detention schemes, providing emergency phone numbers for call-out purposes, or a referral service to solicitors or law centres. A youth worker might also provide personal support, contact the parents of arrested young people or contact the police station. There were also interventions in the courts providing personal support and attempting to divert young people from custodial disposals.

Another area of youth worker involvement was concerned with trying to work with Police Community Liaison Officers, for example, in order to try to influence the way in which operational policing was carried out in a particular area. In addition, there is the question of the involvement of youth workers in the training of police officers.

The final area of current practice to which we would want to draw attention is with those attempts to improve police accountability. This could include attempting to influence police operations through contact with individual police officers or through Police Liaison Committees. Other approaches involved, for example, providing information to a Police Committee or a Police Committee Support Unit if one existed, or providing information to youth officers or youth workers who may be able to influence what is happening between young people and the police. And finally, youth workers being involved in the establishment and running of defence campaigns or police monitoring groups or police accountability groups. From this list it can be seen that there is an enormous range of current practice in relation to youth workers, young people and the police.

In trying to pattern this range of interventions and to take account of some of the recurring themes highlighted by youth workers, particularly related to expressions of powerlessness, we developed a framework. Implicit in this framework is our belief that the scope for manoeuvre by youth workers in relation to this aspect of youth work is fairly limited and the scope which exists is very much at the level of the youth worker and the Local Authority. We envisaged the role of the youth worker and the role of the police officer as overlapping and saw this area of overlap as a grey, hazy border. It is in this borderland that potential conflicts or mutual benefits are negotiated. The approach to this area of negotiation varies markedly. For some, there is a non-acceptance of the existence of potential conflict and a belief in the mutual benefits of interaction. For those people there is nothing to negotiate. For others, there is a belief that the conflict of interests is so great that the mutual benefits are minimal and the odds so stacked there is no point in negotiating at an individual level. Between these two positions are responses based on the acceptance of the inevitability and necessity of negotiation and where the emphasis is on knowing what can be negotiated.

An important point to note is that there is a price in seeing the relationship between the youth worker and the police officer as anything other than a happy meeting of common purposes. That price is vulnerability. Negotiation involves risk-taking with the degree of risk dependent on one's bargaining power. Hence *youth workers* often voiced expressions of powerlessness and vulnerability. A number of factors contributed to this vulnerability with the key element being the relative degrees of authority, status and resources invested in the police force and the Youth Service. This is highlighted by those situations which individual youth workers and police officers negotiate. Examples of these will include entry into the youth club and the stopping and searching of young people with whom the worker is in contact. In these cases youth workers have little or no formal authority and their intervention is at the level of a concerned citizen. The police officer does not simply exist as an individual but as an embodiment of the power and authority vested in the police. This imbalance in the power relationship is a source of vulnerability. A youth worker illustrated this by comparing the reaction of his Management Committee to his criticisms of agencies such as the housing authority with his criticisms of the police. In the case of the former, he stated that there was an openness to act on what was said and an acceptance of his judgement. In the latter, there was reluctance and cross-examination. It is almost the case that raising questions in relation to the police is not seen as legitimate and it invites a heightened level of scrutiny and sense of powerlessness.

It may be helpful to consider two areas in detail in order to explore the complexity of the terrain. The first area is that of police access to youth clubs. It became clear during the consultative work with youth workers that many of them experienced considerable difficulty in deciding what the appropriate response should be. They were uncertain of the legal position governing police rights of entry under different circumstances and the best ways of dealing with these encounters. The premise that the role of the youth worker is to act in the interests of young people until and unless it interferes with the role of the police officer in carrying out his/her legal duties is insufficient in itself to provide clear guidance on response. This is because of the complex process by which the national law on an issue such as conditions of entry is translated into policy for a particular force and then subsequently into a range of practice on the part of individual officers. The result can be that the youth worker is uncertain when the police themselves are acting lawfully. A further complication arises when one considers the variation in policy within local authorities on this. So a local authority policy on co-operation with the police where at all possible can provide the youth worker with an additional set of expectations. These may be at odds with those arising from the interpretation of the job of youth work in such a situation. The potential for conflict and miscommunication in the juggling of the expectations arising from police, employer and young person is considerable. The expectations of the least powerful party, the young people, are likely to lose out, and whatever decision is reached the vulnerability of the youth worker at the point of negotiation is apparent.

A second area which helped to pinpoint the issues is that of voluntary youth work by police in Youth Service provision. This is one of a number of forms in which the police take on a youth work role. Some youth workers have argued against police involvement in youth work at all levels in the following ways:

- There is a dual role involved for police officers are police officers first and youth workers second.
- Following from this is the issue of confidentiality in youth work relationships and the conflicts this could pose for police officers.
- The essence of youth work is a commitment to an open non-judgemental relationship which the police either cannot offer or offer with a view to exploiting.
- Police involvement has implications for how youth work is

perceived in the eyes of young people, and hence for the links between youth workers and young people.
- Youth work is a body of knowledge and skills encased within certain attitudes to young people, therefore there is a need for professional training; it is different from police work.

Based on these arguments, some youth workers have constructed a case against police-run youth provision and paid police involvement in other provision (Potter, 1982). While such a case may be understood and accepted within parts of the Youth Service, for those outside it can be seen as youth workers protecting their professional self-interest. Furthermore, it raises the question that with police-run youth provision young people know what they are buying into. If they choose to do that, then that is their choice. In fact, it has been argued that this type of police involvement is possibly less detrimental than when the police officer in a voluntary capacity acts as a youth worker. In this latter case the roles which are being played out are not very clear. And because of this and because of the difficulty of defining Youth Service boundaries in a Service predominantly made up of voluntary and part-time workers the case to be argued is even more complex.

Within the Youth Service, sections of the field argue for the benefits and good intentions of voluntary youth workers and question the identification of the police as a particular or distinct grouping. Others argue about the detrimental effects of having the police involved at any level in the Service. A further complication arises when one considers that, as a result of varying police force policies, the 'voluntary involvement' of a police officer in free time in youth work may, in practice, mean quite different things. The spectrum ranges from it being precisely a voluntary involvement in an individual's free time; as something formally to be encouraged or discouraged according to force policy; as contributing to a favourable assessment of officers' potential by supervisers; and as entitling an officer to time off in lieu. At some point along that spectrum, the question 'when does voluntary work cease to be voluntary?' arises. There is a need for clarification of this area.

The exploration of these two examples raises broader questions about the general policy position and the implications for this whole area of youth work practice. What follows is an attempt to spell out some important aspects of the process of policy interventions in respect of policing and youth work.

The main policy aims identified in the example of police access to youth clubs were to do with the accountability of the police and the relative powerlessness of youth workers and young people. To a large degree these are two different ways of looking at the same thing. For accountability is essentially about control whilst powerlessness is essentially a condition of the absence of the ability to exercise control (Simey, 1984). So calls for accountability arise out of the context of a lack of control. To achieve a greater accountability of the police in relation to the Youth Service is part and parcel of a process of moving the youth worker from a position of relative powerlessness to one of greater power. This is one reason why calls for accountability in whatever form will always be resisted by the police.

The problem of accountability and powerlessness in the Youth Service arises out of the broader issue of the accountability of the police to the public and the power of the public in some institutional form to control the actions of the police. In the absence of this broader accountability any changes within the Youth Service, important as they may be, can only have a limited impact. The real and overriding need is for reform of the existing arrangements of accountability in order to achieve effective public control over police actions and to ensure that they are answerable to the people they are supposed to serve.

In relation to policing and the Youth Service two areas of work were identified during our consultation as needing development. One of these was the dissemination of information resources for youth workers and young people. These should provide information about the law, and about effective youth work practice, on issues including rights on arrest, detention in the police station, police rights of access to clubs and the various responsibilities of youth workers.

Information alone is not sufficient. Knowledge is not power, nor does it provide control. Support bases are needed if information is to be used effectively and these constitute the second area of work needing development. If the youth worker is to avoid isolation then alliances must be created with other workers, with young people and with the local community. Alliances of these types provide support bases from which to work and add a collective power and legitimacy to the actions which youth workers take.

The final and probably most difficult task is the translation of these policy objectives into practical arrangements. Information resources can provide guidelines for practice in order to help workers decide on the most effective actions and what the implications of these actions might be. They are, nonetheless, difficult to develop and implement. Alliances can provide support and legitimacy. Creating them, though, is not easy and within any community or body of workers there will reside many points of view and differences of interest.

In practical terms these problems must be taken on and confronted. Outside the Youth Service there are growing demands for a much needed accountability of the police to the public. Within the Service it is crucial that these demands are paralleled by a drive towards developing the resources and support that we need. For the problems will not go away if we turn our backs, and sidestepping the issues now could undermine the cause of youth workers and young people for many years.

From the level of practice it is important to recognise that these developments can be double-edged. They can offer protection, support, guidance and strength to workers acting within the policy and practice framework which they determine. On the other hand, they can also be restrictive, reduce freedoms, cut into areas of discretion and increase the accountability of youth workers themselves. In other words, any policy or practice development has costs and benefits. Who pays the costs and who benefits is largely determined by the specific character of the policies which are formulated and this, in turn, pivots around the question of who is involved in the policy process overall. If youth workers wish to see the development of policy and practice which truly reflects the conditions of their day-to-day work then they must be directly involved in the process of policy making. It isn't enough for it to reside in the hands of the senior officers. For no matter how well-intentioned they are, the bureaucratic structure of the Service distances them from the realities of daily youth work. Moreover, the increasing emphasis on managerial efficiency and corporate approaches to local authority provision combined with a growing politicisation of youth issues, especially issues of policing, leads automatically to compromise and trade-off. If the Youth Service and young people are to get the policies they need and deserve then the development of policy and practice must extend into the very roots of youth work.

As a concluding note it is important to recognise that in contemporary Britain the police have an escalating and expanding set of roles and the issue of the police and youth work is developing and growing. To date the Youth Service has paid little attention to the range of issues or to the need to develop policy and practice responses to them. To continue to ignore these important factors in youth work today could lead to the Youth Service and youth workers paying a high price. To begin to formulate policies and develop practice will not let the Youth Service off the hook. There is always a price to pay. One key part of the whole task, though, is to make sure it is not a high one.

10
Professionalism or Trade Unionism? The Search for a Collective Identity

BERNARD DAVIES

Professional or trade unionist? This is a question which for many years seems to have preoccupied full-time youth workers. Often, moreover, the debate has been conducted as if it involved a straight either-or choice as if this were new to the 1970s and 1980s.

Yet, as this chapter will argue, key elements of what we know of as professionalism may in present circumstances within youth work be relevant to a redefined notion of trade unionism. While an examination of youth workers' attempts over the last fifty years to organise themselves reveals a much more complex picture than some more recent debates would suggest.

In some important respects developments in the later 1970s and early 1980s evoke strong echoes from the past. These include the conversion in 1983 of the Community and Youth Service Association (CYSA) into the Community and Youth Workers' Union (CWYU) and the abortive attempt to bring CYWU and the National Association of Youth and Community Education Officers (NAYCEO) closer together, if not actually to merge them. Not least they have prompted sharp controversies over definitions and approaches to collective action which go back at least to the 1940s.

For on the one hand, it has been argued, youth workers are or need to see themselves as relatively autonomous professionals possessing special and even esoteric skills and knowledge which, guided by an explicit code of ethics, are to be devoted to offering a 'client-oriented' service. On the other hand there have been those who first and foremost see themselves as workers and employees – who by definition have very limited control over their work situation and work processes and who must therefore combine as trade unionists if they are to combat the power and conflicting interests of their employers.

This confrontation of definitions and self-perceptions is not new, even within youth work. However its intensity and the precise balance achieved between the two positions has varied over time. In this changing scenario three broad periods of Youth Service development can be distinguised: the early 1940s to the publication of the Albemarle Report (HMSO, 1960); 1960 to the advent of Britain's 'crisis' in the mid-1970s; and the mid-1970s to the mid-1980s.

Youth Service decline and youth worker insecurity

In 1958 a senior Ministry of Education official finally acknowledged that 'the Youth Service is one which it has been definite policy for some time not to advance' (Potts, 1961, p. 16). Economic factors did much to produce this swing away from what had been very firm war-time commitments to youth work. United States aid to the Labour Government of the period was explicitly conditional on the curbing of its social expenditure programmes (Coates, 1975, pp. 68–9). These pressures were greatly increased by bad winters and balance of payments crises. Against such a background and in the context of the appalling housing and health problems inherited from the war, youth work was hardly likely to be seen as a top priority.

Influential ideological factors shaping social policy also helped to define youth work as marginal. For much of this period rather crude economism operated. Labour governments in their pursuit of a Parliamentary route to socialism and Conservative governments committed to one-nation strategies primarily emphasised the material goals identified by the Beveridge Report (HMSO, 1942) – for example full employment, guaranteed income and greater occupational opportunities through an improved education system as well as better housing and health. Moreover, once war-time disruptions to family and community ended, policy-makers' fears, especially about the unruliness of youth, were significantly reduced. To young people above all, the new 'welfare state' seemed to promise most, so that their more general socialisation was not seen as a high priority.

In such a climate it was difficult to make a convincing case for a service relying on an ill-defined partnership between the state and a myriad of philanthropic organisations and providing something as amorphous as 'youth work'. For the Service's small body of full-time workers (according to the Albemarle Report no more than 700 in 1958), the benign neglect which resulted inevitably meant considerable personal and occupational insecurity.

A club leaders' association sponsored initially by the National Association of Girls' Clubs had existed at least since 1938. By the mid-1940s this had become the National Association of Youth Leaders and Organisers (NAYLO). Its membership, always small, amounting to 239 in 1944–5 of whom only 165 were full members (Cooke, 1942, p. 173), had declined to 45 by 1956 (Potts, 1961, p. 5). Its negotiating rights and the machinery for implementing these remained minimal. Moreover with the state's direct role in youth work continuing to be limited, certainly in comparison to the 1960s and 1970s and even today, many of those concerned worked for independent, isolated and often very reactionary voluntary management committees made up of local worthies who regarded what their workers did as a vocation.

Contracts laying down resignation and dismissal procedures, working hours, holiday entitlements and even salaries were thus entirely unregulated and often non-existent. As the report of the 1948 NAYLO annual conference noted, under a sub-heading 'starvation wages': 'Many leaders find it impossible to live on the salaries they receive. They have to act as caretakers, stokers and handymen. Some clubs spend more on the wages of the cleaners than on the salary of the Leader' (*The Youth Leader*, Summer 1948, p. 4). Perhaps not surprisingly, therefore, proposals for organising along trade union lines were first made in this period, at least by those youth workers lacking the comparative security of the new local authority 'youth officers'. These officers had, certainly from 1940 onwards, been drawing together in a national conference which apparently did not become an association until the early 1950s. NAYLO's interest in trade unionism may well have had its roots in earlier anti-elitist gestures, as when in 1943 its

Policy Committee asked: 'Are we to take cognisance of the part-time helper or leader, voluntary or paid?. . . . To wilfully blind ourselves to the existence of hundreds of voluntary workers in youth work seemed at the moment to be criminal' (Potts, 1961, p. 5). The 1948 annual conference does however seem to have been a crunch moment. Significantly, perhaps, it was addressed by the National Women's Officer of the Transport and General Workers' Union who was also the Chair of the TUC's General Council. When in the šame year NAYLO was confronted with a member's alleged wrongful dismissal it for the first time began actively to consider registering as a trade union. This registration was not actually achieved until 1953, by which time Youth Service decline and government indifference were unmistakable. Harsh economic reality, allied to a dominant social policy ideology which gave youth work little credence as a necessary or useful element of the welfare state, apparently helped to persuade face-to-face youth workers to define their collective identity much more in trade union terms.

Youth Service expansion and the swing to professionalism

Despite often contrary interpretations, this commitment to trade unionism was never completely eliminated, even during the 1960s and early 1970s when notions of professionalism seemed to dominate. In his Presidential address to the 1960 NAYLO annual conference, for example, Charles Smales starkly described 'clubs where the leader is still regarded as a glorified caretaker and paid that kind of salary . . . or where the leader's main job was that of raising the funds required, including his own salary' (Smales, 1960, p. 2). NAYLO's identification with trade union principles was also reasserted in 1961 when its Secretary explicitly distanced himself and his national executive from reservations expressed by Don Potts, the Association's historian, over the 1953 decision to register NAYLO as a trade union.

During this period, too, a new unity was achieved amongst workers which was to have important pay-offs for their collective strength. Mergers took place most notably in 1963 between NAYLO and the relatively recently formed National Association of Youth Leaders in Local Education Authorities (NAYLEA) to form the Youth Service Association (YSA). A potentially highly competitive situation was thus avoided between the rapidly growing body of state youth workers and those in voluntary organisations. Equally significant the new body also became a 'central association' of the National Union of Teachers (NUT) since NAYLEA made what was for them a continuing affiliation to the latter a condition of the merger.

The LEA officers' body, now renamed the National Association of Youth Service Officers (NAYSO), remained aloof from these mergers, though they also quickly followed YSA into the NUT. Significant differences of philosophy and of self-perception especially over status helped to keep the two associations apart. However conflicts of material interest were probably most divisive, especially once these were embodied in distinct salary scales and negotiating machinery.

For YSA the establishment in 1961 of a Joint Negotiating Commitee introduced nationally agreed salary scales and conditions of service for 'youth leaders and community centre wardens'. It also provided a major incentive for developing youth workers' collective strength and organisation. The Committee required the creation of an 'employees' panel' to negotiate with employers, so that despite all the subsequent professional rhetoric, key elements of trade union practice eventually became embedded in the YSA structure.

Nonetheless Potts' view expressed in 1959, that NAYLO's 1953 decision to register as a trade union was 'misjudged', was an important sign of the times, as were the arguments he used to justify this conclusion: 'Within a profession that is essentially manned [sic] by individualists, many with a strong sense of vocation, the words 'Trade Union' are repugnant. They are an affront to the individualist who may recognise the value of Trade Unions in other spheres but certainly not in his own' (Potts, 1961, p. 5). Moreover in seeking models for its own development, NAYLO was looking increasingly even in the 1950s to a 'kindred' organisation like the Association of Hospital Almoners. This was mirrored later by developments in NAYSO which published a rather basic list of youth officer tasks which it chose to call 'professional responsibilities' (*Youth Service*, March/April 1972, p. 2). Indeed, in the period after Potts was writing, a swing to professionalism occurred to the point where this rather than a trade union frame of reference came to be the dominant rationale.

However this development can only be properly explained by locating it in the wider social policy thinking and orientation of the period. By the early 1960s it was generally agreed that 'never-had-it-so- good' Britain had eliminated poverty and so could afford increased expenditure on social and education programmes, including post-Albermale youth work. Such public investment was also justified on the grounds that everyone, but especially the young, should be adequately equipped to exploit fully this new opportunity society (Davies, 1980). In 1963, in a revised edition of his book, *The Future of Socialism*, Crosland, the leading exponent of socialist revisionism and a key figure in later Labour governments, repeated his 1955 assertion that in future 'The tone of social expenditure may be set less by old age pensions than by the Family Planning Association, child care committees, home visitors, almoners and mental health workers' (Crosland, 1963, p. 96). His views were shared by others on the left, including academics with considerable political clout such as David Donnison and Mary Stewart, who were advocating for the child care and juvenile justice field, 'a body of well trained professional social workers [whose] development must not outrun the growth of an appropriate code of professional conduct' (Donnison & Stewart, 1958, p. 7). The basic questions of economic growth and class division had, it was assumed, been settled. Overtly political goals, for 'clients' but also for workers themselves, could therefore be abandoned in favour of humanising a given, comprehensive welfare state.

In such a situation, socially skilling the population for a new, expansionist consensual era became a, perhaps the, priority. Youth work, especially as 'social education' for the majority and 'counselling' for a 'disturbed' minority, could clearly contribute to this new social engineering strategy. Confidently, and reasonably convincingly, expert 'human relations' technicians could therefore ensure that much untapped personal, social and even economic potential could be released, especially in those (like young people) who had increasing leisure- time available to them (HMSO, 1960, para. 350).

All this seemed to point to a much more highly developed professional frame of reference for youth workers. This certainly was the message of Edward Sidebottom, Principal of the recently established National College for the Training of Youth Leaders, in his address to the first YSA annual conference in 1963. Though it was, he noted, 'a time when occupations are growing into professions . . . no group becomes professional by making claims. Status is earned' (Sidebottom, 1963). In spelling out how this could happen he encapsulated the professional ethos of the period, particularly emphasising the need for youth leaders:

- to be 'carefully selected';
- to undergo 'a particular kind of education';
- to develop their 'professional ethics';
- to extend 'the body of knowledge on which all [their] work is based'; and
- to have 'supervision' available, especially in their first full-time year in post, to preserve and deepen their trained skill.

Part-time workers, too, he believed should aspire to and might even achieve professional standards. However as they were most likely to do this 'intuitively' it was overwhelmingly to full-timers that Sidebottom looked for professionalisation.

As other writers of the time elaborated the same messages (Matthews, undated; Davies & Rogers, 1972; NAYLEA, 1960, ch. 4) the balance of thinking and rhetoric tipped unmistakably in favour of such depoliticised professional notions of youth work. However as John Holmes' subsequent research into youth workers' careers vividly demonstrated, integrating such ideas into practice remained extremely elusive (Holmes, 1981, pp. 28–33). For the organisation of youth workers there were nonetheless some important practical implications. In contrast to the position in the early 1950s, part-timers were specifically excluded from membership of YSA. Both YSA and NAYSO energetically pursued precisely those objectives which Sidebottom had advocated. They pressed for qualifying courses lasting two years (achieved in 1970) and even three years, a demand made by NAYLEA as early as 1960 (NAYLEA, 1960, p. 13). In the early 1970s YSA set up a national network of 'supervision panels' to provide full-time workers with greater support and staff development opportunities. Intensive inter-professional co-operation was also sought for example, through NAYSO's proposed 'social education association' for all 'professionally concerned with such practice' (NAYSO, 1970).

Much work was also done in the 1970s and beyond to articulate and enforce a code of professional conduct. Proposals were presented to YSA's successor body in 1978 by one of its leading executive members, Bill Barnett, which seemed to envisage the equivalent of a Hippocratic Oath for youth workers and the establishment within the organisation of a disciplinary committee (Barnett, 1977). Parallel proposals were developed in 1978 by students at Brunel University (Brunel, 1978); and in 1983–4 by two youth officers, one of whom was an ex-chair of the British Association of Counselling (Casemore, 1983).

Finally in the 1970s both the main youth worker organisations, for the best of declared reasons, executed what could be seen as classic pieces of professional aggrandisement by colonising the newly fashionable concept of 'community'. In 1971 YSA became the Community and Youth Service Association (CYSA) and in 1975 NAYSO transformed itself into the National Association of Youth and Community Education Officers (NAYCEO). Indeed, in 1973 David Glassman used the framework of a management consultant's report for the CYSA to argue strongly for a new association 'comprising professional workers in the middle ground between formal education and social work' and in particular merging CYSA and NAYSO (Glassman, 1974).

However achieving professional status, and especially the equivalent of the doctor's clinical freedom from close managerial oversight, only partly depended on the intrinsic strength of the youth worker's claims to being appropriately trained and skilled and to having a code of ethics. For one thing youth work 'skills', unlike those of a surgeon wielding a scalpel, were extremely difficult to demonstrate. However, even a licence to practice as if such skills did exist, which to some extent youth workers were granted in the 1960s and early 1970s, largely depended on wider political and economic conditions and dominant ideas. Here the given assumptions about the availability of public resources for such work were particularly important. In the 1960s, though the rate of growth for these was frequently held back, such resources continued to be seen as, and to be, expandable and their use for 'soft' purposes like personal and social education acceptable. In other words these purposes could provide a worthwhile societal as well as individual return on investment.

Certainly this investment in education including youth work was required to have an economic justification. As we saw earlier, the Albemarle Report did not overlook this possibility while Sidebottom echoed it in his address to the YSA in 1963 when he talked of youth workers' ability to render 'a service of considerable economic advantage to the nation' through the 'help they can give the young to grow into happier, less strained and more vital adults' (Sidebottom, 1963, p. 8). However the motivation here was also and perhaps even predominantly to 'win' young people to a basic commitment to their society since, for governments of both parties at the time, managing social relations and the values and attitudes which kept them harmonious was almost as important as managing the economy. While these social policy priorities and the ideological and material conditions which sustained them survived, youth work professionalism had a quite widely endorsed rationale and perhaps therefore an even chance of establishing itself. Once those basic conditions changed the odds lengthened enormously.

Retrenchment, managerialism and the re-emergence of active trade unionism

Underlying doubts about professionalism's relevance in youth work were never wholly dispelled even in its heyday and may well have helped to tip the balance against it from the mid-1970s. As we saw Sidebottom, even as he sought to inspire the full-time Youth Service vanguard to a more confident professionalism, felt the need to reassure himself and his audience that the part-timer could be as skilled as the fully trained full-timer (Sidebottom, 1963, p. 1). Joan Matthews too insisted that through good supervision professional skill could be spread to 'voluntary club leaders and helpers' (Matthews, undated).

No doubt these accolades to the part-timer were very sincerely meant. However lurking within them was apparently a recognition that if the special expertise of part-timers who were 'demonstrably doing the greater part of the work' (Sidebottom, 1963, p. 1) was not convincingly demonstrated the very enterprise of youth work as a 'professional' activity might well to the outsider be totally undermined.

Such scepticism strengthened considerably once the social democratic vision of a fully open and participatory society faded. Small and even large-scale grass-roots campaigns and rebellions generated or increased identification amongst workers with 'the consumer' rather than with some inward-looking professional interest group. This orientation was, at least rhetorically, semi-advocated officially in 1970 by the Report, *Youth and Community Work in the 70s*. This emphasised 'the active society' (DES, 1969) though as Holmes points out, in recommending that full-timers' training be extended to two and even three years for reasons of 'status and parity of esteem, the report somewhat contradictorily endorsed professionalisation' (Holmes, 1981, p. 32).

Such professionalisation was now also attacked explicitly by youth workers. In 1972 for example Robert Hamilton, in an article entitled 'Don't join the professionals: that would kill youth work', equated professionalism with abandoning 'the weak' and identifying with 'the powerful' – all in the name of acquiring 'money, status and even a little power'. For him its only morality was 'the one that is commonly accepted', expounded in the name of objectivity in support of employers. His conclusion was that 'it is impossible for the full time youth and community workers to build up a profession while identifying with and trying to analyse the problems facing their constituents' (Hamilton, 1972). The ideological assault on professionalism seems to have been fuelled by the experience and philosophies of two sharply contrasting groups of full time workers recruited in the previous decade. One comprised the new, especially social science, graduates; another, workers from industry who had often been active trade unionists. Both these groups in their contrasting ways challenged the traditional notion of youth work as a vocation and were often highly critical of youth workers' employment conditions. For both groups therefore neither the rhetoric of professionalism nor its style and philosophy or organising seemed appropriate.

The perspectives and approaches of these groups were also interwoven in this period with another new influence: that of women workers strongly committed to feminist ideas. Though few in number, they made a significant impact on youth work thinking, above all through their highly critical analysis of the Youth Service's response to girls, young women and women workers and officers. By making questions of power and conflicts of interest central to this analysis, they echoed and indeed substantially developed many of the key trade unionist and anti-professional themes then re-emerging within youth work, and contributed much to the embodiment of these within CYSA and later CYWU.

Within mainstream youth work, however, there remained one notable 'absence': the active and collective involvement of black youth workers. Such an organisation did develop but largely separate from existing bodies even where these adopted a firmer trade union orientation, with the CYWU in particular continuing to struggle to reflect its stated anti- racist positions in its own internal structures and operations.

As we have seen, this grass-roots scepticism about professionalism, together with a more positive preference for a trade union approach, were not new. It took significant changes in the basic conditions of youth work and in the dominat ideologies underpinning national and local policies to produce the later 1970s' surge to trade unionism. This occurred particularly as the post-war economic boom collapsed and with it the political consensus which it had encouraged especially around social policies. Dramatic events at home and abroad – coal strikes, mass pickets and three-day weeks, huge oil-price rises, runs on the pound and public spending cuts demanded by the IMF, clearly marked these changes. In the resultant conditions of sharply reduced profitability and international recession, the actual problems of young people and popular and public expectations of what 'society' should do with them also underwent a fundamental change.

In the educational world in which youth workers still mainly operated, the ideological shifts were most forcibly signalled by James Callaghan's Ruskin speech in October 1976 when, as Prime Minister, he launched the 'great education debate'. This unambiguously demanded that education should much more directly serve 'the national interest' – a theme explicitly given a Youth Service interpretation by Barney Baker, the senior DES civil servant then servicing the ill-fated Youth Service Forum. Using his attendance at the joint CYSA/NAYCEO conference in April 1978 as his prompt, Baker, in a paper written for Forum members, at least implicitly challenged the capacity of client-centred work to win young people's allegiance to their society and therefore the rationale for investing in it. Rather, he insisted, a client-centred approach 'must be complemented by an assessment of needs in relation to society's as well as young people's interests' even though the former 'may be defined in terms more or less unpalatable to young people'. Not surprisingly, perhaps, his conclusion was that by 1978, with so many competing claims on public funds, it was necessary to 'attempt to make the case for expenditure on the Youth Service principally by reference to the social objectives it serves' (Baker, 1978).

Given that this was Baker's priority it is at least questionable whether youth work, conceived professionally as a personalised service to clients, any longer represented a supportable social provision. Indeed as the decade progressed, and especially under Mrs Thatcher's Conservative Government, this seemed to be increasingly the official view. Locally Youth Service resources and staffing were steadily reduced (D. I. Smith, 1979; 1980). Nationally, the Government all but ignored the recommendations of the Thompson committee (HMSO, 1982) while at the same time deliberately and, in the case of the MSC massively, increasing its commitment to forms of 'youth work' conceived in narrowly vocational and/or law-and-order terms (Davies, 1981).

As well as undermining youth worker's professional ethic, these ideological shifts increasingly challenged their claims to professional autonomy. Emphasis was now more and more on worker accountability and the cost-effective use of public funds as measured by a 'societal' and especially an economic return on them (DES, 1985b, paras 4 & 5). These expectations were not of course new. Post-Albemarle the state's role as direct employer or (for 'voluntary' organisations) as financial guarantor grew, and youth workers found themselves working for agencies under increasing pressure to demonstrate a commitment to 'the national interest' and to adopt managerialist strategies for getting staff to deliver these promises. This managerialism developed particularly from the mid-1970s onwards following local government reorganisation in 1974, and the increasing adoption of corporate management techniques by local authorities (Benington, 1976). This was matched by a growing political concern, locally as well as nationally, to manage the upsurge of community activism (Cockburn, 1977).

Youth workers thus faced increased demands that they operate as workers often in relatively de-skilled ways which assumed that their first obligation was to fulfil laid down administrative requirements and policy objectives. Clearly as youth workers could no longer (if they ever could) rely on their employers to treat them, individually or collectively, as professionals, they had better begin to identify and organise themselves as employees.

Given youth work's dispersed settings and its informal approaches managerialism's reach was bound to remain somewhat limited. Moreover the Youth Service's small number of full-timers could never expect to generate as much collective strength as other groups of public service staff such as health workers, teachers or even social workers (Winchester, 1983). Trade union activism and coherence were therefore always likely to be curtailed and were restricted still further by the withdrawal of many long-standing, professionally- oriented practitioners into quiescence or even isolated individualism.

Nonetheless trade unionism did advance within the Youth Service, leading most significantly to the painful reconstruction of CYSA in 1983 into CYWU and the latter's rejection of merger or even closer liaison with what was seen as the 'bosses' organisation NAYCEO. Other more general trade unions, most notably NALGO, also increasingly recruited youth workers, especially in the London area; while in 1985 as an indication of the strength of the trade union tide running within CYWU, a motion at it Annual Conference committed to seek amalgamation with another larger union, as yet unspecified. Though this contributed to a major internal crisis in the Union in 1985–6, after carrying out an inquiry it survived and showed signs of recovery and renewed unity.

Professionalism and trade unionism in conditions of crisis

Two basically conflicting sets of assumptions and orientations have run through the youth workers' search for a collective identity and organisational base. Yet, the question needs to be asked: are there points of accommodation between the two, especially at a time when neither professionalism nor trade unionism on its own seems adequate to protect workers or clients against the loss of some important 'progressive' advances?

In the 1980s Britain's crisis has deepened. Mrs Thatcher's social policies either destroyed or radically restructured whole tracts of the welfare state, including the Youth Service, in order to protect a narrow set of ruling class interests. This threatened youth workers to the point where often their very jobs were at risk. It left old-style professionalism, resting as it does on notions of workers' political neutrality and objectivity, in tatters. Indeed, as salaries and conditions of service deteriorated, it also made less tenable the would-be professionals' claims, whether implicit or explicit, to having established themselves at different (that is, superior) points in the occupational hierarchy. In some respects the gap between youth workers' own interests and even material conditions and those of their clientele narrowed and degrees of shared concern and experience emerged which conflicted with the basic tenets of professionalism.

In the conditions of the 1980s a trade union framework thus seems essential. This is true despite the unresolved dilemmas over designing tactics capable of hurting employers rather than an 'innocent' and perhaps even 'vulnerable' clientele. Yet the Thatcher revolution may have made certain so-called professional positions much more defensible. Contradictory though it undoubtedly is alongside commitments to consumer and political perspectives the notion of 'professional autonomy' may carry within it in the conditions of the 1980s important progressive possibilities, especially if it is redefined as worker control.

For, what the authoritarian and centralising thrust of Mrs Thatcher's policies has done, despite the rhetoric about market forces and even parental choice in education, is not to break the power of the professionals in the interests of working class consumers. Rather, as has been illustrated by the role of civil servants in the day-to-day implementation of MSC youth programmes, it has substituted for professional power the power of state functionaries. Such people have no first-hand experience of the realities of face-to-face practice, no training for such practice and no commitment utlimately to the perspectives or demands of the young people on the receiving end of their programmes. Defensive, and indeed offensive, alternative strategies for combatting this bureaucratic intrusion in the interests of Baker's 'social objectives' need to be fashioned. A politicised interpretation by trade unionists of professional autonomy as workers' control, based on confident assertions of who can establish the greatest legitimacy and credibility with 'consumers', is therefore vital.

In similar fashion, some up-dated use of the professional's service ethic may also have a place in hard-headed defensive and offensive responses to Thatcherism. Restricted trade union perspectives which concentrate exclusively on members' jobs and wages are in this context in need of urgent extension. In a situation where services and facilities are being systematically destroyed or reorientated, a concern about the quality of 'the product' is needed which for trade unionists in other settings may be totally inappropriate. In part out of self-interest, but also as an essential political intervention, some of the traditional professional preoccupation with the standard of service being offered may therefore be required.

None of this should be seen as an nostalgic reaching back for an elitist professionalism which in youth work was always based on foundations of sand. Social workers at least have their own 'British Association'. Teachers, though never quite achieving a general council outside of Scotland, have managed to restrict entry to those acceptably trained and qualified. Youth workers have done neither of these things. Youth work, though undoubtedly requiring considerable self-awareness, some sophisticated social skills and insights and some hard practical competences, has never been able to substantiate its claims to esoteric professional skill or an exclusive professional ethic. For thousands of young people, probably the vast majority using the Youth Service, many 'ordinary' women and men act as youth workers on the basis of no or very minimal training and without knowingly meeting any restrictive professional criteria. Given such 'dilution', pretensions to professional standing alongside doctors or lawyers, assuming that even they merit such status, are surely entirely illusory.

What has not been illusory however in the circumstances and climate of the 1980s has been the need both for a specific defence of youth workers' jobs, wages and conditions of service and for a more outgoing alternative strategy for developing a consumer-led service. Here, trade unionism refined and reshaped for a people-centred occupation operating in an increasingly oppressive society is essential. Given the history of youth worker organisation over some forty years, it would no doubt be dangerous to predict that the professional–trade union debate has been settled once and for all in favour of the latter. However, in the present juncture, though trade unionism will almost certainly remain weak in such a marginal state service, it would seem to provide the only viable basis on which a relevant collective response can be mounted.

11
Training the Professional Worker

YUSUF AHMAD and RON KIRBY

Following the 1983 JNC resolution that unqualified workers will not be employed in full-time posts in the Youth and Community Service except as trainees questions about training have attained new significance. Further, a teaching qualification will not constitute an automatic entry route into the occupation after 1988. As a result a Service where, at the moment, only 27 per cent of full-time staff have received specialised training (Kuper, 1985, p. 15), will apparently be moving to a situation where all new recruits will be trained. Consequently initial training is in the process of becoming a prime agency for the socialisation of youth workers and, therefore, also a crucial influence upon the future quality and direction of the Youth Service. It is in this context that we look at the influences and policies that have shaped the form and content of initial training.

In order to throw light on the contemporary debates around training we initially look at the historical background. On the one hand, training was and is funded by the state as the mechanism through which it can produce suitable personnel to address its definition of the 'youth problem'. Consequently the state has always sought to exercise control over the process. Training is also the vehicle through which an insecure and relatively new occupational group could acquire the skill and legitimation required to achieve professional status (Holmes, 1981; Larson, 1981). On the other hand, training like any other social process has been subject to modification and change by the participants in the process. In this case the resistance of groups of both trainers and trainees to the imperatives laid down by state and profession must be acknowledged. This is an uneven process wherein the contest for the control of meaning and content is far from over.

Prior to 1939 the bulk of youth work was organised and run on a voluntary basis. Training, such as it was, was ad hoc and uncoordinated (Evans, 1965). However the war years witnessed a rapid expansion of the Youth Service. This was accompanied by various debates regarding the shape and form that the Service would take after the war. McNair (Board of Education, 1944) was the first offical report devoted to the subject of full-time training. It identified the need for an adequate supply of trained full-time leaders and posited the need for professionals whose training would be distinct from that of teachers and other kinds of social workers. The foundations for the development of a new occupational group had been laid. McNair also suggested a training programme which should include possibilities of personal development and practical work. Several courses were set up at various universities but all, save one, had ceased operating by 1953 (Milson, 1970). Two further reports produced in this period had implications for training – Jackson (Ministry of Education, 1949) and Fletcher (HMSO, 1951). The former attempted to locate full-time youth work centrally within the teaching profession while the latter, in calling for youth leaders from a wide variety of backgrounds and experience, suggested separate and specialised training courses endorsing the McNair recommendations. None of these reports made any real impact in terms of an expansion of provision for the separate training for youth leaders. In the immediate post-war period 'youth' had ceased to be perceived as an urgent problem and was not on the state's agenda of priorities. At a time when welfare expenditure was beginning to rise in terms of other groups, the Youth Service was actually experiencing cuts (HMSO, 1951). These reports are relevant to the present discussion in terms of the training courses they proposed. Fletcher proposed a curriculum which had three components:

1. Background Studies:
   a) some study of the economic and social structure of modern Britain.
   b) Human relationships – the psychology of the individual, the family and the group – health and sex education.

   c) Some study of the religious, political and philosophical ideas of western civilisation as a background to modern society.

   d) Consideration of the educational, moral and religious problems which confront the youth leader in his work.

   e) A study personally chosen which continues the general education of the student.

2. Specialised Studies:

   a) The aims of organisation of and relationships within the youth service.

   b) Methods and problems of group work.

   c) The psychology of the adolescent.

   d) The transition from school to work and from adolescence to adult life.

3. Practical Work:

This should be done under the guidance and supervision of an experienced worker in youth service. The work should be planned so as to:

   a) give experience of at least two different types of youth service;

   b) give some experience of continuous though necessarily restricted responsibility;

   c) show possibilities of some of the commoner activities in clubs, e.g. drama, music, physical training, art, handicrafts, etc. (HMSO, 1951, p. 12).

In examining the structure and content of contemporary courses it is interesting to note the extent to which this format has been retained. In essence, Fletcher's mix of personal development, study of the human sciences and fieldwork can be found in all contemporary courses. Reasons for this continuity are partly institutional. Training is a comparatively recent phenomenon and a relatively small group of trainers have been responsible for the development of programmes. Inevitably this group have enjoyed close personal and professional contact. Perhaps a more important reason for the longlevity of the Fletcher format is that it reflected the liberal tradition in which youth and community work training is firmly rooted. From its inception youth work was conceived of as a type of social work that involved presenting young people with an 'admired type' of adult leader (Brew, 1957, p. 173). Training has essentially been about the socialisation of this admired type. Whilst subsequent developments have added to the range of techniques available, for example, training in groupwork and management, the central idea of the production of an 'admired type' remains.

The period after the war actually saw a drop in the numbers of full-time leaders from an estimated 1800 in 1948 to around 700 in 1960 (Jeffs, 1979, p. 89). In the period of post-war reconstruction the Youth Service did not merit the same attention as it had during the war. The marginality of youth work was underlined by the Ministry of Education Annual Report for 1952 which, in announcing cuts in expenditure on the Youth Service commented: 'Some useful but not essential work has to be given up' (Ministry of Education, 1952, p. 2).

This decline created within the Youth Service a sense of depression and panic (Milson, 1970, p. 12). During the 1950s initial training for youth workers, which was recognised for grant purposes by the Ministry of Education, was being provided by only two courses – those located at University College, Swansea, and Westhill College, Birmingham (HMSO, 1960, para. 254, p. 73).

It was in a context of malaise and relative inactivity that the Albemarle Report (HMSO, 1960) was written. The implications of Albemarle for the Youth Service are well documented elsewhere (see Jeffs, 1979, p. 31–45). We shall be looking at the Report in terms of its relation to the training of youth workers. The significance of Albemarle lies not so much in what was being said, because much of it was simply a reiteration of what had more-or-less been said in previous reports. Rather, in the context of a media-led panic about young people it was actually implemented forthwith by the government of the day. The impact of the Report on training can be perceived in two main ways. Firstly, in arguing for and justifying the expansion of the Youth Service with the requisite increase of full-time youth leaders it created an immediate demand for training. Secondly, the form and content of this training was very much influenced, if not constructed, by the definitions and views Albemarle put forward both explicitly and implicitly about what constituted youth work practice.

The terms of reference of the Report arose out of a widespread and acute concern about the state of the nation's youth. This concern focused around 'deviant practices' of youth as manisfested in police crime figures and perceived aberrant behaviour. Albemarle located the malaise of youth in terms of lack of leadership and confusions arising out of a rapidly changing, complex, technological society with rising levels of income. The Youth Service was charged with providing the missing leadership and creating a practice that would enable the resolution of such confusion.

This, then, was the justification of the role of the Youth Service as an agency for the control of adolescent deviance and of a person-centred practice as a method of implementation. It recognised that earlier methods based on moral exhortation were unlikely to achieve this and so a youth leader who was able to communicate in an effective and relevant manner with the young was required. It could be argued that to achieve this did not entail specialist training but only appropriate selection. Albemarle operated in a period when a belief in the ability of the welfare state to cure social problems via 'professional' intervention was dominant, producing a growth in the employment of specialist 'people-workers'. For the Youth Service and youth worker to have legitimacy it would have to professionalise. The vehicle for this was to be training. However, Albemarle proposed this in a way which did little to enhance the status and credibility of youth workers as a discrete professional grouping. In noting that even with the planned expansion, youth work as such could offer a life-long career for but a few, Albemarle devised a training strategy which, in effect, formalised the status of youth work as being allied to teaching. A major form of training was to be within youth options in teacher training. Qualified teachers were seen as a major source of long-term supply. In addition, the Report suggested three other training routes:

1. youth work be incorporated into a scheme of training for social work as recommended by the Younghusband Report (Ministry of Health, 1959) – i.e. students follow a social science course at university followed by a year's professional training;
2. three-month training courses for qualified teachers, social workers and others professionally qualified to enable them to 'transfer' to youth work;
3. two-year training course for mature students who, while not

possessing formal qualification, would have displayed an aptitude for youth leadership.

The first stage in this last option was the recommendation to set up, as part of an emergency plan, a one-year training course for mature students. This came to fruition as the National College, Leicester, in 1961. It is on this, and various other specialised courses that were subsequently set up, that the rest of this chapter focuses.

The thrust of the National College scheme was informed by an ideology of professionalism. Owen Watkins, one of the staff associated with the college, wrote:

> the training for youth work is professional training in that the youth worker can act professionally. This implies, among other things, certain principal methods and skills are common, irrespective of personalities and working situations . . . it also means that to practice professionally the youth worker must display certain personal characteristics, such as the ability to plan ahead, express himself effectively, to exercise emotional control, etc. (Watkins, 1970, p. 8)

Training was to enable this process to happen. We would argue that this perspective stamped the training process and product, in a manner which is visible even today, in two ways. It determined certain practices, skills and methods as being crucial to professional youth work practice. Central to this was the concept of social group work. This skill fitted in admirably with the Albemarle imperative to 'communicate' with young people. Secondly, in identifying the possession of personal characteristics by the worker as being central, it ensured a certain affective learning model – a behaviour modification package often to the detriment of a process of cognitive learning and understanding. Other things arising from this perspective, which have since come to be enshrined as central tools of youth and community work training, are techniques such as fieldwork placement recordings. But often these 'innovations' were experienced in the field as 'restrictive' structures and procedures (Davies, 1980).

The curriculum content of the National College course was organised around the framework initially suggested by the Fletcher Report and developed by Albemarle, containing as it did a core unit called principles and practice of youth work. This comprised an investigation into the history of the Youth Service and the development of methods mentioned above. This was supported by two other strands organised around social studies and human growth and development. These were offered in conjunction with a programme of individual personal development and fieldwork placement. The methods of instruction at the National College stressed student participation and integration of theory and practice (Watkins, 1972, ibid., pp. 18–40).

The National College played a central role in creating a relative legitimacy for youth leaders as a profession. Equally, its person-centered strategy contained within it progressive and humane elements. However, its obsession with the ideology of professionalism deflected from its ability to enable students to have a comprehensive and critical view of the world. There was for instance no recognition of the fact that 'youth', as a category, experience the world from their location within the structures of gender, race and class. Further, by its tendency to stress the refinement of technique in order to achieve a superior professional status over all else, it often had the consequence of distancing the full-time from the part-time workers (Jeffs, 1979, pp. 50–7).

Throughout the 1960s, the National College constituted the main source of supply of qualified youth leaders. This period also witnessed the massive expansion of statutory Youth Service provision. In spite of this the Service was not seen to be making a noticeable impact on the behaviour of the nation's youth (ibid., p. 85).

The Fairbairn-Milson Report, published a decade later, again sought a formula to make the Youth Service 'relevant' to the needs of young people. Its central significance for training was that it argued for a wider remit in order to 'bring professional workers operating separately in the youth and community field into a more effective relationship with each other and to enable them to fill the much more demanding roles which future developments would require' (DES, 1969, p. 109). In effect this Report attempted to forge an organic link between the areas of youth work and community work and carried an implicit criticism of Albemarle in that youth were not a separate category in the community. Thus it advocated the introduction of community work training to youth work courses. Whilst the Report was not taken up by the government, its impact on courses' was immediate in that they added the word community to their prospectus. Significantly, the DES ruled that whatever their title they should continue to restrict themselves 'to the training of youth workers and community centre wardens' (Jeffs, 1979, p. 61). The CETYCW guide lists over half of initial training courses as 'Community and Youth Work Courses' whilst in its most recent formulation Leicester Polytechnic describe their course as a 'Certificate in Youth and Community Development' (1984a).

Fairbairn-Milson also proposed an extension of the training period from one to two years. Further, it suggested that these proposed courses be located within social studies departments of colleges of education and polytechnics; that is, it came out against monotechnic institutions like the National College. This shift has some current significance in so far as youth and community courses are regarded as social science courses by the National Advisory Board for Higher Education. The social sciences are regarded by Mrs Thatcher's Government as an area ripe for cutting back. Thus we have a situation where the supply of trained workers is likely to be restricted at the very time when more will be needed to replace the loss of teacher entrants. This significant, for the teacher-trained staff in the workforce increased from 27 per cent in 1972 to 43 per cent in 1983. Consequently, the ratio of teacher-trained to specialised-trained workers entering the service between 1978 and 1983 was nearly 3 to 1 (Kuper, 1985, p. 16).

During the 1970s there took place a rapid expansion of training with the establishment of 12 institutions (Holmes, 1981, p. 16). Most of these were two-year certificate courses with mainly mature entrants, although two catered for primarily graduate entrants and were of one-year duration. Some geographical areas are not covered by the spread of courses, notably the South, South-West and East Anglia. Intake on the courses initially reflected the nature of the profession; that is, overwhelmingly white and male. Recent evidence demonstrates the extent to which courses have redressed the balance. The 1984 intake for two-year courses was composed of 176 male and 166 female students, of whom 72 were Afro-Caribbean and 16 Asian. One-year courses had 30 male and 28 female entrants, none of whom were from ethnic minorities (Parr, 1985).

A problem for both intending students and training agencies

themselves is the fact that grants by LEA's for attendance on these courses remains discretionary rather than mandatory. As Parr notes, it is enormously difficult for training agencies to determine how many offers should be made in order to reach intake targets. The discretionary grant system acts as a second line of selection and has become so unpredictable as to make it impossible for reasonable estimates of offers to be made (Parr, 1985).

Estimating the future supply of trained youth and community work staff is thus a hazardous process. To the 401 students who commenced two and one-year courses in 1984 must be added those on the part-time in-service course at Avery Hill and the distance-learning course run by YMCA National College and those students taking a B.Ed. course in youth and community studies. It is estimated that 400 trained entrants are needed each year simply to replace those that leave youth and community work (Kuper, 1985, p. 16). However, these figures refer only to those in education-based youth and community work who appear on the DES register. It is known that at most only half the output of training agencies actually take up employment in the education-based service. This is reflected, of course, in the current concern regarding the 'export' of trained youth and community workers to other professions. Apart from the narrow view of youth and community work that this approach demonstrates, it is a reflection of somewhat crass departmentalism which argues that since the DES 'paid' for their training the DES should reap the benefit of the products of training courses.

We now go on to look at the content and structure of current courses. Available evidence suggests not only that the structure of courses has remained largely unchanged over the last forty years, but that the basic syllabi on most courses are similar (Hogarth, 1983). In both the one and two-year courses roughly 40 per cent of the time is spent on placement. In terms of academic content, we can see similar clusters of units around principles and practice of youth and community work (which may include group work and counselling, history of the Youth Service, community development, management studies) and related to what may be called background studies which draw from the discipline areas of sociology, social policy, psychology and social psychology (CETYCW, 1984). Given the wide range of areas and the constraints of time available, one of the charges that training courses are open to is of superficial eclecticism arising out of the attempt to integrate mutually exclusive and often ill-digested theories with practical work situations. As Hogarth comments, 'Training sometimes seems to manage to deprive people of their native commonsense; if this is happening, there is something amiss in the way that theory is being taught and the links that are being made with practice' (Hogarth, 1983, p. 37).

Leaving aside the dangers of eclecticism, the question is raised as to the assumptions that underpin what is selected and used. It is very clear from the experiences documented of earlier courses, particularly that of the National College (Watkins, 1972), that the dominant view of youth work intervention was derived from a social pathology model which looked to the amelioration of defined social problems in an individually person-centred youth work practice. This can be located within a generalised strategy of depoliticisation – the privatisation of public ills whereby important and central issues of social concern are removed to the realms of 'neutral' experts and social engineering (Galper, 1975). The other point to stress here is that by giving a 'scientific' gloss to features of youth work practice, such as group work and counselling, training is lending support for youth work's claims to professional and expert status.

It is perhaps important to locate the developments of such perspectives within training in the context of the 'you've never had it so good' period of British capitalism in the 1950s and 1960s. The visible improvements in health, education and welfare provision, of rising living standards and an expansion of opportunities, enabled youth workers to argue that the residue of individuals who constituted problems could only be understood in terms of their particular personalities. The role, then, of youth work was to help young people to realise this vast potential. This perspective seems to have held sway within dominant sections of the occupation and within training, even in the face of drastic social and economic evidence to the contrary.

In the 1970s, with the expansion of training courses, the recruitment of a new generation of students and the prevailing climate of social, political and economic upheaval, these assumptions came under increasing attack. Critiques of youth work as an agency of social control began emerging from practitioners and trainers (Davies, 1980). The methods and practices came under closer

scrutiny and criticism on some courses with
community work and community developmen
lowing Fairbairn-Milson. Community work, wi
structural analysis, challenged traditional you
(ACW, 1983). The social sciences, which for
knowledge based for training, were experiencing a radical upsurge
which also found its way into the content of training. The questions being posed were predicated upon a growing awareness of
the failure of the welfare state to fulfil its promises and a declining
confidence in the ability of social democracy to bring about an
egalitarian society. These were concerns that youth work training
could not avoid. One of the main implications for training was that
views of society based on conflict, and resolvable only by drastic
social change, posed a threat to the very foundations on which the
youth work project was conceived. Many students on courses
holding these views found themselves in a precarious situation in
that their thinking was in conflict with the dominant ideology of
youth work. Consequently large numbers of students either opted
out of the field altogether or worked in situations outside the
statutory sector where the contradictions were perceived to be less
stark. As Holmes notes: 'Partly because of the reputation of
courses and partly because of what occurred during training the
students on some courses were more sceptical of youth and community service jobs and more imbued with the community work
ideology' (Holmes, 1981, p. 85).

Both the state and the power elite within youth work itself
articulated their concern over such developments. Dissatisfaction
was expressed by organisations such as NAYCEO who felt that
training agencies were failing their central task, which was defined
as preparing students for centre-based youth work: 'Training
agencies set up . . . to train youth leaders and community centre
workers have been moving away from their specific objective and
now want to drop it completely' (NYB, 1975, p. 18).

The Thompson Report (HMSO, 1982) had implications for
initial training in two main ways. Firstly, in locating the problems
of the Youth Service in poor management arising out of the lack of
training of workers in management tasks, the responsibility for the
perceived failure of the Youth Service was placed centrally in the
arena of training. Secondly, in order to rectify this situation it
advocated the setting up of a national body to be 'concerned with

nature, quality and extent of training available for those seeking qualified status and for all full-time personnel in the youth and community service' (HMSO, 1982, p. 97). The Report, in recognising certain structural features of contemporary British society such as unemployment, racism, sexism and homelessness (HMSO, 1982, p. 10), posits a theme of participation and emancipation by and of young people, while at the same time it is also concerned with the integration of young people into the existing social and economic order. By focusing specifically on the Youth Service, the Report drops the word 'community' from the agenda. Cartlidge sees this as 'basically an attempt to de-radicalise an increasingly policised youth and community work field' (Cartlidge, 1983, p. 13). He further suggested that the proposed national supervisory body would possibly be the mechanism that would ensure that this would happen.

By focusing on the mismatch between employer needs and training agency products, the Report was posing a direct challenge to those agencies which have adopted a radical approach to youth and community work (Cartlidge, 1983). While the Report refrains from suggesting any detailed curriculum, by concentrating on management and administration as being the priorities, it poses an implicit model of training which David Marsland is quick to identify as 'effective training towards optimal performance' (Marsland, 1983, p. 30).

The recommendation to set up a national supervisory body was implemented by the creation of the Council for Education and Training in Youth and Community Work (CETYCW) in February 1983. The overall impact of the Council is still to be assessed, however it is perhaps necessary to note the disproportionate presence of employers' representatives on it. Further, despite the noises that Thompson made about race and gender there were only three women (out of a panel of 22) and no black representation when it was first established. This is explained by a spokesperson for the Council who notes that 'our constituent organisations have not on the whole selected women to represent them. By the same token there are no representatives of ethnic minorities, again none have been selected by our member organisation' (Kuper, 1984, p. 8). Some voices are, therefore, conspicuous by their absence on the Council. Included among these is the Association of Community Workers, which has argued the case for community work training on youth and community work courses and has suggested that this might affect not only the content but the way in which courses are taught (ACW, 1983). This omission may be explained indirectly by Kuper who very diplomatically, but clearly, argues for the separation of community work training from that of youth work on the basis that it (community work) is a separate profession and therefore ought to have its own national body (ibid., p. 7).

The Council has made its impact felt on the training primarily through its role of endorsing existing and new training courses. In order to achieve professional validation (and JNC recognition), courses have had to follow a set guidelines, which are fairly prescriptive (CETYCW, 1984). This centralised control of training is something new for youth and community work. In the past, courses have been validated by variety of academic bodies including the CNAA, local universities and colleges themselves. But this validation has taken place with clear notions of academic freedom and no predetermined agenda. While the arrival of CETYCW can be perceived as an attempt to ensure the quality and relevance of training, equally it has given rise to fears about the excesses of centralised control.

The Thompson Report and the setting up of CETYCW have encouraged the perennial debate within both training agencies and the field as to the nature and purpose of youth work. This debate is being conducted within training agencies in the context of severe cutbacks in higher education. In the debate the ideology of vocationalism has almost become a prerequisite for the existence of any form of learning. In this situation the entry of CETYCW with its remit for professional licensing is welcomed by training agencies as further legitimising their existence.

In looking at the training agencies we find that initial training in youth and community work is an essentially contradictory process. The contradictions can be seen as existing on a number of different levels. On a philosophical level the training agency is faced with a number of different types of training and educational imperatives. These range from a perspective which sees youth work as involved in the task of character building and morally uplifting the nation's youth, through to a radical political practice leading to the self-emancipation of working-class youth (Butters, 1981). The mix that emanates from any training agency at any given moment in time depends on the ideological composition of both staff and students and the political environment within which the training agency operates. Many courses operate through discrete strands which are often ideologically opposed – this manifesting itself in both the content and the method through which training takes place.

In practice the debate continues to be one between a perspective which in recognising social disadvantage and inequality goes on to seek the amelioration of these in personal change. In training terms the skills that take precedence are those of person-centred practice, mainly the techniques of group work or counselling. The dominance of this pathological model cannot be underestimated. It reappears in various radical guises, at the moment particularly in the form of race and sex 'awareness training' (Gurnah, 1984). This tradition is counterposed by one which locates social problems within structures and seeks to attack these through collective action brought about through a learning process which enables the working class to have a consciousness of their own history and cultural strengths. Agencies where such views are prevalent are viewed with guarded alarm by the Youth Service establishment. It is ironical that it is the very agencies which anticipated Thompson in their handling of issues of race, gender and participation that are identified (by the use of the euphemism 'experiential') as being those which are not training students to meet employer needs (Cartlidge, 1983).

In purely training terms, even if there had been consensus about the general direction and purpose of training, agencies still have to face the problem of the great diversity of jobs that students are recruited to (each with very distinct needs and expertise). Thompson is very clear about this issue in that it sees initial training as mainly being about training for the Youth Service. Be that as it may, students' needs and aspirations still lie elsewhere. In fact, this is one of the major criticisms of existing training, that it is seen as lacking direct relevance to centre-based work, which is the mainstay of the statutory Youth Service. The implication of this is that greater emphasis must be placed on the teaching of management and administration and the supervision of staff. Trainers are clearly split about this in that there are those like Marsland who welcome this as a way forward to the clarification and consolidation of the role of the Youth Service. On the other hand there are those like Cartlidge who see these more as a ploy aiding those who wish to establish professional control. The future of training is, in our opinion, going to be determined very much by the extent to which training agencies can defend the perspectives and principles of radical practices from any onslaught from the Council. Any attempt to remove elements of the community work focus, as being suggested by Kuper (1984, p. 84) and others, must be resisted. However, within training agencies themselves there is a great need to re-evaluate and reassess both structure and content of courses. To that extent we need always to ask to what degree a training package devised in the 1940s remains an appropriate vehicle for late 1980s.

12

The Promise of Management for Youth Work

TONY JEFFS and MARK SMITH

Writers of youth work textbooks and handbooks have generally felt or been obliged to include a chapter on 'management'. Much is promised following the application of its precepts. Early commentators such as Stanley were not only concerned to expedite the efficient administration of the club, but also to establish the correct relationship between Lady Managers and their superintendents (1890). Russell & Rigby stressed the importance of leaving a very high degree of discretion with the worker or leader (1908, p. 77) and the significance of attention to detail in the design of youth work plant (ibid., pp. 40–52). The cult of efficiency and the rise of Taylorism (Taylor, 1911) was much in evidence and by 1919 Baker had devoted an entire book to a '*Course on the Scientific Management of Clubs for Boys*'. A number of later writers continued in these traditions (Henriques, 1933; Brew, 1943; Leighton 1972; Matthews, 1975) and by the late 1970s, management was vaunted in most official utterances and reflected in the publications aimed at youth workers. However, it did not consistently achieve such prominence.

Influential books concerning practice produced in the confident after-glow of the Albemarle Report (HMSO, 1960) gave little direct space to the area (Matthews, 1966; Davies & Gibson, 1967; Goetschius & Tash, 1967). The Albemarle Report (HMSO 1960) contains a small section on administration and planning, the em-

230

phasis, as far as the worker was concerned, being placed upon face-to-face work with young people. Much of the blame for the parlous state of the Service at that time was attributed to under-resourcing and an over reliance on traditional practices. Fairbairn-Milson mention the worker's role as manager (DES, 1969, p. 110), but they make little reference to this in their deliberations, preferring to concentrate upon questions of co-ordination and partnership. At similar moments of apparent confidence in the work, such as during the Second World War, official reports carry only the barest mention of the subject (Board of Education, 1943; Board of Education, 1944; Ministry of Education, 1945). Whilst there might be questions concerning coordination, the purpose of youth work appeared clear.

The contrast with the 1980s is stark. Management has been a major theme in the youth work literature. Official reports such as Thompson (HMSO, 1982), numerous local authority reviews (DES, 1987), HMI Reports (Ritchie, 1986) and a whole range of practitioner-directed publications (Arnold *et al.*; 1981; Feek, 1982a; 1982b; 1983; McCaughey, 1984) have extolled its virtues. The high profile it has assumed is only in part to do with the state of youth work practice. It is a metaphor for something much deeper. At one level there has been a decline in confidence and sense of purpose within the Youth Service. However, beyond this, New Right thinking and deeper changes in economic relations have made a fundamental impact. Thus, whilst the promise of management may be efficiency and effectiveness, these are not neutral free-floating notions. For they can mean radically different things, for example, to the providers of youth work, the potential and actual users and the funders. Traditionally, advocates of management in youth work have rarely set their concerns in context.

The nature of Youth Service organisations

Reference has already been made in Chapter 3 to the shape and nature of youth work organisations. Front-line units, with few exceptions, enjoy considerable freedom of initiative; their work can be undertaken largely independently of other units; and there are considerable obstacles to direct supervision (D. Smith, 1965).

Such units usually constitute organisations in themselves, with their own legal and charity status and financial systems. Frequently they have an associational structure with an elected management committee. Even within the more clearly structured voluntary organisations which possess a coherent and shared identity, such as the Scouts and Guides, the local or front-line unit retains considerable discretion as to its conduct. However, this chapter focuses on management in what might be called 'open' or 'non-uniformed' youth work, as it is here where there are areas of considerable debate and imprecision. The front-line phenomenon is particularly marked in this sector. In the youth club or project the locus of identity for part-time workers, members of advisory or management committees, members and users and even full-time workers is likely to be the unit itself rather than some broader institution such as the Youth and Community Service or NAYC. School-based work may be something of an exception. Such work tends to look to the school or a defined area within it. Indeed much of the opposition within the Youth Service to school-based work, is based on the premise that schools may constrain the freedom of the worker, rather than impede the delivery of a service to clients (See Chapter 5).

From this it is quickly apparent that tensions concerning management will arise in three main arenas at the local level. Firstly there are the conflicts at what might be termed the 'centre' of particular youth and community services. The Youth Service has traditionally been placed within education departments, although a number of authorities have changed the location to Leisure Services. Inevitably there are the usual run of inter- and intra-departmental divisions concerning the share of resources and the direction of work. Similarly there will be tensions between the various sections within the Service. Usually Services are organised according to locality, often following LEA administrative boundaries. Some authority-wide specialist services such as training and the Duke of Edinburgh Award Scheme are also usually present. Area or divisional officers will have to assume such specialist responsibilities in addition to their local work in many authorities.

Secondly, there tend to be considerable tensions in the front-line unit including, 'conflicts between the needs of the organisation and the needs of the members; between the lay committees and the professionals. There are conflicts between clubs and organisations themselves and between members and adults' (Eggleston, 1976, p. 5). In all this the full-time worker in those units where there is one, plays a pivotal role. Eggleston argues that perhaps the key to the Youth Service's survival lies in this central absorbing role (ibid.).

Lastly, the relationship between the centre of the local authority service and the front-line unit is fraught with difficulties. These are not simply attributable to the usual range of conflicts between managers and workers or resourcers and recipients, but are also concerned with the peculiar administrative arrangements involved. Here we must note that the practice of local authority secondment of full- and part-time workers to local, largely autonomous bodies means that neither body has an overall picture of finance and that local authorities have considerable difficulties in carrying through co-ordinated and coherent policy initiatives at the point at which youth work is delivered (see Chapter 3). A similar position arises in relation to school-based youth work and Youth Service Officers, where the senior manager is in effect the Headteacher. Even where workers are directly line-managed by local authorities such as is usually the case with area workers and in some centre-based or detached work, there are considerable impediments to central management.

The state of management in the Youth Service

A devastating commentary upon the current state of management within youth work is provided by Smith in his survey of local authority reviews of the Youth Service since the Thompson Report. These documents represent the public persona of local authority Youth Services and, as such, are likely to be set to catch the current ideologocial wind. For example, one authority identified:

a. a lack of clear objectives;
b. policies and priorities unclear or conflicting;
c. little systematic collection of management information;
d. poor forward planning;
e. outdated systems for allocating budgets, which do not adequately reflect needs;

f. confusion and uncertainty in management structure (D. I. Smith, 1987, p. 8).

The significance of this list isn't that one authority could have this range of problems, but that most people involved in the Youth Service reading it would probably assent to the main points in connection with their own Service and organisation. Beyond Smith, there lies a wealth of material which underpins the critique. For example, little effective attention has been paid to questions of purpose (M. Smith, 1988); management committees and questions of democratic control have been neglected (Moore & Rogers, 1979; Cauldwell, 1985); youth work qualifying courses do not prepare students for the realities of management (Forbes, 1984; Hoggarth, 1983) and trained workers find management, maintenance and administration, 'very frustrating and difficult, especially in first jobs' (Holmes, 1981, p. 155); there has been a lack of attention to staff development (INSTEP, 1985) and to team development and management (Feek, 1982b); part-time workers are 'largely excluded from discussion and decision-making processes, which results in a inevitable sense of alienation' (Harper, 1985, p. 15); those engaged under temporary employment schemes such as CP have been similarly exploited and have laboured under totally unrealistic expectations (Dooney & Watson, 1985); and the structure, location and direction of services have failed to accord with the expressed needs of the young people they are supposedly directed at (Willis *et al.*, 1985). More than this there are control questions, for example regarding the extent to which workers and officers make illegitimate use of the resources placed at their disposal. In the course of undertaking the research for this book, the editors came across a number of examples of the flagrant and conscious misuse of resources by workers and officers. The most common of these being the utilisation of youth work equipment and monies for private gain or pleasure. It has also been our experience that the examination of such failings and the retelling of accounts of others' dishonesty play a significant role in the discourse of workers. However, little has been written about this area and it would appear to be a case of 'the truth that does not speak its name'. A further demonstration of such problems is the apparent failure on the part of a significant body of workers to fulfil contractural requirements in respect of the amount of face-to-face work undertaken or facilitated. Here there are qualitative as well as quantitative considerations, perhaps best expressed in the tendency towards working with those groups of young people that the worker feels comfortable with, rather than those that have prioritised needs.

HMI Reports on youth provision have made frequent reference to the state of youth work management. What is unknown is the extent to which this is a recent phenomenon. Prior to the rationalisation and systemisation of HMI information-keeping in 1978, little general can be said. The first published Inspections of named youth work organisations only appeared in the early 1980s. Most of these Reports devote a special section of 'management'. A typical example arises from the inspection of provision in two areas of Bedfordshire:

> Much of the work seen by HMI was categorised as responsive. While workers and officers were all well able to articulate their philosophy and policy, which were commonly in line with the stated policies of the LEA, their translation into effective strategies for planning and programming work was less successful. One consequence of this was an excessive workload for many of the staff, which appeared largely to stem from a common failure to agree priorities and set work targets. Another consequence is that initiatives when taken, are not always the result of planning at unit or are level and so do not always therefore appear to contribute to a coherent programme (DES, 1983d, p. 22).

Here the problem would appear to be presented as being less about purpose than organisation; a matter of technical concern. In contrast, D. I. Smith states that it was apparent from the local authority reviews that, 'services and workers were confused about their aims and objectives. Policies and priorities were non-existent, unclear, confused or made irrelevant by the passage of time and changing circumstances' (1987, p. 8). From this it would not be too strong to suggest that what workers and officers are 'all well able to articulate' is professional rhetoric, as the peculiar uses to which the notion of social education is put demonstrates (M. Smith, 1988). The language and theory of youth work has not provided a fertile soil in which the cultivation of a clear sense of purpose and mission can flourish (Jeffs & Smith, 1987, pp. 1–9). Setting priorities and work targets can only be done once the purpose is known.

In another report, this time on detached work in Sheffield, the peculiar relationship between officers and advisers and workers is highlighted. The field workers believed they could exercise their professional judgement without undue direction from managment:

> consulting advisers only as and when they feel necessary. The effect is a rich diversity of professional practice and initiative which may not be known by those who determine and are responsible for implementing authority policy, because the detached workers and the advisers interpret their professional roles and individual initiatives differently . . .

> The lack of formal reporting, of information and of observations from the field to the Youth and Community Advisers responsible for management, has a serious and two-fold consequence. Lack of accurate and up to date reports from the field leave responsible committees without sufficient material on which to make policy decisions and determine priorities . . . Furthermore, and just as important, the lack of regular professional supervision leaves some workers feeling isolated in their professional tasks and not able to learn so much they might from the collective and developing experience of the service as a whole (DES, 1984a, p. 9).

Whilst the Inspectors rightly identify outcomes of the process, these are again presented as arising from a technical problem – the lack of appropriate systems of accountability and collective meetings. This may indeed be a contributory factor, but there is something rather more at work here. Within the occupational culture of the youth work lies a deep-seated resistance to 'being told what to do'. Something of the frontier spirit remains, with the lone cowboy or cowgirl opening up new territories or simply going where the trail takes them. This may indeed lead to a 'rich diversity of practice', but it may also expresses a pandering to the individual ego. Whilst some nurses may see in health visiting and district nursing an escape from the ward, and some social workers flee from the rigours of casework into community work and more indulgent forms of therapy, youth work is still perceived as offering the opportunity to maximise freedom and minimalise accountability. This is an attitude which is not significantly challenged in the operation of a number of training agencies (Scottish Education Department, 1986, p. 14; DES, 1987a).

The concern with self, and the fairly general resistance to external management combine, as the Inspectors note, to make 'support' and 'consultancies' the new holy grail. There is a peculiar blind spot here. Having striven to avoid being managed, there is a failure to recognise the costs and responsibilities entailed by such actions. When this is added to the lack of concern with purpose and theory, the position becomes understandable. The problem is that most commentators fail to get below the surface. In youth work, we are told by one group of writers, 'we all need support, since it can be a very lonely business' (Akehurst *et al.*, 1984). This point is also underlined by Booton when he argues that professional isolation is a traditional characteristic of the job and that professional support is inadequately realised (1987, p. 112). Whilst this may all be true, it is necessary to look beyond the simple equation of physical isolation with the need for this elusive and apparently magical quality 'support'. We must recognise that some workers have lacked basic competencies. These may in part be the outcome of poor selection, inadequate management and resourcing, mis-directed training and the operations of the relationships and structures workers are placed in; however, deficiencies cannot be totally passed-off onto structure. Individual workers have to take responsibility for their actions or lack of them, but they do so in an area of welfare which has singularly failed to address purpose and theory and hence the appropriate relations of practice. 'Independence' may be the attraction of youth work, but it can quickly become an albatross.

One of the major reasons given by workers for rejecting or attempting to minimise attempts to influence their activities concerns the inadequacy of line-managers. It is apparent that Youth Officers have not been held in very high regard by workers. Indeed their track record hasn't been inspiring, as the various HMI reports demonstrate. Up until the late 1980s there were no consistent specialist training opportunities for the roles they have to undertake. Some experimental courses did exist (Gibson 1970), but such efforts soon evaporated. Further problems have apparently arisen from the lack of career structure for officers and the mixing of administrative, management and advisory roles and consequent blurring of boundaries (HMSO, 1982, p. 91). This form of arguing has a long history, and has yet to be subjected to sustained analysis. Firstly there are questions concerning the way in which boundaries are drawn around notions such as career structure. Is the structure simply defined by those of the Youth Service or can be officer or worker realistically look beyond these to other arenas? Given that approaching 50 per cent of those now entering youth work are qualified teachers, it would appear that a significant proportion of the labour force have some potential to transfer. Secondly, there is an inbuilt tendency in all competitive occupational structures, for those who have not 'advanced', to complain of their lack of opportunity to do so. This points to questions concerning the way in which notions such as 'career structure' can be quantified. Thirdly, and still further into the unknown, there arises the question of the relative standards of competence of individual youth workers and officers and those in parallel and competing occupational groupings. In other words there may not be a problem with the physical career structure. Rather, the difficulty may lie in the nature of the occupational culture or in some other facet of these groupings.

Beyond surface debates concerning adequacy, fundamental questions arise as to the nature of management and to the serious under-representation of women and certain ethnic groups in middle- and higher-management. Concerns about the former have perhaps been best expressed in feminist critiques of the competitive, masculine and hierarchical assumptions and practices prevalent within local authorities and voluntary agencies and the impact this has upon people operating within them. As Webster has argued, whilst many workers may favour a corporate or co-operative style of working, as they move 'upward' in the hierarchy, 'they seem less likely to want to validate the style. Perhaps this is because "moving up" means that the system starts to work for them' (1985, p. 6). The impact of equal opportunity policies, where they exist, is still to be fully experienced within youth work. Lacking any reliable statistical information as to the make-up and structure of the Youth Service work force, we have to rely on impressionistic and limited material. For example, when we examined the occupancy of positions of overall responsibility for local authority Youth Services, we found that of the 108 identified, only 10 of the senior officers were female. In terms of middle management, some authorities such as ILEA do appear to have made some progress in the appointment of women and of those from unrepresented racial groups. However, the position remains weighted in favour of white men.

Also problematic has been the general failure by workers and officers to attend fully to questions of local and community accountability. Such debates had a degree of fashionability in the first half of the 1970s, perhaps influenced by the tensions experienced in community work, but they have faded somewhat since. In part the lack of attention has risen from a reluctance to recognise and accept the political nature of youth work practice (Caldwell, 1985, p. 14). Attempts are made to keep issues contained within a technicist framework. There is also a problem concerning the inability of many workers and officers to appreciate the nature of work with adults. For example, this can be illustrated in relation to the operation of management committees, where there is often considerable resistance by workers, to any attempts to make such bodies work. First, as the Inspectors note, workers do not provide managers with the sorts of information that makes for informed decision. Reports are often verbal and even where written, short and tabled 'on the night'. Second, many workers fail to appreciate their educational/community development responsibilities *vis-à-vis* their committees.

> Workers have sometimes come to scorn management committees, treating them as an obligation and waste of time. Often this is because the workers feel they could run the agency and exercise greater influence on the local community if they 'went it alone'. This of course, directly contradicts one of the main reasons for workers being involved in the Youth and Community Service (Feek, 1982a, p. 1).

In sum, the state of management within the Youth Service would appear to be a matter of some concern. However, it is an area that is, at present, beyond quantification and there is the danger of both overlooking areas of good practice and of failing to make comparison with other welfare agencies. We can find similar debates repeated in education, personal social services and the health service. More than that, as stressed at the outset, the very notion of 'management' cannot be treated as unproblematic.

What is management?

Whilst 'management' may have achieved prominence, there remains a lack of clarity about what the term actually means.

Displaying the confidence of the huckster, rather than the hesitancy of the scholar, the Review Group on the Youth Service in England asserts that there is 'no real mystery about good management' (HMSO 1982, p. 74). It has four basic aspects:

defining objectives, assigning roles, allocating resources and monitoring performance. These four activities change in nature and scope according to the level at which management is carried out, and therefore take one form at national level and another at local level. Where an appropriate structure combined with the will and the skill to make it work, exists, the Service will function effectively; but where any of these is lacking, it will not (ibid.).

To what extent this is an adequate description of management is a matter of some debate and interest. It is useful to examine this portrayal of management as it accords with much that is written about the subject in the youth work context. We might begin by contrasting it with Drucker's popular explication wherein three tasks, equally important but essentially different, face the management of every institution:

• to think through and define the specific purpose and mission of the institution, whether business enterprise, hospital or university;
• to make work productive and the worker achieving;
• to manage social impacts and social responsibilities (1979, p. 36).

On two immediate counts there are problems. The notion of 'objectives' does not satisfactorily cover both those of 'purpose' (the reason for which something is done, created or exists) and of mission (the paramount objective for the immediate future). In addition, the Review Group's vision of management does not explicitly deal with handling the social impacts of the work. Other writers may stress leadership (Adair, 1983); setting goals and praising and reprimanding subordinates (Blanchard & Johnson, 1983); or winning as a matter of style (Goldsmith & Clutterbuck, 1985). Thus at this minimal level there are competing notions as to what makes for 'good' management. However, as soon as we pass beyond such cookbook notions of management, a more complex and deeply political process is revealed. At one level the process may be viewed as comprising the technical functions connected with activities such as planning, organising and integrating the activities that occur within an enterprise. At another, management is a structure of control, a means of ensuring the compliance of subordinates who do not necessarily share the same interests as their institutional superiors. Those charged with managing such processes, if they are to be effective, have to be able to draw upon a sophisticated ability to read and understand organisations (Morgan 1986) and a particular kind of political clarity. As Reed has argued, organisational theory, 'has presented management with a stock of 'moral fictions'' (such as managerial effectiveness) that disguise the social reality of contemporary management practice and the institutional structures through which it is carried on' (1985, p. 95). Thus, there can only be 'no mystery about good management' for as long as questions about social reality are blissfully ignored.

Further, the Review Group's view of management when placed firmly in the context of youth work organisation, has the appearance of whistling in the wind. Firstly, there are immediate questions about structure. Given the relative sophistication of large individual organisations such as the Boys' Brigades, Girl Guides and Woodcraft Folk and the integrity of their structures it is difficult to conceive of anything but a loose consultative or administrative arrangement linking these organisations at either a national or local level. The two areas where voluntary youth organisations have come together have been in the provision of fairly low level activities such as football leagues and in the allocation of reasonably small amounts of monies funnelled through community chest schemes and the like. Secondly, there are linked questions about 'will'. People's working relationships and youth work identity are formed and maintained within particular institutions such as those of Scouting, frequently lay considerable stress on the boundaries between 'them and us'. Born of different traditions, expressing divergent ideologies and emphasising contrasting practices, youth work organisations will tend to look to their own.

Beyond this, when such a view of management is interrogated more closely, it manifests a common collapsing of administrative tasks into the domain of management. For example, the practice of 'management work' is described as follows:

Work with other staff, full-timers, part-timers and volunteers, in varying capacities including being colleagues in a team, participating in collaborative activities, leading and directing, supervising and training, and so on.

Administration and finance, whether concerned with youth work in general in an area, or with a particular centre of project, including the preparation and processing of plans and budgets, consultation with management and other committees, the care and maintenance of premises, and all the paperwork and telephoning that these processes inevitably involve (HMSO, 1982, p. 87).

The split that appears to have been made here is between handling people and handling paper. Certainly an emphasis on administration is one echoed by many officers and trainers. When complaints about initial training are analysed, statements about the inability of workers to manage often can be reduced to concerns about the ability of workers to write reports, complete forms and accounts and to be in the office during set hours in the morning. As Forbes has commented 'budgeting and book-keeping are not regarded by youth workers as their forte' (1984, p. 17). A brief investigation of the curriculae of so called 'management courses' in higher education reveals substantial sections on accounting, law, marketing, systems analysis, writing for business, computing and so on. Herein lies the danger. The 'brief' acquaintance leads to a confusion of administrative competencies that may help the manager in her or his task with management itself.

It may be that many workers and officers have a cavalier attitude to the execution of basic administrative tasks, and that they are lacking in writing, book-keeping and time-keeping skills. If these things are necessary to the work then they must be done and done effectively. However a more fundamental question must be asked in relation to this phenomenon – why are workers and officers required to prepare or complete ever-increasing numbers of reports, memos, forms, accounts and returns and what are the implications of this for the quality of face-to-face work for which they are responsible? The inability to set management in context, the tendency to view it merely as a matter of technical concern, is perhaps the most worrying aspect of the current vogue for the subject. There is indeed a failure in many of the texts to take proper account of the 'ideological and political tensions embedded in any management of human purposes' (Scott, 1981, p. 28) and an 'appallingly naive understanding of the roles of management and the implications of particular societal models' (ibid., p. 27). In what remains of this chapter we want to attempt to set the current concern with management in time and place.

Cutbacks and the concern with management

Part of the reason for 'management' becoming such a rallying call derives from the continuing cutbacks in public expenditure. Policy-makers have had little option but to be more concerned about the effective use of resources. To achieve this it was seen as essential to extend their degree of control over the work they fund. However, the rhetoric surrounding such slogans as 'efficiency, effectiveness and economy' can all too easily flounder when brought into engagement with the real world of hidden transfers and voluntary involvement. The basis for making even rudimentary judgements about the use of resources in youth work is often lacking. That said, even in this time of relative scarcity and under-resourcing there remain substantial examples of waste within a number of Youth Services as HMI reports have indicated (DES, 1982a; DES 1986c).

With cutbacks in resources, workers and officers have had to turn to other, often short-term, sources of funding which have had major implications for the nature of their work. Getting hold of such monies or resources usually involves substantial amounts of correspondence and proposal writing as well as the inevitable round of meetings. Having gained the money, reports have to be written and grants reapplied for. Similarly involvement in anything connected with the MSC brings with it the same administrative mountain. This heightening of the youth worker's administrative function has tended to direct attention to management. A trend further underlined by the generalised shift towards the provision of leisure activity. It is usually the case that workers who adopt a 'provision' orientation, that is to say those who seek to provide a substantial programme of ready made activities, are more likely to be engaged in a larger round of paperwork than are those who seek to work with young people in the construction and running of their own group and activities.

The discussion and cutbacks cannot, of course, be taken in solation

244 The Promise of Management for Youth Work

from the political doctrines and concerns that have underpinned their execution. The emphasis upon profit, entrepreneurship and individual effort, and the supposedly disruptive and debilitating effects of the collective organising of the labour movement has, in New Right thinking, led to a growth in the heroic status of the manager. Constraints upon the ability of managers to manage must be removed. Red tape and restrictive practices must be cut through. The market must be free. Whilst the manager may be king (and the language invariably sexist), the manager is not a bureaucrat hidebound by unnecessary rules and procedures. The model is the entrepreneur and in this there are important implications for the way in which concerns with management have been experienced within youth work. For it is very easy to equate the activities of the individual worker in charge of particular piece of work or plant with the commercial entrepreneur (Ingram, 1987). With much of the rhetoric of management being derived from capitalist activity and with the bulk of the training materials and texts being similarly grounded, it is hardly surprising that a rather narrow and technical conception of management has taken root in youth work.

Crucially the general growth in concern about management when set against the apparently poor record of youth work in this respect may have been a further factor in the shift of resources away from the key areas of Youth Service endeavour into school-based work and IT. The comparatively clear management structures and systems of accountability within schooling has some appeal to those wishing to control the activities of youth workers more closely (See Ch. 5). Similarly the location of youth work with personal social service departments in the form of IT has meant that more direct forms of management were available and that this area of work had to justify itself. The resulting emphasis upon evaluation and writing-up, whilst producing the expected quota of dross, has also established a partial means by which management can be exercised. By using measures such as reconviction rates, IT has at least taken a shaky step beyond what passes for evaluation within the bulk of youth work. Whilst there may be disputes about what the figures actually mean, at least there is some recognition of the importance of empirical evidence.

Centralisation and management

Alongside the rise of the manager, there is at present a concerted attempt by both local and central employers and funders to gain a more direct control over the activities of youth workers. This broad drift to centralisation was masked in the first half of the 1980s by the rhetoric of liberalism, of 'setting the people free'. Within youth work, at a national level, this process was reflected in the establishment of CETYCW. This body acquired responsibility for the accreditation of in-service training and courses of initial training for full-time youth work. More recently it took on a responsibility to 'encourage' the development of training opportunities for part-time workers. The enhanced role for the Council has, to a considerable extent, flowed from a desire on the part of employers to re-orientate training. Much of the motivation for this being to ensure that newly qualified workers will be more disposed to employment within established forms of provision such as the club and less inclined to seek out what they perceive to be more radical and community-orientated posts (Smith, 1982; Hoggarth, 1983). Also at a national level we have seen a strengthening of the Youth Service Inspectorate, an effective limitation of the terms of reference of the National Youth Bureau and the establishment of a Youth Service section within the DES. All this has to be put in the context of a general growth in power of the DES at the expense of local authorities and the unions (Salter & Tapper, 1981) and the declining autonomy of local authorities (Chapter 4).

At the local level there was a related trend – the rise of managerialism. Encouraged by bodies such as CETYCW through its In-Service Training and Education Panel (INSTEP) and by the Review Group Report (HMSO, 1982), there was a growth in emphasis on management. As already noted, these trends are part of broader developments within local government. 'Management' and its accoutrements have tended to be presented as a cure-all. Somehow, by adopting spells and potions offered by management experts and consultants, the ills of youth work would disappear. Youth centres would be full, social education would happen, young people would develop. There is positive side to the development, the possession and use of certain managerial skills for workers can lead to increased effectiveness and possibly job satisfaction. But there should be no illusions as to why the siren call of the 'science of management' has met with ready acceptance from Youth Service policy makers. For through the interjection of regular work reviews, performance appraisals and more detailed job specifications there arises the possibility of enhancing the control of the central manager.

In-service training has also been seen as having potential as a control mechanism. As with initial training, in-service training has been perceived as an opening through which a set of prepackaged norms and practices can better be imposed. The internalisation of these norms and methods ensuring the control of workers in settings where intense managerial supervision is not a realistic option. The growing interest in in-service training on the part of Youth Service managers can be interpreted as an expression both of a desire to simultaneously raise and modify practice, better to coincide with established policies. Given that a significant degree of discretion remains in the hands of front-line workers, training, rather than direct line-management, becomes an attractive option.

Some authorities have attempted to dispense with the services of local management or advisory committees. At one level this may have been borne of a desire to clear away some of the confusion that exists, at another it is a further expression of centralism and technicism. This development clearly has consequences for the individual worker. Where, formerly, a worker may have been seconded to a voluntary management committee or directly employed by that committee (and funded by the authority), they may now find themselves with split responsibilities (to a voluntary committee for the club work, and to the youth and community officer for the area work), or transferred to the exclusive control of the local authority officer.

Workers, it should not be forgotten, have often colluded with this destruction of local management and area committees. Sometimes this has been because of the amount of effort that was required to service such bodies; sometimes that the control exercised by 'amateurs' was felt to be an affront to the worker's ego; and in other cases the existence of the committees was seen to undermine claims of youth work to professional status. More than this, such bodies can often operate to seriously disadvantage young people, whether through naked self-interest, paternalism, sexism or racism (Lacey, 1987, pp. 48–51). To some workers and officers it appeared that a 'professional' solution would combat such tendencies.

A by-product of this process of centralisation has been a significant increase in time spent by full-time workers and officers in meetings. The expansion in the time consumed may flow from a conscious desire on the part of participants to develop a corporate mode of working, a wish to rationalise provision and coordinate the organisation of events and activities. However, frequently such meetings are little more than an arena for the articulation of concerns that were formerly the province of voluntary area advisory committees and their equivalent. Or simply a means of self-justification for those managers, officers and workers who choose to measure their effectiveness in terms of the number of meetings they attend. In effect the process of centralisation, through a variety of devices, has drawn full-time workers away from face-to-face work into more intermediate roles. This in itself need not necessarily be a bad thing. However, it is difficult to escape the conclusion that full-time workers now spend too much time talking to each other and not enough time working with young people, part-timers, community groups and voluntary managers.

The polarisation of skill and youth work

It is necessary to set the changes already discussed alongside an analysis of the wider restructuring of the relationships in and to work. In this century the trend in job design, particularly for those people in operative jobs such as machinery, assembly, maintenance, clerical and secretarial work, has been towards the imposition of greater specialisation and a reduction in the degree of discretion they have over their work (Braverman, 1974). Whilst Braverman's thesis has been subjected to some critical attention (Thompson, 1984; Salaman, 1986), on the basis of the limited evidence available there would appear to have been a restructuring of the labour process which has further encouraged the polarisation of skill. This has entailed the wholesale upgrading of certain jobs and the deskilling of others (Woods, 1985, p. 101). The increased division of labour, of which the polarisation of skill is a central feature, has eroded the relative freedom of groups of workers to decide how and what they do. The education and welfare services have not been immune from this restructuring. It has involved decreasing the autonomy of the worker by introducing a variety of measures designed to ensure greater conformity to

agency policy and prescribed practices; and for example, concerted attempts to standardise and centralise certain elements of
youth work.

The almost evangelical conversion to the mystical qualities of
'line-management' has fed the growth in the number of posts that
acquire some notional area responsibility where the worker is
expected to service, supervise and develop units or initiatives
within a specified locale. Such units and initiatives are usually
staffed by part-time and voluntary workers who either are managed or serviced by the full-timer. In this example we can see a
possible process of deskilling at work. Area appointments are
frequently created by the removal of workers from a full-time
commitment to a particular club and group of young people. The
extent of this removal can range from complete withdrawal to the
specification that a certain amount of the workers time must be
spent on area work. In effect some of the face to face work that
was previously undertaken by trained full-timers is now transferred to part-timers.

Holmes (1981) hints at a further area of deskilling in his survey
of ex-students from youth and community work courses. He found
that a substantial number of people interviewed had rejected entry
into club-based work because of the lack of face-to-face contact
and because the management and administration of a centre was
perceived in terms of low status activities. These included going
round with a big bunch of keys, taking the money on the door,
putting toilet rolls in the toilets, and routine paperwork (Holmes,
1981, p. 75). Activities that were seen as somewhat removed from
the practice skills students felt they had acquired in their training.
The imposition of line-management appears to have done little to
change the situation outlined by Holmes. As Stone (1987) points
out, the range of financial, role and organisational pressures that
currently are experienced by workers is, to a significant extent, an
end-product of the confused expectations of both employers and
managers.

Perhaps the most blatant attempt at deskilling has been the use
of people on the MSC's Community Programme to undertake
tasks formally the province of the full-time worker. Whilst there is
some evidence that CP workers are treated as 'mere menials, on
hand to do any heavy, unpleasant or tedious tasks that the professionals would not do themselves' (Dooney & Watson, 1985,

p. 18), a large number of them are not so employed. Many are engaged on so called 'community development' tasks, a large number undertake substantial face-to-face work with young people. Deskilling occurs through the operation of temporary contracts (of one year) and the fact that these posts effectively substitute low paid, largely untrained personnel for professional staff, both full- and part-time. Even then on such schemes there is a general lack of emphasis upon appropriate specialist training.

It is not only workers and lay-people who serve on local management bodies who have been affected by these trends, middle management, i.e. youth and community officers and the like, have also experienced some changes in their functions. With increased centralisation there would be a natural assumption that the role of middle management would become more significant – after all someone has to take on the supervisory functions that were formerly in the hands of local committees or that had previously not been exercised. However, when we examine the work of officers it is probably true to say that they also have had to operate with a decreased degree of discretion. The amount of funding at their disposal has frequently diminished in relative terms and there has been an increased concern with the minutae of policy at higher levels.

Middle management is being obliged to process more paperwork without there necessarily being any increase in the appropriate clerical support (or in their own capacity to undertake this work). We also need to bear in mind that middle management has been required to undertake a representative function on those local management committees that remain and on other 'professional' bodies. They have also had to 'manage' directly an increasing number of front-line workers. The combined effect of this has been to squeeze their time. In many respects their position is now similar to 'supervisors' in industry and commerce, a position which has traditionally been regarded as problematic.

> Supervisors often have a wide range of shop floor or office responsibilities to cover, though these may be relatively minor. A substantial part of their job can consist in handling a stream of different 'disturbances' in the course of the workflow going smoothly. . . On the other hand their discretion has usually become very limited so that they cannot be said to be exercising managerial authority, whether this be over employees, over the

planning of workflows or over technical matters. The combination of wide responsibility within the confines of their department or section, and severely limited discretion has been found to bother many supervisors (Child, 1984, p. 48).

Increased division of labour has been experienced both vertically and horizontally. Vertically there has been a process of deskilling and increased centralisation. However, there are major structural and operational impediments to this process, particularly when we come to examine the point where youth work is delivered (see Chapter 3). The role and function of middle-management is riven with contradictory demands. They are literally caught in the middle. Again, whilst full-time workers may have been increasingly removed from face-to-face work, this does not mean that the quality of the work has suffered. Here we not only have to consider to the competence of part-time workers but also, rather more fundamentally, the lack of clarity about purpose and the inadequacy of theory. Questions of skill are largely irrelevant in the absence of theory and purpose.

The 'horizontal' division of labour has been expressed in the development of other agencies who offer services for young people. As we have seen, personal social services, probation, intermediate treatment, schooling, further education, youth training, and recreation and leisure, have each articulated a particular rationale for their work with young people. They have also displayed a growing regard for theory making and sound research alongside a desire to be seen as professional. Significantly, within the Youth Service, it is these professionals, particularly those trained as teachers, who are ascendant in the full-time labour force. They are advantaged in terms of career development and, uniquely in the welfare professions, they out-number those who are specialist trained. With changes in JNC regulations and the introduction of new funding arrangements for the in-service training of teachers and youth workers (DES, 1986) it may be that a higher proportion of the labour force will be specialist trained in some way. However, it is still likely that those who train via the teacher route will be considerably advantaged and that Albemarle's cadre of 'certificate trained' workers will remain second-class citizens within welfare (Jeffs & Smith, 1987a).

Increasing 'horizontal' specialisation and division of labour has also been experienced in other ways. Club and centre-based employment within youth work has been augmented by the development of detached work, project work, counselling and advice services, drop-in centres, youth houses, play provision, neighbourhood work, preventative and diversionary work, outdoor pursuits, homelessness and hostel work, and specialist activity work. These, amongst others, have contributed to a broadening of the range of job opportunities within youth and community work and have substantially altered the nature of the experience of those presenting themselves for specialist training. Whilst all this may have created a degree of diversification, a price has been extracted in terms of the equilibrium of youth work. The funding basis for a significant proportion of this work has been short or limited term. In addition, many of these developing specialisms can be readily associated with the movements in other welfare agencies described above.

The promise of management

Whilst management may be viewed as a process, what increasingly appears to be the case in youth work is that it is perceived as a job in itself. Changes in the organisation of youth work seem to be creating a tier of full-time managers whilst denuding youth work of full-time face-to-face workers. Much of the debate concerning management in youth work has been inappropriate and ill-informed. It has been technicist and has failed to place the growth of concern with management within the context of broader ideological and concrete shifts in welfare and the division of labour. One of the consequences of this has been a failure to take proper account of the dynamics of front-line organisations; another has been the stress laid upon inappropriate competitive, professionalised and entrepreneurial notions of management. Whilst efficiency and effectiveness may be management's promise, fundamental questions remain as to whose interests may be served by its disconnected application.

13

Conclusion

TONY JEFFS and MARK SMITH

The future of the Youth Service is far from secure. It has been squeezed and jostled by larger and more vigorous forms of welfare provision directed at young people. Schooling, the MSC, and further and higher education along with those services that un-ashamedly deal with treatment and punishment at one extreme and leisure at another have left it with fewer and fewer opportunities to sustain an identity of its own.

Although the Youth Service may be in the autumn of its years, it never enjoyed a glorious summer. At different times the sun did threaten to break through. Various official and semi-official reports and ground swells of support did at times lead to optimism and an air of expectancy. But it was never to be. It lacked the essential unity in action and clarity of purpose that could have given it a role and secure future. The Youth Service therefore remains something of a rhetorical device, a League of Nations. The voluntary organisations never seriously considered negotiating away their independence, whilst the statutory sector never developed beyond a Balkanised state. There was never the slightest hope that this disperate gathering could hammer out a clear and constructive policy, let alone breath any life into it. In the end the posturing centre stage became irrelevant. Individual workers, individual units and individual organisations carried on, survived and developed as best they could. Given the lack of central direction, the appalling low quality of training, the absence of research, the paucity of resources and poor management, it says a great deal about the commitment of many individual workers, full- and part-time, that it is possible to see practice which addresses the

252

lived experiences of young people. However that practice is all the more visible because of the murk that surrounds it.

The Youth Service has shown itself to be irrelevant to the majority of young people, who traverse adolescence encountering neither trauma nor mishap; who reject its provision as a locale for their leisure and who rarely see it as an agency capable of offering help of any value. For it is a service that possesses neither the resources, nor more importantly the expertise, to do more than tinker at the fringes of the more serious difficulties, dilemmas and questions young people may encounter or pose. The best the Youth Service and youth workers can do in these circumstances is to put those young people in touch with the 'experts' such as health visitors, IT officers, social workers, probation officers, sympathetic solicitors, drug counsellors, consultants and advice workers; or to engage in some form of preventative education. However, this again often merely entails the importation of an external 'expert'. The quality of the training and education, along with the historically low standards required for 'professional' certification mean that, at this level, intervention rarely rises above exhortation and rhetoric, or the commonsense solutions available in the bus queue.

The Youth Service encounters increasingly sophisticated young people who perceive little of value in the quality and content of the bulk of youth work. This reality, needless to say, has not escaped the attention of those state agencies who provide funding. The Youth Service, in their eyes, however, has one saving grace – it is cheap. It garners in large numbers of voluntary workers and consumes very little in the way of capital resources. Even the bill for the training of the full-time staff is so often subsidised by the participants. The Service also, for a minimal cost, offers the state a legitimacy of sorts. In particular, for a government to be seen to close down the Youth Service would entail a degree of electoral risk, not because large numbers of young people would suffer or be disadvantaged, but because opponents could exploit such an act as 'evidence' of a callous turning away from deprived young people. So like the charity donations of multinational firms and the sponsorship of school prizes by local worthies, the state continues to maintain a minimalist Youth Service. It has no enthusiasm for the task, but it is an easier option than to cut the lifeline in one fell swoop. The Youth Service therefore limps on, a remnant from an earlier age of more robust charity and voluntarism. It is the ghost at the educational banquet, the product of an era when the overwhelming majority of young people aged 14–21 were in full-time employment, when there was an arguable requirement for an informal educational agency to meet their 'social education' needs. The massive expansion of higher education, which post-Robbins saw a six-fold increase in student numbers; the raising of the school leaving age and the growth in voluntary staying on; and, more recently, the rise of the MSC, have all eroded a need for a safety-net agency such as the Youth Service.

Albemarle's twin vision of a Youth Service catering for the 'social education' of the majority of young people and the control and rehabilitation of a deviant or troublesome minority has been overtaken by events. Even the leftover role of leisure provider has been increasingly constrained by the expansion, on one hand, of commercial provision, and on the other, of local authority leisure departments. The former has, of course, always provided a ready alternative to statutory and voluntary youth provision and remains a recurrent motif in the inventory of fears articulated by youth workers. This has been partly expressed in relation to the extent to which the success of their own enterprises may suffer from competition from the commercial sector, yet also in terms of the 'harm' that may befall those young people lured into its clutches. The self-limiting impact of the commercial stratum has always been the price of entry and availability to the individual young person. The extent to which this disincentive will continue to operate in favour of the youth club or unit may be diminishing. Changes in the nature of leisure provision, especially concerning the development of home-based forms of activity; the apparent attraction of such provision to young people (and their readiness to pay a 'premium' for its consumption); and the narrowing gap in terms of pricing as a consequence of financial constraints within the public sector, have all contributed to an altered balance in the market.

The threat posed by the renaissance of municipal leisure is of a different order, and, perhaps, in the long term will prove potentially more damaging to the Service than the historic threat of the commercial sector. This partially relates to its courting of those very young people whose attraction to sports and activities has, in the past, made them something of a bedrock of Youth Service affiliates. However, the threat is not unidimensional, for it is entwined with the development of a new 'leisure science', in turn linked with the appearance of advanced training to degree level of middle and upper management in leisure departments. As a consequence, within the local authority sector there has emerged a new cadre of managers that is self-confident in the use of leisure activity for its own sake and which is unencumbered by grand designs of improvement and rescue. Currently the provision of leisure centres is even more patchy than that of youth centres and wings. The DES (1983) survey found that distance from leisure centres was a major factor in constraining attendance, but as the gaps in provision are filled so this will alter. Despite their paucity in many localities, the same survey found the 29 per cent of young people interviewed who affiliated to youth clubs and provision compared unfavourably with the 47 per cent who were sports/leisure centre users. Thus the final redoubt of leisure and activity of and for itself appears to under serious threat. The Youth Service, having lost most of its historical functions, faces questions as to what role it might conceivably be left to play in the future.

The major voluntary youth organisations, with their unique identities and resourcing in the main from non-state sources, may continue to evolve, though not necessarily grow. However, it is important at this stage not to conflate the Youth Service with youth work. The former may be in serious difficulties, but that should not imply that all youth work is in a highly problematic position. Whilst the state may place little concrete value upon the Youth Service, a whole range of institutions and groups do perceive a benefit from informal work with young people. Churches wish to socialise their young, as do groups of neighbours or members of political parties. There will therefore always remain a substantial body of popular youth work, gaining its identity and purpose from a wide range of institutions, groupings and organisations (Smith, 1988). Indeed such is the scope of this form of youth work, and the sharp ideological differences built into its various traditions, that although it may survive and even prosper, it will, as always, by its very nature be fragmented. All attempts to coerce or coalesce this into a cohesive whole must fail. Popular youth work exists because it is manifested in forms that are independent and exist to be independent. Some individual units within these traditions have long histories, although these are often fractured by moments of decline, but in the main they have a relatively short shelf-life. They may take money from the state, borrow premises or use equipment, but such support rarely ensures the survival of the individual unit, or the flowering of such groups where the ground is not fertile.

Squeezed on all sides by the growth of other agencies, and unable to effectively service popular youth work with its variegated requirements, 'professional' youth workers have been reduced to little more than the beachcombers of welfare, collecting the driftwood thrown overboard by other agencies. Up to now, little discernable attention has been paid to purpose and theory, and the way in which these can be made to inform practice. Other state workers will continue rightly to intervene in the lives of young people, their focus reflecting their base within education, leisure, training, policing or casework. Their predisposition to expansion can only further weaken the ability of the statutory Youth Service to sustain a separate corporate identity. An indication of this is the fact that Scotland and several LEAs such as Birmingham no longer have an identifiable youth service linked to education. Welfare services don't usually disappear overnight. They slip away through a combination of merger, neglect and professional and public indifference. The Youth Service is experiencing elements of all of these. The demise of the statutory Youth Service, as or when it occurs, will be neither dramatic, nor cataclysmic for all the reasons we have given. Rather it will be as Richard Jefferies, writing in the 1830s, described the death of Hodge, the old labourer pushed aside by new technology and scientific farming. Deposited in the workhouse to await his death; 'the end came very slowly, he ceased to exist by imperceptible degrees like an oak tree' (1959, p. 310).

Notes on the Contributors

Robert Adams lectures in social work at Humberside College of Higher Education. He studied at Manchester, Leeds and York Universities. He worked in the penal system before becoming project director for Barnardo's. He has researched and written mainly on youth and crime.

Yusuf I. Ahmad is employed as a lecturer at Bristol Polytechnic. He previously worked in the Department of Applied and Community Studies at Bradford and Ilkley Community College, in an action-research programme with young unemployed people, and as part of a community arts team. He is currently involved in a research project on the situation of young people in Bradford.

Bernard Davies is Training Officer for the Youth Service in Sheffield. He was formerly senior lecturer in applied social studies, University of Warwick. He is experienced in youth work, teaching and social work, and in professional training for all three occupations. Currently member of the Continuing Education Subcommittee of Warwickshire Education Committee. Publications include *The State We're In: Restructuring Youth Policies in Britain* and *Threatening Youth: Towards a National Youth Policy*.

Tony Jeffs is a lecturer in social policy at Newcastle Polytechnic in the Department of Social Work and Social Policy. He was until 1987 the editor of the journal *Youth and Policy*. He now edits with Pam Carter and Mark Smith the *Social Work as Social Welfare Yearbook*.

Ron Kirby taught on community and youth work courses at Bradford and Ilkley Community College. Previously he was involved in community education in Coventry and London. His current research interest is a major survey of young people in Bradford. He has recently begun working at Plymouth Polytechnic.

Mary Marken was working at the National Youth Bureau when she wrote Chapter 9 (with Doug Smith). She has co-authored various publications on youth work practice. Currently she is the Assistant Education Officer (youth and community work), Sheffield City Council.

Neil Ritchie works for Neighbourhood Energy Action. When helping to write this chapter he was an information officer at the National Youth Bureau.

Duncan Scott is a lecturer in social policy in the Department of Social Administration, University of Manchester. He has chaired national initiatives concerning the education and training of voluntary and part-time youth and community workers and co-authored *Starting from Strengths* (with Steve Bolger).

Keith Shaw is a lecturer in government at Newcastle Polytechnic. He previously worked in the Department of Social Science at Sunderland Polytechnic.

Douglas Smith has worked as Research Officer at the National Youth Bureau since 1978. He is author of various publications concerned with young people and the Youth Service and is series editor of NYB's research publications.

Mark Smith is a tutor at the Centre for Professional Studies in Informal Education, YMCA National College, London. With Pam Carter and Tony Jeffs he edits the *Social Work and Social Welfare Yearbook*.

Howard Williamson is a practising youth worker and an Honorary Research Fellow in the Social Research Unit, University College, Cardiff. He has published widely on youth and community work, delinquency and juvenile justice, and training and employment initiatives. Between 1979 and 1982 he was involved in a major research project on the impact of the Youth Opportunities Programme.

Bibliography

Aberdeen University (Unpub.) 'Community Education in the Grampian Region', Report 5, Aberdeen, University of Aberdeen.

ACW (1983) Talking Point No. 47, London, Association of Community Workers.

ADSS (1985) *Children Still in Trouble. A Report of an ADSS Group*, London, Association of Directors of Social Service.

Abercrombie, N., Hill, S. and Turner, B. (1980) *The Dominant Ideology Thesis*, London, Allen & Unwin.

Adair, J (1983) *Effective Leadership. A Modern Guide to Developing Leadership Skills*, London, Pan.

Adams, R. (1982) '*Organisation and development of intermediate treatment*, M. Phil. unpublished, University of York.

Adams, R. (1984) 'Contradictory face of IT practice', *Youth and Policy*, no. 10, pp. 9–15.

Adams, R. *et al.* (1981) *A Measure of Diversion?*, Leicester, National Youth Bureau.

Adler, R. and Dearling, A. (1986) 'Children's rights – a Scottish Perspective' in Franklin, B. (ed.) *The Rights of Children*, Oxford, Basil Blackwell.

Akehurst, M. *et al.* (1984) *Fieldwork. An Aid to the Support of Youth Workers*, Leicester, National Association of Youth Clubs.

Allen, G. *et al.* (1987) *Community Education*, Milton Keynes, Open University Press.

Altaver, E (1978) 'Some problems of state interventionism' in Holloway, J. and Picciotto, S. (eds) *State and Capital: a Marxist Debate*, London, Arnold.

Arnold, J. *et al.* (1981) *The Management of Detached Work. How and Why*, Leicester, National Association of Youth Clubs.

Asquith, S. (1983) *Children and Justice. Decision-making in Children's Hearings and Juvenile Courts*, Edinburgh, Edinburgh University Press.

Association of County Councils (1984) *Juvenile Courts*, ACC Working Party Report, London, Association of County Councils.

Atkinson, P., Rees, T., Shone, D. and Williamson, H. (1982) 'Social and life skills. The latest case of Compensatory Education' in Rees, T. L. and Atkinson, P. (eds) *Youth Unemployment and State Intervention*, London, Routledge & Kegan Paul.

Auld, J., Dorn, N. and South, N. (1984) 'Heroin Now: bringing it all back home', *Youth and Policy*, no. 9.

259

Baden-Powell, R. (1918) 'The responsibilities of citizenhood', *The Scouter*, June.

Bacon, R. and Eltis, W. (1976) *Britain's Economic Problem. Too Few Producers*, London, Macmillan.

Bakal, Y. (ed.) (1973) *Closing Correctional Institutions*, London, Heath.

Baker, M. R. (1978) 'The future role of the Youth Service: note by the Secretary', Youth Service Forum of England and Wales, unpublished.

Baker, S. H. (1919) *Character Building for Boys. The Scientific Management of Clubs for Boys*, London, YMCA Boys' Department.

Baker, B. (1986) *Rescuing the Comprehensive Experience*, Milton Keynes; Open University Press.

Barker, R. (1986) 'Rise of the great pretenders', *Times Higher Educational Supplement*, 4 April 1986.

Barnard, E. (1986) 'A new approach to juvenile crime', *Christian Action Journal*, Autumn.

Barnett, W. R. (1977) 'Code of professional conduct', Manchester, Community and Youth Service Association (unpublished).

Bedfordshire County Youth Officer (1984) 'Report by H. M. Inspectors – preliminary comments on the issues raised', Bedford, Bedfordshire County Council.

Bell, D. (1982) 'The social effects of the closure of village schools in Northumberland', Morpeth, Community Council of Northumberland.

Ben-Tovim, G. *et al* (1986) *The Local Politics of Race*, London, Macmillan.

Bendix, R. (1964) *Nation-building and Citizenship*, New York, Wiley.

Benington, J. (1976) *Local Government Becomes Big Business*, London, Community Development Projects Information and Intelligence Unit.

Benyon, J. (1984) *Scarman and After. Essays Reflecting on Lord Scarman's Report, the Riots and their Aftermath*, Oxford, Pergamon.

Bernstein, B. (1977) *Class, Codes and Control*. Vol. 3, *Towards a Theory of Educational Transmission* (2nd ed.), London, Routledge & Kegan Paul.

Birch, A. (1959) *Small Town Politics*, Oxford, Oxford University Press.

Blackmore, L. (1973) 'Intermediate treatment – ridiculous', *Youth Service*, vol. 12.

Blanch, M. (1979) 'Imperialism, nationalism and organized youth' in Clarke, J., Critcher, C. and Johnson, R. (eds) *Working Class Culture. Studies in History and Theory*, London, Hutchinson.

Blanchard, K. and Johnson, S. (1983) *The One Minute Manager*, London, Fontana.

Board of Education (1939) *The Service of Youth*, Circular 1486, London, HMSO.

Board of Education (1940) *The Challenge of Youth*, Circular 1516, London, HMSO.

Board of Education (1943) *The Youth Service after the War*, London, HMSO.

Board of Education (1944) *Teachers and Youth Leaders*, Report of the Committee appointed by the President of the Board of Education to consider the Supply, Recruitment and Training of Teachers and Youth Leaders (*'The McNair Report'*), London, HMSO.

Bolger, S. and Scott, D. (1984) *Starting From Strengths*, The Report of the Panel to Promote the Continuing Development of Training for Part-time and Voluntary Youth and Community Workers, Leicester, National Youth Bureau.

Bolger, S. *et al.* (1981) *Towards Socialist Welfare Work*, London, Macmillan.

Bone, M. and Ross, E. (1972) *The Youth Service and Similar Provision for Young People*, London, HMSO.

Booton, F. (1980) 'Deschooling the Youth Service' in Booton, F. and Dearling, A. (eds) *The 1980s and Beyond*, Leicester, National Youth Bureau.

Bottoms, A. E. (1974) 'On the decriminalisation of English juvenile courts' in Hood, R. (ed.) *Crime, Criminology and Public Policy. Essays in Honour of Sir Leon Radzinowicz*, London, Heinemann.

Bourdieu, P. (1977a) *Outline of Theory and Practice*, Cambridge, Cambridge University Press.

Bourdieu, P. and Passerson, J. C. (1977b) *Reproduction in Education, Society and Culture*, London, Sage.

Bowles, S. and Gintis, H. (1976) *Schooling in Capitalist America. Educational Reform and the Contradictions of Economic Life*, London, Routledge & Kegan Paul.

Boyd, D. *et al.* (1985) 'Caught in the Act', *Youth in Society* No. 98.

Brah, A. (1986) 'Unemployment and racism: Asian youth on the dole' in Allen, S., Waton, A., Purcell, K. and Wood, S. (eds) *The Experience of Unemployment*, London, Macmillan.

Braverman, H. (1974) *Labor and Monopoly Capital. The Degradation of Work in the Twentieth Century*, New York, Monthly Review Press.

Breakwell, G., Harrison, B. and Propper, C. (1984) 'Explaining the psychological effects of unemployment for young people: the importance of specific situational factors', *British Journal of Guidance and Counselling*, vol. 12, no. 2, pp. 132–40.

Brenton, M. (1985) *The Voluntary Sector in British Social Services*, London, Longman.

Brenton, M. and Ungerson, C. (eds) (1986) *Yearbook of Social Policy in Britain 1985*, London, Routledge & Kegan Paul.

Brew, J. McAlister (1943) *In the Service of Youth*, London, Faber.

Brew, J. McAlister (1957) *Youth and Youth Groups*, London, Faber

Bridge, K. (1984) 'Local government finance in a period of change', paper given to PAC Annual Conference.

Brittan, L. (1979) Address to IT Conference, Sheffield, 9–11 July 1979.

Broadfoot, P. (1986) 'Power relations and English education: the changing role of central government', *Journal of Education Policy*, vol. 1, no. 1.

Brody, S. (1966) *The Effectiveness of Sentencing*, Home Office Research Study no. 35, London, HMSO.

Brooke, P. (1984) Address (as Under-Secretary of State for Education and Science) to NCVYS AGM, 13 November 1984.

Brunel University (1978) 'A professional code of ethics for the Youth and Community Service. A discussion paper', Uxbridge, Brunel University.

Brynin, M. (1987) 'The Young Homeless', *Youth and Policy*, no. 20.

Burch, M. and Moran, M. (1985) 'The changing British political elite 1945–83', *Parliamentary Affairs* Winter 1985.

Burney, E. (1985) *Sentencing Young People: What Went Wrong with the Criminal Justice Act 1982*, Farnborough, Gower.

Buswell, C. (1985) 'Skill, corporatism and the curriculum: the case of youth training schemes', paper presented at the International Sociology of Education Conference, Westhill College, Birmingham, 1985.

Butters, S. with Newell, S. (1978) *Realities of Training. A review of adults who volunteer to work in the youth and community service*, Leicester, National Youth Bureau.

Byford, L. (1984) 'Crime and punishment', *Education*, January.

CETYCW (1984) *Guidelines to Endorsement. 1: Initial training in youth and community work provided in two-year full-time courses*, Leicester, Council for Education and Training of Youth and Community Workers.

CETYCW (1984a) *Initial Training Courses in Youth and Community Work*, Leicester, Council for Education and Training of Youth and Community Workers.

CSE State Group (1979) *Struggle over the State*, London, Conference of Socialist Economists.

Caldwell, T. (1985) 'Local people and local management', *Youth and Policy*, no. 13.

Callow, F. (1983) 'A tradition of exploitation', *Youth in Society*, no. 85.

Calouste Gulbenkian Foundation (1973) *Current Issues in Community Work. A Study by the Community Work Group*, London, Routledge & Kegan Paul.

Campbell, B. (1985) *The Road to Wigan Pier*, London, Virago.

Cane, T. (1983) *MSC Funded Youth Work Schemes and Implications for INSTEP*, Leicester, Council for Education and Training in Youth and Community Work.

Cantor, L. and Roberts, I. (1979) *Further Education Today. A Critical Review*, London, Routledge & Kegan Paul.

Carlen, P. (1983) 'On rights and powers. Some notes on penal politics' in Garland, D. and Young, P. (eds) *The Power to Punish. Contemporary Penality and Social Analysis*, London, Heinemann.

Carpenter, V. and Young, K. (1986) *Coming in From the Margins. Youth Work with Girls and Young Women*, Leicester, NAYC.

Cartlidge, R. (1983) 'Review of the Thompson Report', *Youth and Policy*, vol. 1, no. 4.

Casemore, R. *et al.* (1983) 'A Code of Practice: for all youth and community service personnel', unpublished.

Castells, M. (1977) *The Urban Question*, London, Arnold.

Cattermole, F. (1986) Speech to NCVYS AGM, London, 11 November.

Caul, B. *et al.* (1983) *The Juvenile Justice System in Northern Ireland*, Belfast, Ulster Polytechnic.

Central Statistical Office (1981) *Economic Trends* no. 327, London, HMSO.

Central Statistical Office (1985) *Economic Trends* no. 381, London, HMSO.

Chibnall, S. (1977) *Law and Order News. An Analysis of Crime Reporting in the British Press*, London, Tavistock.

Child, J. (1984) *Organization. A Guide to Problems and Practice*, London, Harper & Row.

Clarke, J. and Critcher, C. (1985) *The Devil Makes Work. Leisure in Capitalist Britain*, London, Macmillan.

Coates, D. (1975) *The Labour Movement and the Struggle for Socialism*, Cambridge, Cambridge University Press.

Coates, D. (1984) *The Context of British Politics*, London, Hutchinson.

Cochrane, R. and Billig, M. (1983) 'Youth and politics', *Youth and Policy*, vol. 2, no. 1.

Cockburn, C. (1977) *The Local State*, London, Pluto Press.

Cockburn, C. (1987) *Two Track Training. Sex Inequalities and the YTS*, London, Macmillan.

Cockburn, C. (1987a) 'Positive action for young women in YTS', *Youth and Policy*, no. 19.

Cockerill, G. F. (1983) *National Youth Bureau. Report of Review*, London, DES.

Coffield, F., Borrill, C. and Marshall, S. (1986) *Growing Up at the Margins*, Milton Keynes, Open University Press.

Cohen, P. (1984) 'Against the new vocationalism', in Bates, I., Clarke, J., Cohen, P., Finn, D., Moore, R. and Willis, P., *Schooling for the Dole?*, London, Macmillan.

Cohen, P. (1984a) 'Losing the generation game?' in Curran, J. (ed.) *The Future of the Left*, Cambridge, Polity.

Cooke, D. (ed.) (1942) *Youth Organisations in Great Britain, 1944–45*, London, Jordan.

Comber, L. (1981) *The Social Effects of Rural Primary School Reorganisation*, Birmingham, University of Aston.

Cornish, D. B. and Clarke, R. V. G. (1975) *Residential Treatment and its Effects on Delinquency*, London, HMSO.

Corrigan, P. (1979) *Schooling the Smash Street Kids*, London, Macmillan.

Corrigan, P. (1979a) 'The local state: the struggle for democracy', *Marxism Today*, July.

Critical Social Policy (1983) Privatising local government: the case of Birmingham, *Critical Social Policy* Issue 8 Autumn.

Croft, S. and Beresford, P. (1986) *Whose Welfare*? Brighton, Brighton Polytechnic.

Crosland, C. A. R. (1963) *The Future of Socialism*, London, Schocken Books.

Cross, M. (1987) 'Black youth and YTS: the policy issues' in Cross, M. and Smith, D. I. (eds) *Black Youth Futures*, Leicester, National Youth Bureau.

Crouch, C. (1979) 'The state, capital and liberal democracy' in Crouch, C. (ed.) *State and Economy in Contemporary Capitalism*, London, Croom Helm.

Curtis, S. J. and Boultwood, M. E. A. (1960) *An Introductory History of English Education since 1800*, London, University Tutorial Press.

DES (1966) *A Second Report on the Training of Part-time Youth Leaders and Assistants*, Report of the Review Committee of the Youth Service Development Council, December 1965, London, HMSO.

DES (1969) *Youth and Community Work in the 1970s*, ('*The Fairbairn-Milson Report*'), London, HMSO.

DES (1975) *Provision for Youth, Discussion paper*, London, Department of Education and Science.

DES (1980) *Report by H.M. Inspectors on Educational Provision by Inner London Educational Authority*, London, DES.

DES (1982a) *Three Lambeth Youth Clubs, ILEA. Report by HM Inspectors*, London, DES.

DES (1982b) *Youth Training Scheme. Implications for the Education Service, Circular 6/82*, London, DES.

DES (1982c) *Survey of Shared and Extended Use of Schools in 1978–9. DES Statistical Bulletin*, London, DES.

DES (1983) *Young People in the 80's. A Survey*, London, HMSO.

DES (1983a) *The Work of HM Inspectorate in England and Wales*, London, DES.

DES (1983b) *Educational Provision by the London Borough of Sutton. Report by HM Inspectors*, London, DES.

DES (1983c) *Education Provision in the Darlaston Area of the Metropolitan Borough of Walsall. Report by H. M. Inspectors*, London, DES.

DES (1983d) *Youth Service Provision in Two Areas of Bedfordshire. Report by H.M. Inspectors*, London, DES.

DES (1983e) *Police Liaison with the Education Service. A Report of an enquiry carried out by HM Inspectors of Schools in July 1982*, London, HMSO.

DES (1984a) *Some Detached Youth and Community Work in Sheffield. Report by HM Inspectors*, London, DES.

DES (1984b) *Memorandum on Headquarters Grants to NVYOs under the Education (Grant) Regulations, 1983*, London, DES.

DES (1984c) *Draft Circular to All Local Education Authorities and National Voluntary Youth Organisations*, London, DES.

DES (1985a) *1984 Annual Report*, London, DES.

DES (1985b) *Circular 1/85*, London, DES.

DES (1985c) *Survey of Shared and Extended Use of Schools in 1983. DES Statistical Bulletin*, London, DES.

DES (1986) *Local Authority Training Grants Scheme. Financial Year 1987–88, Circular 6/86*, London, HMSO.

DES (1986a) *Report by HM Inspectors on Youth Service in Cornwall*, London, DES.

DES (1986b) *Report by HM Inspectors on the YMCA National College*:

Two Year Certificate Course in Youth and Community Work, London, DES.

DES (1986c) *Report by H.M. Inspectors on Aspects of the Work of the Youth Service in Wigan*, London, DES.

DES (1987) Press Notice 23/87 'Education department publishes Youth Service analysis', London, DES.

DES (1987a) *Report by HMI: Manchester Poly. Qualifying Training in Youth & Community Work*, London, HMSO.

DOE (NI) (1986) *Youth Service Expenditure 1984/85*, Belfast, Department of Education (Northern Ireland).

Dale, J. and Foster, P. (1986) *Feminists and State Welfare*, London, Allen & Unwin.

Davies, B. (1967) *School-based Youth Work in Debate. A Collection of Professional Papers*, Leicester: Youth Service Information Centre.

Davies, B. (1979) *In Whose Interest? From Social Education to Social and Life Skills*, Leicester, National Youth Bureau.

Davies, B. (1980) 'Policies and priorities in Youth and Community Work. A review of two decades' in Booton, F. and Dearling, A. (eds) *The 1980's and Beyond*, Leicester, National Youth Bureau.

Davies, B. (1981) *The State We're In. Restructuring Youth Policies in Britain*, Leicester, National Youth Bureau.

Davies, B. (1982) 'Juvenile justice in confusion', *Youth and Policy*, vol. 1, no. 2, pp. 33–5.

Davies, B. (1986) *Threatening Youth. Towards a National Youth Policy*, Milton Keynes, Open University Press.

Davies, B. (1986a) 'Towards an integrated view of youth policy', *Youth and Policy*, no. 18.

Davies, B. (1986b) 'The death knell tolls?', *Community Education Network*, vol. 6, no. 5.

Davies, B. and Gibson, A. (1967) *The Social Education of the Adolescent*, London, University of London Press.

Davies, B. and Rogers, J. (eds) (1972) *Working with Youth*, London, BBC Publications.

Davies, M. (1985) 'The pathology of Reaganomics', *New Left Review*, no. 149.

Dawson, P. (1981) *Making a Comprehensive Work. The Road from Bomb Alley*, Oxford, Blackwell.

Dearlove, J. (1979) *The Reorganisation of British Local Government*, Cambridge, Cambridge University Press.

Donnison, D. and Stewart, M. (1958) *The Child and the Social Services*, London, Fabian Society.

Dooney, S. and Watson, R. (1985) 'MSC, Community Programme and the Youth Service', *Youth and Policy*, no. 12, pp. 17–20.

Drake, K. (1986) *Public Funds for 16–19 Year Olds*, London, Public Finance Foundation.

Drucker, P. (1979) *Management*, London, Pan.

Dunleavy, P. (1980) *Urban Political Analysis*, London, Macmillan.

Dunleavy, P. (1981) *The Politics of Mass Housing in Britain 1945–74. A Study of Corporate Power and Political Influence in the Welfare State*, London, Clarendon Press.

Dunleavy, P. (1984) 'The limits to local government' in Boddy, M. and Fudge, C. (eds) *Local Socialism*, London, Macmillan.

Dunleavy, P. and Rhodes, R. (1986) 'Government beyond Whitehall' in Drucker, H. *et al.* (eds) *Developments in British Politics* (2nd ed.), London, Macmillan.

Dunlop, S. (1985) 'The role of the Youth Tutor', *Youth and Policy*, no. 12.

Dybeck, M. (1981) *The Village College Ways. An Approach to Community Education*, Coventry, Community Education Development Centre.

Dyhouse, C. (1981) *Girls Growing Up in Late Victorian and Edwardian England*, London, Routledge & Kegan Paul.

EEC Economic and Social Committee (1983) *Youth Unemployment*, Brussels, European community.

Eggleston, J. (1976) *Adolescence and Community. The Youth Service in Britain*, London, Edward Arnold.

Elcock, H. (1982) *Local Government. Politicians, Professionals and the Public in Local Authorities*, London, Methuen.

Elcock, H. (1983) 'Young voters 1988: will they break the mould?', *Youth and Policy*, no. 10.

Empey, La Mar T. (1984) 'The American experience. The implications of research and theory for diversion programmes' in *Diversion. Corporate Action with Juveniles*, Proceedings of a Conference on Crime Prevention, Birmingham, 4–6 December 1983, Lancaster, Centre of Youth, Crime and Community, University of Lancaster.

Evans, W. M. (1965) *Young People in Society*, Oxford, Blackwell.

Ewen, J. (1972) *Towards a Youth Policy*, Leicester, MBS Publications.

Ewen, J. (1975) *A Positive Future for the Youth Service*, Leicester, National Youth Bureau.

Fairbairn, A. (1969) 'Youth Service in Community Colleges', *Adult Education*, vol. 41.

Fairbairn, A. (1978) *The Leicestershire Community Colleges and Centres*, Nottingham, University of Nottingham.

Fairbairn, A. (1980) *The Leicestershire Plan*, London, Heinemann.

Fairbairn, A. (1971) *The Leicestershire Community Colleges*, London, National Institute of Adult Education.

Farrington, D. P. (1978) 'The effectiveness of sentences', *Justice of the Peace*, vol. 142, February 4.

Feek, W. (1982a) *Management Committees. Practicising Community Control*, Leicester, National Youth Bureau.

Feek, W. (1982b) *The Way We Work. Making Staff Teams Effective*, Leicester, National Youth Bureau.

Feek, W. (1983) *Steps in Time. A Guide to Agency Planning*, Leicester, National Youth Bureau.

Field, S. and Southgate, P. (1982) *Public Disorders. A Review of Research and a Study in One Inner City Area*, London, Home Office.

Finn, D. (1984a) 'Britain's mis-spent youth', *Marxism Today*, February, pp. 18–24.

Finn, D. (1984b) 'Leaving school and growing up Work experience in the juvenile labour market' in Bates I. *et al.* (eds) *Schooling for the Dole?*, London, Macmillan.

Finn, D. (1987) *Training without Jobs. New Deals and Broken Promises*, London, Macmillan.

Fisher, G. and Day, M. (1983) *Towards a Black Perspective*, A report of an experimental Afro-Caribbean training project for part-time youth and community workers, London, Commission for Racial Equality.

Fletcher, C. (1984) *The Challenge of Community Education*, Nottingham, University of Nottingham.

Fletcher, C. *et al.* (1985) *Schools on Trial*, Milton Keynes, Open University Press.

Forbes, Y. (1984) 'Management training. Are we getting a raw deal?', *Youth in Society*, no. 92.

Foreman, A. (1987) 'Youth workers as Redcoats' in Jeffs, T. and Smith, M. (eds) *Youth Work*, London, Macmillan.

Forsythe, D. *et al.* (1983) *The Rural Community and the Small School*, Aberdeen, Aberdeen University Press.

Foster, C. D. *et al.* (1980) *Local Government Finance in a Unitary State*, London, Allen & Unwin.

Francis, D., Henderson, P. and Thomas, D. N. (1984) *A Survey of Community Workers in the United Kingdom*, London, National Institute for Social Work.

Franklin, B. (1986) 'Children's political rights' in Franklin, B. (ed.) *The Rights of Children*, Oxford, Blackwell.

Freeman, M. D. A. (1979) *Violence in the Home*, Farnborough, Saxon House.

Galper, J. H. (1975) *The Politics of the Social Services*, London, Prentice-Hall.

Garland, D. and Young, P. (1983) 'Towards a social analysis of penality' in Garland, D. and Young, P. (eds), *The Power to Punish. Contemporary Penality and Social Analysis*, London, Heinemann.

Garner, W. and Gillespie, N. (1986) 'Youth work in West Belfast', *Youth and Policy*, no. 18.

General Household Survey 1981 (1984) in *Social Trends*, no. 14, London, HMSO.

George, V. (1983) 'The aims and consequences of social policy' in Bean, P. and MacPherson, S. (eds) *Approaches to Welfare*, London, Routledge & Kegan Paul.

Gibson, A. (1970) *The Youth Service Officers Course 1968–69. Record of an Experimental Approach*, Leicester, Youth Service Information Centre.

Gillis, J. R. (1974) *Youth and History. Tradition and Change in European Age Relations 1770–Present*, New York, Academic Press.

Gilroy, P. (1987) *There Ain't No Black in the Union Jack*, London, Hutchinson.

Ginsburg, N. (1979) *Class, Capital and Social Policy*, London, Macmillan.

Giroux, H. A. (1983) *Theory and Resistance in Education*, London, Heinemann.

Gittins, D. (1985) *The Family in Question. Changing Households and Familiar Ideologies*, London, Macmillan.

Gladstone, F. (1979) *Voluntary Action in a Changing World*, London, Bedford Square Press.

Glasman, D. (1974) 'Professional association or trade union?' *Youth Service*, May/June, pp. 14–15.

Glennerster, H. (1985) *Paying for Welfare*, Oxford, Blackwell.

Goetschius, G. W. and Tash, J. (1967) *Working with Unattached Youth. Problem, Approach, Method*, London, Routledge & Kegan Paul.

Golding, P. and Middleton, S. (1982) *Images of Welfare*, Oxford, Martin Robertson.

Goldsmith, M. (1985) 'The Conservatives and local government, 1979 and after' in Bell, D. (ed.) *The Conservative Government 1979–84. An Interim Report*, London, Croom Helm.

Goldsmith, M. and Newton, K. (1984) 'Central–local government relations: the irresistable rise of central power' in Berrington, H. (ed.) *Change in British Politics*, London, Frank Cass.

Goldsmith, W. and Clutterbuck, D. (1985) *The Winning Streak. Britain's Top Companies Reveal Formulae for Success*, Harmondsworth, Penguin.

Gordon, P. (1983) *White Law: Racism in the Police, Courts and Prisons*, London, Pluto Press.

Gordon, T. (1986) *Democracy in One School?*, Lewes, Falmer Press.

Gough, I. (1979) *The Political Economy of the Welfare State*, London, Macmillan.

Greenwood, R. (1982) 'The politics of central–local relations in England and Wales 1974–81', *West European Politics*, July.

Gurnah, A. (1984) 'The politics of Race Awareness Training', *Critical Social Policy*, no. 11, pp. 6–19.

Gyford, J. and James, M. (1983) *National Parties and Local Politics*, London, Allen & Unwin.

HMI (Wales) (1984) *Youth Service Provision in Wales. Education Survey* 13 (2 vols), London, HMSO.

HMSO (1942) *Social Insurance and Allied Services*, ('*The Beveridge Report*'), London, HMSO.

HMSO (1951) *Report of the Committee on the Recruitment and Training of Community Centre Wardens* ('*The Fletcher Report*'). London, HMSO.

HMSO (1960) *The Youth Service in England and Wales* ('*The Albermarle Report*'), London, HMSO.

HMSO (1963) *Higher Education. Report of the Committee appointed by the Prime Minister* ('*The Robbins Report*'), London, HMSO.

HMSO (1964) *Children and Young Persons: Scotland* ('*The Kilbrandon Committee*'), London, HMSO.

HMSO (1967) *Committee on the Management of Local Government*, vol.

1 ('*The Maud Report*'), London, HMSO.

HMSO (1969) *Royal Commission on Local Government in England. Written Evidence of Commercial, Industrial and Political Organisations. Research Study 10*, London, HMSO.

HMSO (1972) *The New Local Authorities*: *Management and Structure* ('*The Bains Report*'), London, HMSO.

HMSO (1975) *Eleventh Report from the Expenditure Committee. Children and Young Persons Act 1969*, London, HMSO.

HMSO (1976) *Children and Young Persons Act 1969. Observations on the Eleventh Report from Expenditure Committee*, London, HMSO.

HMSO (1982) *Expenditure and Participation. Report of the Review Group on the Youth Service in England* ('*The Thompson Report*'), London, HMSO.

HMSO, (1983a) *Local Government Finance. The Rate Support Grant Report, England 1983/4*, House of Commons Paper HC 149, London, HMSO.

HMSO, (1983b) *Study of HM Inspectorate in England and Wales* (Lord Rayner), London, HMSO.

HMSO (1984) *Northern Ireland Assembly. Report on the Youth Service*, Belfast HMSO.

HMSO (1986) *Paying for Local Government*, London, HMSO.

HMSO (1987) *Annual Abstract of Statistics*, No. 123. London, HMSO.

Hadley, R. and Hatch, S. (1981) *Social Welfare and the Failure of the State. Centralised Social Services and Participatory Alternatives*, London, Allen & Unwin.

Hadley, R. and McGrath, M. (eds) (1980) *Going Local. Neighbourhood Social Services*, London, Bedford Square Press.

Hall, G. Stanley (1904) *Adolescence. Its Psychology and its Relation to Physiology, Anthropology, Sociology, Sex, Crime, Religion and Education* (2 vols), New York, Appleton.

Hall, J. and Jones, D. C. (1950) 'Social grading of occupations', *British Journal of Sociology*, vol. 1, no. 1, pp. 31–51.

Hall, M. P. (1965) *The Social Services of Modern England*, London, Routledge & Kegan Paul.

Hall, P. (1983) 'The Community College flexible response system?' in Troyna, B. and Smith, D. (eds) *Racism, School and the Labour Market*, Leicester, National Youth Bureau.

Hall, P., Marks, C., Street, P. and Clifford, A. (1984) *Going Community for Secondary Schools*, Coventry, Community Education Development Centre.

Hall, S. (1984) 'The rise of the representative/interventionist state' in McLennan, G., Held, D. and Hall, S. (eds) *State and Society in Contemporary Britain*, Cambridge, Polity.

Hall, S., Critcher, C., Jefferson, T., Clarke, J. and Roberts, B. (1978) *Policing and the Crisis*: *Mugging, the State, and Law and Order*, London, Macmillan.

Handy, C. B. (1985) *Understanding Organisations*, 3rd ed., Harmondsworth, Penguin.

270   *Bibliography*

Hanmer, J. (1964) *Girls at Leisure*, London, London Union of Youth Clubs.

Harper, B. (1983) *Better than Bessey? A review of the training provision for part-time and voluntary youth workers in the statutory sector in England and Wales*, Leicester, National Youth Bureau.

Harper, B. (1985) *People Who Count. Youth Work Resources in Local Authorities*, Leicester, National Youth Bureau.

Harris, R. and Seldon, A. (1979) *Over-ruled on Welfare*, London, Institute of Economic Affairs.

Hebdige, D. (1979) *Subculture. The Meaning of Style*, London, Methuen.

Heidenheimer, A. J. *et al.* (1983) *Comparative Public Policy*, London, Macmillan.

Henderson, J., Robins, L. and Wormald, E. (1980) 'Trained for unemployment: a note on passivity among unemployed teachers', *Journal of Further and Higher Education*, vol. 4, no. 2.

Hendricks, H. (1986) 'Personality and psychology. Defining Edwardian boys', *Youth and Policy*, no. 18.

Hendry, L. (1986) 'Young people, school and leisure. Developing meta-cognitive skills? in Haywood, L. (ed.) *Leisure & Youth*, Conference Papers 17, London, Leisure Studies Association.

Hendry, L., Brown, L. and Hutcheon, G. (1981) 'Adolescents in Community Centres. Some urban & rural comparisons', *Scottish Journal of Physical Education*, vol. 8 (3).

Henriques, B. L. Q. (1933) *Club Leadership*, Oxford, Oxford University Press.

Higgins, H. E. (1967) *The Essentials of Boys' Club Leadership*, London, National Association of Boys Clubs.

Hobbs, G., Foxall, S., Schofield, Y. and Burfield, N. (1983) 'Making the best of YTS', *Youth in Society*, no. 78.

Hodson, R. (1983) *Worker's Earnings and Corporate Economic Structure*, New York, Academic Press.

Hogarth, L. (1983) 'Against the odds. Training youth and community workers', *Youth and Policy*, vol. 2. pp. 34–8.

Holland, J. (1976) 'Parental involvement in an evolving Community School', unpublished B. Phil., University of York.

Holmes, J. (1981) *Professionalisation. A Misleading Myth?*, Leicester, National Youth Bureau.

Holmes, J. (1986) 'Women students in youth and community work courses', *Youth and Policy*, no. 17.

Home Office (1976) *IMPACT. The Results of the Experiment*, London, HMSO.

Home Office (1979) *Report of the Children and Young Persons Review Group ('The Black Report')*, Belfast, HMSO.

Home Office (1983) *British Crime Survey 1983*, London, HMSO.

Home Office (1984) *Tougher Regimes in Detention Centres. Report of an Evaluation by the Young Offender Psychology Unit*, London, HMSO.

Horobin, J. C. (1980) *Community Education Statistics. A Report Commissioned by the Scottish Council for Community Education*, St Andrews, Univerity of St Andrews.

Hudson, B. (1984) 'Femininity and adolescence' in McRobbie, A. and Nava, M. (eds) *Gender and Generation*, London, Macmillan.

Hughes, S. (1986) 'How London will fare under rates reform plan', *Municipal Journal*, February.

Humble, S. (1982) *Voluntary Action in the 1980's. A Summary of the Findings of a National Survey*, Berkhamsted, Volunteer Centre.

Humphries, J. (1980) 'Class struggle and the working class family' in Lamsden, A. H. (ed.) *The Economics of Women and Work*, Harmondsworth, Penguin.

Humphries, S. (1981) *Hooligans or Rebels? An Oral History of Working-class Childhood and Youth 1889–1939*, Oxford, Blackwell.

Hutchinson, A. (1985) 'Community uprising or riot? Handsworth', *Youth and Policy*, no. 15.

ILEA (1984) *The Youth Service. A Fair Deal for Girls?*, London, ILEA.

INSTEP (1985) *Guidelines to a Staff Development Programme*, Leicester, CETYCW.

Ingram, G. (1987) 'Youth workers as entrepreneurs' in Jeffs, T. and Smith, M., *Youth Work*, London, Macmillan.

Issac-Henry, K. (1984) 'Taking stock of Local Authority Associations', *Public Administration*, summer.

Ives, R. (1986) 'Children's sexual rights' in Franklin, B. (ed.) *The Rights of Children*, Oxford, Blackwell.

Jefferies, R. (1880) *Hodge and His Masters*, London, Smith & Elder.

Jeffs, T. (1979) *Young People and the Youth Service*, London, Routledge & Kegan Paul.

Jeffs, T. (1982) 'Youth and Community Service and the cuts', *Youth and Policy*, vol. 1, no. 1.

Jeffs, T. (1984), *Youth Conscription*, London, Youthaid.

Jeffs, T. (1987) 'Youth and Community Work and the Community School' in Allen, G. *et al.* (eds) *Community Education. Agenda for Educational Reform*, Milton Keynes, Open University Press.

Jeffs, T. and Smith, M. (eds.) (1987) *Youth Work*, London, Macmillan.

Jeffs, T. and Smith, M. (1987a) 'What future for Initial Training?' *Youth and Policy*, no. 20.

Jephcott, P. (1967) *A Time of One's Own*, Edinburgh, Oliver & Boyd.

Jervis, M. (1986) 'RATs tales', *Social Services Insight*, vol. 1, no. 28.

Jewell, H. (1972) *English Local Administration in the Middle Ages*, Newton Abbot, David & Charles.

Jones, A. (1972) 'The all purpose all age Community School', *Youth Review*, no. 22.

Jones, C. (1983) *Social Work and the Working Class*, London, Macmillan.

Jones, P., Williamson, H., Payne, J. and Smith, G. (1983) *Out of School. A Case Study of the Role of Government Schemes at a Time of Growing Unemployment*, Sheffield, Manpower Services Commission.

Judge, K. (1983) 'Public opinion and the privatisation of welfare. Some theoretical implications', *Journal of Social Policy*, vol. 12, no. 4.

Judge, K. (1984) *A Generation of School*, Oxford, Oxford University Press.

Karabel, J. and Halsey, A. H. (1977) 'Educational research A review and introduction' in Karabel, J. and Halsey, A. H. (eds) *Power and Ideology in Education*, New York, Oxford University Press.

Kaufmann, F-X. (1982) *Towards a Sociological Theory of Political Intevention*, Bielefeld; University of Bielefeld, Center for Interdisciplinary Research.

Kaufmann, F-X. (1985) 'Major problems and dimensions of the welfare state' in Eisenstadt, S. N. and Ahimeir, O. (eds) *The Welfare State and its Aftermath*, London, Croom Helm.

Keating, P. J. (ed.) (1976) *Into Unknown England 1866–1913. Selections from the Social Explorers*, London, Fontana.

Kelly, G. (1979) 'Social work in the courts in Northern Ireland' in Parker, H. (ed.), *Social Work and the Courts*, London, Edward Arnold.

Kendra, N. (1985a) 'The demythologisation of part-time Youth Work training', *Youth and Policy*.

Kerr, C. *et al.* (1973) *Industrialism and Industrial Man*, Harmondsworth, Penguin.

Kidd, H. (1972) 'All in it together', *Youth Review*, No. 22.

King, A. (1986) *Partnership in Youth Work. A Survey of Voluntary and Statutory Practice in Scotland*, Edinburgh, SSCVYO.

King, M. and Petit, M-A. (1985) 'Thin sticks and fat carrot. The French juvenile justice system', *Youth and Policy*, no. 15.

King, R. (1986) *The State in Modern Society*, London, Macmillan.

Kirby, R. (1986) 'Democracy and control in Community Education', *Youth and Policy*, no. 15.

Kirkhan, S. (1985) 'Jobless fear may affect health of the young', *Times Education Supplement*, August 16.

Klein, R. and O'Higgins, M. (1986) 'Social policy after incrementalism' in Klein, R. and O'Higgins, M. (eds) *The Future of Welfare*, Oxford, Blackwell.

Kuper, B. (1984) 'Youth and community work. Training and community work', *Youth and Policy*, no. 10.

Kuper, B. (1985) 'The supply of training', *Youth and Policy*, no. 13.

Lacey, F. (1987) 'Youth workers as community workers' in Jeffs, T. and Smith, M. (eds) *Youth Work*, London, Macmillan.

Larson, M. (1981) 'Monopolies of competence and bourgeois ideology', in Dale, R., Esland, G., Ferguson, R. and MacDonald, M. (eds), *Education and the State*, vol. 1: *Politics, Patriarchy and Practice*, Lewes, Falmer Press.

Lawrence, E. (1982) 'Just plain common sense. The "roots" of racism' in Centre for Contemporary Cultural Studies, *The Empire Strikes Back. Race and Racism in 70s Britain*, London, Hutchinson.

Lawrence, J. (1986) 'Is big business moving into caring?' *New Society*, February 10.

Leat, D., Tester, S. and Unell, J. (1986) *A Price Worth Paying? A Study of the Effects of Governmental Grant Aid to Voluntary Organisations*, London, Policy Studies Institute.

Lee, G. and Wrench J. (1983) *Skill Seekers. Black Youth, Apprenticeships and Disadvantage*, Leicester, National Youth Bureau.

Leighton, J. P. (1972) *The Principles and Practice of Youth and Community Work*, London, Chester House.

Lerman, P. (1975) *Community Treatment and Social Control. A Critical Analysis of Juvenile Correctional Policy*, Chicago, Chicago University Press.

Leys, C. (1983) *Politics in Britain*, London, Heinemann.

Linell, J. (1983) 'Looking after the early leavers', *Youth in Society*, no. 80.

Lipton, D. *et al.* (1975) *The Effectiveness of Correctional Treatment. A Survey of Treatment Evaluation Studies*, New York, Praeger.

Little, A. (1984) 'Feminism and Youth Work in practice', *Youth and Policy*, vol. 2, no. 4.

London Edinburgh Weekend Return Group (1980) *In and Against the State* (rev. ed.), London, Pluto Press.

Lowe, J. (1973) *The Managers. A survey of Youth Club management, its Structure, Function and Effectiveness*, London; ILEA.

MSC (1982) *Youth Task Group Report*, London, Manpower Services Commission.

MSC (1985) *Development of the Youth Training Scheme*, Sheffield, MSC.

MSC (1985a) *Annual Report 1984–5*, Sheffield, MSC.

MacPherson, C. B. (1966) *The Real World of Democracy*, Oxford, Clarendon Press.

Mack, J. and Lansley, S. (1985) *Poor Britain*, London, Allen & Unwin.

Maddison, B. (1980) *The Meaning of Social Policy. The Comparative Dimension in Social Welfare*, London, Croom Helm.

Manaster, G. et al (1985) 'Youth's outlook on the future', *Youth and Society* (USA), vol. 17, no. 1.

Marken, M. (1985) 'Management in the Youth Service', *Working with Girls Newsletter*, no. 25.

Marsh, C. (1986) 'Social class and occupation' in Burgess, R. G. (ed.) *Key Variables in Social Investigation*, London, Routledge & Kegan Paul.

Marshall, T. H. (1950) *Citizenship and Social Class*, Cambridge, Cambridge University Press.

Marsland, D. (1978) *Sociological Explorations in the Service of Youth*, Leicester, National Youth Bureau.

Marsland, D. (1978a) 'Youth's problems and the problem of youth' in Day, M. and Marsland, D. (eds), *Black Kids, White Kids, What Hope?*, Leicester; National Youth Bureau.

Marsland, D. (1980) 'Novelty, ideology and Reorganisation' in Anderson, D. (ed.) *The Ignorance of Social Intevention*, London, Croom Helm.

Marsland, D. (1983) 'Dreams or strategies. The future of the Youth Service', *Youth and Policy*, vol. 1, no. 4.

Marsland, D. (1985) 'Youth workers and unemployment. Talk or action?' paper presented at the International Sociology of Education Conference, Westhill College, Birmingham 1985.

Marsland, D. (1986) 'Young people, the family and the state' in Anderson, D. and Dawson, G. (eds) *Family Portraits*, London, Social Affairs Unit.

Marsland, D. and Anderson, D. (1981) 'Escape from bureaucratic serf-dom. A positive perspective on economic stringency', *Rapport*, vol. 6, no. 2.

Marsland, D. and Day, M. (1975) *The Youth Service and its Continuing Development*, Leicester, National Youth Bureau.

Marx, K. (1974) *Capital*, vol. 1, London, Lawrence & Wishart.

Mathieson, T. (1974) *The Politics of Abolition*, Oxford, Martin Robertson.

Matthews, J. (undated) *Professional Skill*, London, National Association of Mixed Clubs and Girls' Clubs.

Matthews, J. E. (1966) *Working with Youth Groups*, London; University of London Press.

Matthews, K. R. (1975) *A Guide to Youth Club Leadership. Principles and Practice*, London, Elek.

Mays, J. (1965) 'The role of social work' in Kellmer Pringle, M. (ed.) *Investment in Children*, London, Longman.

McCabe, S. and Treitel, P. (1983) *Juvenile Justice in the United Kingdom. Comparisons and Suggestions for Change*, London, New Approaches to Juvenile Crime.

McCaughey, B. (1984) *Management and Evaluation. A Selective Bibliography for the Youth Service*, Leicester, National Youth Bureau.

McLennan, G. (1984) 'The contours of British politics' in McLennan, G., Held, D. and Hall, S. (eds.) *State and Society in Contemporary Britain*, Cambridge, Polity Press.

Middlemas, K. (1979) *Politics in an Industrial Society*, London, André Deutsch.

Millham, S. *et al.* (1975) *After Grace – Teeth*, London, Human Context Books.

Milson, F. (1970) *Youth Work in the 1970s*, London, Routledge & Kegan Paul.

Ministry of Education (1945) *The Aims and Purpose of the Youth Service*, London, HMSO.

Ministry of Education (1949) *Report of the Committee on the Recruitment, Training and Conditions of Service of Youth Leaders and Community Centre Wardens* ('*The Jackson Report*'), London, HMSO.

Ministry of Education (1952) *Annual Report, 1951–2, London, HMSO.*

Ministry of Education (1962) The Training of Part-time Leaders and Assistants. Report of the Working Party Appointed by the Minister of Education in July 1961, London, HMSO.

Ministry of Health (1959) *The Working Party on Social Workers in Local Authority, Health and Welfare Services* ('*The Younghusband Report*'), London, HMSO.

Mishra, R. (1973) 'Welfare and industrial man', *Sociological Review*, vol. 21, no. 4.

Mishra, R. (1986) 'The Left and welfare', *Critical Social Policy*, no. 15.

Moore, R. and Rogers, A. (1979) 'Out of sight, out of mind. Youth Work's neglected management committees', *Youth in Society*, 37.

Monks, T. (1968) *Comprehensive Education in England and Wales*, Slough, National Foundation for Educational Research.

Morgan, D. H. J. (1986) 'Gender' in Burgess, R. G. (ed.) *Key Variables in Social Investigation*, London, Routledge & Kegan Paul.
Morgan, G. (1986) *Images of Organization*, Beverly Hills, Sage.
Morris, H. (1924) *The Village College*, Cambridge; Cambridge University Press.
Morris, K. (1984) *Local Authority Expenditure of Intermediate Treatment 1984–5*, Leicester; National Youth Bureau.
Morrison, I. (undated) 'Curriculum issues in youth and community work training', unpublished research for M. Phil. thesis, Brunel University.
Muncie, J. (1984) *'The trouble with kids today', Youth and Crime in Post-war Britain*, London, Hutchinson.
Mungham, G. (1982) 'Workless youth as a "Moral Panic"' in Rees, T. L. and Atkinson, P. (eds) *Youth Unemployment and State Intervention*, London, Routledge & Kegan Paul.
NACYS (1986a) *Revised Memorandum of Procedure*, London, DES.
NACYS (1986b) *The Place of the Youth Service*, London, DES.
NACYS (1986c) *Future Work Programme*, London, DES.
NACYS (1986d) *Training Issues*, Note of DES (NACYS 86/9), London, DES.
NAYC (1981) *A Submission to the Youth Service Review*, Leicester, National Association of Youth Clubs.
NAYC (1985) *Annual Report 1984/85*, Leicester, National Association of Youth Clubs.
NAYLEA (1960) *A Pattern for the New Youth Service*, London, National Association of LEA Youth Leaders.
NAYSO (1970) Open letter published by the National Association of Youth Service Officers and signed by the then Chairman D. Spink.
NCVYS (1983) *Partnership in the Youth Service. A Survey of Local Authority Policy and Practice*, Leicester, NCVYS.
NCVYS (1984) *Annual Report 1983–4*, London, NCVYS.
NCVYS (1985) *DES Circular 1/85*, Press Release 25 March 1985, London, NCVYS.
NISW (1982) *Social Workers, Their Role and Tasks* ('The Barclay Report'), London, Bedford Square Press.
NYB (1975) 'Training for full-time youth and community workers. A report of a consultative process', Leicester, National Youth Bureau.
NYB (1978) *Young People and the Police. The Written Evidence of the National Youth Bureau to the Royal Commission on Criminal Procedure*, Leicester, National Youth Bureau.
NYB (1979) 'Comment', *Youth Service Scene*, no. 45.
NYB (1981) *Young People, the Youth Service and Youth Provision. The Written Submission of NYB to the DES Review Group*, Leicester, National Youth Bureau.
NYB (1983) 'Co-operation or conflict', *Youth in Society*, no. 81.
Nava, M. (1984) 'Youth Service provision, social order and the question of girls' in McRobbie, A. and Nava, M. (eds) *Gender and Generation*, London, Macmillan.
Newton, K. and Karran, T. (1984) *The Politics of Local Expenditure*, London, Allen & Unwin.

Nichol, B. (1981) 'Spearhead of the Youth Service', *Rapport*, vol. 6, no. 3.

Nisbet, J., Hendry, L., Stewart, C. and Watt, J. (1980) *Towards Community Education*, Aberdeen, Abberdeen University Press.

Norris, P. (1985) 'Reagan on youth. A realignment?', *Youth and Policy*, no. 15.

Norton-Taylor, R. (1985) 'School Inspectors may ballot over merit pay', *Guardian*, 2 April 1985.

Norton-Taylor, R. (1985a) 'School Inspectors reject performance bonus plan', Guardian, 9 July 1985.

Nozick, R. (1974) *Anarchy, State and Utopia*, New York, Basic Books.

OPCS (1986) *General Household Survey 1984*, London, HMSO.

O'Connor, J. (1973) *The Fiscal Crisis of the State*, New York, St Martin's Press.

Offe, C. (1984) *Contradictions of the Welfare State*, London, Hutchinson.

Owen, R. (1969) *A New View of Society*, Harmondsworth, Penguin.

Parker, H. and Giller, H. (1981) 'More and less the same. British delinquency research since the sixties', *British Journal of Criminology*, vol. 21, no. 3, pp. 230–45.

Parkin, F. (1979) *Marxism and Class Theory. A Bourgeois Critique*, London, Tavistock.

Parkinson, D. (1987) 'Youth club bricks and mortar', *Youth in Society*, no. 123.

Parr, J. (1985) *Community and Youth Work Training Agencies Intake Report 1984/85*, Birmingham, Training Agencies Group.

Pearson, G. (1983) *Hooligan. A History of Respectable Fears*, London, Macmillan.

Pethick, E. (1898) 'Working girls' clubs' in Reason, W. (ed.) *University and Social Settlements*, London, Methuen.

Pinkerton, J. (1983) 'The politics of Black' in Caul, B. (ed.), *The Juvenile Justice System in Northern Ireland*, Belfast; Ulster Polytechnic.

Platt, S. (1986) Recent trends in parasuicide and unemployment among men in Edinburgh' in Allen, S., Waton, A., Purcell, K. and Wood, S. (eds) *The Experience of Unemployment*, London, Macmillan.

Pond, C. (1986) writing in the Volunteer Centre (UK) *Annual Report 1985–6*, Berkhamsted; Volunteer Centre.

Popple, K. (1988) 'Youth work and race' in Jeffs, T. and Smith, M. (eds) *Young People, Inequalities and Youth Work*, London, Macmillan.

Porteous, M. A. and Colston, N. J. (1980) 'How adolescents are reported in the British Press', *Journal of Adolescence*, no. 3.

Posnett, J. (1984) 'A Profile of the Charity Sector', *Charity Statistics 1983/84*, London; Charities Aid Foundation.

Poster, C. (1977) 'Competitors or partners? Community Education and the Youth Service', *Youth in Society*, no. 25.

Poster, C. (1982) *Community Education. Its Development and Management*, London, Heinemann.

Potter, S. (1982) *Police and Youth Work*, Manchester; Community and Youth Workers' Union (Manchester Branch).

Potts, D. (1961) 'Some notes on the history of the National Association of Youth Leaders and Organisers', NAYLO.

Poulantzas, N. (1985) *Classes in Contemporary Capitalism*, London, New Left Books.

Powell, R. (1984) 'Young people and violence in Northern Ireland, *Youth and Policy*, no. 10.

Punnett, R. M. (1968) *British Government and Politics*, London, Heinemann.

Ranson, S. *et al.* (1986) 'Nationalising the government of education' in Goldsmith, M. (ed.) *New Research in Central – local Relations*, Farnborough, Gower.

Redman, W. (1981) *Guidelines to Finding Your Own Support*; Leicester, NAYC.

Reed, M. (1985) *Redirections in Organizational Analysis*, London, Tavistock.

Rees, T. (1985) 'The reproduction of gender relations in the labour markets. The role of the state', paper presented at the University of Wales inter-collegiate symposium, Gregynoog, Wales, 1985.

Rennie, J. (1985) *British Community Primary Schools*, Brighton, Falmer Press.

Rhodes, R. (1979) 'Ordering urban change. Corporate planning in the government of English cities' in Lagroye, J. and Wright, V. (eds) *Local Government in Britain and France*, London; Allen & Unwin.

Riordan, J. (1987) 'Political socialisation and young people's organisations in the USSR', *Youth and Policy*, no. 19.

Riordan, J. (1987a) 'Western influences on Soviet youth culture', *Youth and Policy*, no. 21.

Ritchie, N. (1984) 'School-based youth work', unpublished; NYB memo.

Ritchie, N. (1986) *An Inspector Calls. A Critical Review of Her Majesty's Inspectorate Reports on Youth Provision*, Leicester, NYB.

Roberts, H. (ed.) (1981) *Doing Feminist Research*, London, Routledge & Kegan Paul.

Roberts, K. (1968) 'The entry into employment. An approach towards a general thoery', *Sociological Review*, vol. 16, no. 2, pp. 165–84.

Roberts, K. (1983) *Youth and Leisure*, London, Allen & Unwin.

Robinson, R. (1986) 'Restructuring the welfare state. An analysis of public expenditure 1979/80–1984/85', *Journal of Social Policy*, vol. 15, no. 1.

Rogers, R. (1983) 'HMI – Whose Servant?', Where?, no. 189.

Rojek, C. (1985) *Capitalism and Leisure Theory*, London, Tavistock.

Rooff, M. (1935) *Youth and Leisure. A Survey of Girls' Organisations in England and Wales*, Edinburgh, Carnegie Trust.

Russell, C. E. B. and Rigby, L. M. (1908) *Working Lads' Clubs*, London; Macmillan.

Rutherford, A. (1986) *Growing Out of Crime. Society and Young People in Trouble*, Harmondsworth, Penguin.

Rutter, M. and Giller, H. (1983) *Juvenile Delinquency*. Trends and *Perspectives*, Harmondsworth; Penguin.

Sadler, M. (1981) *Statutory Sources of Funding*, Leicester, National Association of Youth Clubs.

Salter, B. and Tapper, T. (1981) *Education, Politics and the State. The theory and Practice of Educational Change*, London; Grant McIntyre.

Saunders, P. (1983) 'Local government and the state', *New Society*, March 15.

Scarlett, C. (1975) *Euroscot. The New European Generation*, Edinburgh, Scottish Standing Conference of Voluntary Youth Organisations.

'Scarman Report' (1982) *The Brixton Disorders*, London, HMSO.

Scase, R. (1980) *The State in Western Europe*, London, Croom Helm.

Scene (1983) 'GLC backs down on Scouts', *Scene*, no. 89.

Scene (1986) 'Council sets out priorities', *Scene*, no. 119.

Schur, E. M. (1973) *Radical Non-intervention. Rethinking the Delinquency Problem*, Englewood Cliffs, N.J., Prentice-Hall.

Scofield, P., Preston, E. and Jacques, E. (1983) *Youth Training. The Tories' Poisoned Apple*, Leeds; Independent Labour Publications.

Scott, D. (1981) 'Review – the management of detached work', *Youth in Society*, no. 57.

Scott, D. (1986) 'The MSC and the organisation of non-statutory funding' in Brenton, M. and Ungerson, C. (eds) *The Yearbook of Social Policy in Britain 1985*, London; Routledge & Kegan Paul.

Scott, J. (1987) 'Where there's a will . . .', *Youth in Society*, no. 123.

Scott, R. A. (1972) 'A proposed framework for analysing deviance as a property of social disorder' in Scott, R. A. and Douglas, J. D. (eds) *Theoretical Perspectives on Deviance*, New York, Basic Books.

Scottish Education Department (1987) *HM Inspection of Schools: Aberdeen College of Education, Aberdeen*, Edinburgh, Scottish Education Department.

Scout Association (1985) *Annual Report 1984/85*, London, The Scout Association.

Scull, A. (1977) *Decarceration*, Englewood Cliffs, NJ, Prentice-Hall.

Seabrook, J. (1982) *Unemployment*, London, Quartet.

Seabrook, J. (1984) *The Idea of Neighbourhood. What Local Political Should Be About*, London, Pluto Press.

Secondary Headteachers' Association (1979) Report no. 3 (June 1979) of Community Schools Working Party, *SHA Review*, no. 234.

Sharron, H. (1985) 'Rob the poor – give to the rich?, *Social Work Today*, 11 March 1985.

Shaw, K. (1986) 'Economic initiative by local authorities. A critical review', *Teaching Politics*, May.

Shillito, D. (1986) *Survey of Provision for Young Black and White Unemployed Women in Leeds*, Leeds, Women's Committee and Resource Centre.

Short, C. (1983) 'Young and foolish', *Guardian*, Feb 1.

Short, C. (1986) 'The MSC and special measures for unemployment' in Benn, C. and Farley, J. (eds) *Challenging the MSC*, London, Pluto Press.

Sidebottom, E. (1963) *Making the Best Use of Professional Skill*, Youth Service Association.

Simey, M. (1984) *Government by Consent*, London, Bedford Square Press.

Sivanandan, A. (1982) *A Different Hunger*, London, Pluto Press.

Sivanandan, A. (1985) 'RAT and the degration of the black struggle', *Race and Class*, vol. 26, no. 4.

Slaughter (1985) *Marx and Marxism. An Introduction*, London, Longman.

Smales, C. (1960) Presidential Address delivered at the Annual Conference on 8 May, NAYLO.

Smith, C. S. (1966) 'The Youth Service and delinquency', *Howard Journal of Penology and Crime Prevention*, vol. XII, no. 1, pp. 42–51.

Smith, D. (1985) 'No place like home', *Youth in Society*, no. 104.

Smith, D. E. (1965) 'Front-line organization of the state mental hospital', *Administrative Science Quarterly*, vol. 10.

Smith, D. I. (1979) *Local Authority Expenditure on the Youth Service, 1975–80*, Leicester, NYB.

Smith, D. I. (1980) *Local Authority Expenditure on the Youth Service, 1979/80 to 1980/81*, Leicester, NYB.

Smith, D. I. (1983) 'Review of the Thompson Report', *Youth and Policy*, vol. 1, no. 4.

Smith, D. I. (1985) *Expenditure on the Youth Service 1978 to 1983. A Consultative Document*, Leicester, NYB.

Smith, D. I. (1987) *Reshaping the Youth Service. Policy Developments Following the Thompson Report*, Leicester, NYB.

Smith, D. J. (1983) *Police and People in London*, vols I to IV, London, Policy Studies Institute.

Smith, D. M. (1984) 'The problems of youth and the problems of sociology', *Youth and Policy*, vol. 2, no. 4.

Smith, D. R. (1984) *GREA Today: Gone Tomorrow? An analysis of the Public Funding of Youth Work 1981/2 to 1984/5*, Leicester, National Council of Voluntary Youth Organisations.

Smith, G. (1979) *Social Work and the Sociology of Organisations*, London, Routledge & Kegan Paul.

Smith, M. (1982) 'The end of community and the coming crisis in Initial Training', *Rapport*, vol. 7, no. 9.

Smith, M. (1988) *Developing Youth Work*, Milton Keynes, Open University Press.

Smith, N. (1984) *Youth Service Provision for Girls and Young Women*, Leicester, NAYC.

Smith, R. (1987) 'The practice of diversion', *Youth and Policy*, no. 19.

Society of Conservative Lawyers, Committee of (1974) *Apprentices in Crime*, London, Society of Conservative Lawyers.

Solomos, J. (1986) 'Political language and violent protest. Ideological and policy responses to the 1981 and 1985 riots', *Youth and Policy*, no. 18.

Sports Council (1977) *Joint Provision, the School Leaver and the Community*, London, Sports Council.

Spring, J. (1982) *American Education*, New York, Longman.

Springhall, J. (1977) *Youth, Empire and Society. British Youth Movements 1883–1940*, London, Croom Helm.

Springhall, J., Fraser, B. and Hoare, M. (1983) *Sure and Stadfast. A History of the Boys' Brigade 1883 to 1983*, London, Collins.

St John Brooks, C. (1985) *Who Controls Training? The Rise of the MSC*, London, Fabian Society.

Stafford, E. (1982) 'The impact of the Youth Opportunities Programme on young people's employment prospects and psychological well-being', *British Journal of Guidance and Counselling*, vol. 10, pp. 12–22.

Stanley, M. (1890) *Club for Working Girls*, London, Macmillan.

Stein, M. (1983) 'Protest in care' in Jordan, B. and Parton, N. (eds) *The Political Dimensions of Social Work*, Oxford, Blackwell.

Stewart, J. (1974) *The Responsive Local Authority*, London, Charles Knight.

Stokes, G. (1983) 'Out of school – out of work: the psychological impact', *Youth and policy*, no. 10.

Stone, C. (1987) 'Youth workers as caretakers' in Jeffs, T. and Smith, M., *Youth Work*, London, Macmillan.

Stronach, I. (1984) 'Work experience: the sacred anvil', in Varlaam, C. (ed.), *Rethinking Transition: Educational Innovation and the Transition to Adult Life*, Lewes; Falmer Press.

Swain, G. (1983) 'A permanent bridge . . . ', *Youth in Society*, no. 78, May 1983, pp. 10–11.

Tann, S., Gann, N. and Whiteside, T. (1983) 'Youth and the New Leicestershire Community Colleges', *Journal of Community Education*, vol. 2 (2).

Tawney, R. H. (1964) 'An experiment in democtratic education', *Political Quarterly*, repr. in Tawney, R. H. (1964) *The Radical Tradition*, Harmondsworth, Penguin.

Taylor, F. W. (1911) *Principles of Scientific Management* New York, Harper & Row.

Taylor; T. (1987) 'Youth workers as character builders. Constructing a socialist alternative', in Jeffs, T. and Smith, M. (eds) *Youth Work*, London; Macmillan.

Taylor-Gooby, P. (1982) 'Two cheers for the welfare state. Public opinion and private welfare', *Journal of Public Policy*, vol. 2, no. 4.

Taylor-Gooby, P. (1985) *Public Opinion, Ideology and State Welfare*, London, Routledge & Kegan Paul.

Taylor-Gooby, P. (1985a) 'Attitudes to welfare', *Journal of Social Policy*, vol. 14, no. 1.

Teasdale, J. and Powell, N. (1987) 'Youth workers and juvenile justice' in Jeffs, T. and Smith, M. (eds) *Youth Work* London, Macmillan.

Thane, P. (1982) *The Foundations of the Welfare State*, London, Longman.

Thatcher, M. (1977) *Let Our Children Grow Tall*, London, Centre for Policy Studies.

Therborn, G. (1986) *Why Some People Are More Unemployed Than Others*, London, Verso.

Thomas, M. and Perry, J. (1975) *National Voluntary Youth Organisations*, London, Political and Economic Planning.

Thomas, T. (1986) *The Police and Social Workers*, Farnborough, Gower.
Thompson, N. (1983) 'Abraham Moss Centre: The experience of conti-nuing education' in Moon, B. (ed.) *Comprehensive Schools: Challenge and Change*, London, NFER.
Thompson, P. (1984) 'The labour process and deskilling' in Thompson, K. (ed.) *Work, Employment and Unemployment*, Milton Keynes, Open University Press.
Thorpe, D. H. (1983) 'De-institutionalisation and justice' in Morris, A. and Giller, H. (eds) *Providing Criminal Justice for Children*, London, Edward Arnold.
Thorpe, D. H. *et al.* (1980) *Out of Care. The Community Support of Juvenile Offenders*, London, Allen & Unwin.
Titmuss, R. (1968) *Commitment to Welfare*, London, Allen & Unwin.
Troyna, B. and Smith, D. I. (eds) (1983) *Racism, School and the Labour Market*, Leicester, NYB.
Tutt, N. (1974) *Care of Custody*, London, Darton, Longman & Todd.
Tutt, N. (1978) *Alternative Strategies for Coping with Crime*, Oxford; Blackwell.
US Bureau of the Census (1980) *Current Population Reports Series P-20*, Washington, DC, US Government Printing Office.
Venables, E. (1971) *Teachers and Youth Leaders*, London; Evans/ Methuen.
Walker, A. (1986) 'Policies for sharing the job shortage: reducing or redistributing unemployment?' in Klein, R. and O'Higgins, M. (eds) *The Future of Welfare*, Oxford, Blackwell.
Walker, R. (1981) *The Observational Work of LEA Inspectors and Advisers; Final Report*, Norwich, University of East Anglia.
Wallis, J. and Mee, G. (1983) *Community Schools. Claims and Perfor-mance*, Nottingham, University of Nottingham.
Walsh, K. (1981) 'Local government military in Britain and the USA', paper given to the PAC Annual Conference, York, September 1981.
Watkins, O. (1972) *Professional Training for Youth Work. The Develop-ment of Methods Used at the National College for the Training of Youth Leaders 1960–70*, Leicester; Youth Service Information Centre.
Weale, A. (1983) *Political Theory and Social Policy*, London, Macmillan.
Webley, I. (1971) 'The youth wing' in Rogers, T. (ed.) *School for the Community*, London, Routledge & Kegan Paul.
Webster, M. (1985) 'A style of our own', *Working with Girls Newsletter*, no. 25.
Welsh Office (1986a) *Report by HM Inspectors on Youth Wings in West Glamorgan*, Cardiff; Welsh Office.
Welsh Office (1986b) *Report by HM Inspectors on Youth, Community and Adult Education, Ystradgynlais*, Cardiff, Welsh Office.
Welton, J. (1985) 'Schools and multi-professional approach to welfare' in Ribbins, P. (ed.) *Schooling and Welfare*, Lewes, Falmer Press.
Wharton, A. (1986) 'Gender segregation and the dual economy: a study of blue-collar occupation in US manufacturing industries', *International Journal of Sociology and Social Policy*, vol. 6, no. 2.

282   *Bibliography*

Whitehead, P. (1985) 'School-based Youth Work', unpublished report, Leicester, NYB.
Whiteside, T. (1984) 'Youth and Community Education', unpublished; University of Leicester mimeo.
Wiggans, A. (1984) *Making the Past Count. Training Which Builds on Personal Histories*, Leicester; NYB.
Wilensky, H. (1976) *The New Corporatism*, New York, Sage.
Williams; R. (1983) *Towards 2000*, London, Chatto & Windus.
Williamson, H. (1982) 'Client response to the Youth Opportunities Programme', in Rees, T. and Atkinson, P. (eds) *Youth Unemployment and State Intervention*, London, Routledge & Kegan Paul.
Williamson, H. (1983) 'A duty to explain', *Youth in Society*, no. 84, pp. 22–3.
Willis, P. (1977) *Learning to Labour*, Farnborough, Saxon House.
Willis, P. (1984) 'Conclusion: theory and practice', in Bates, I., Clarke, J., Cohen, P., Finn, D., Moore, R. and Willis, P., *Schooling for the Dole?*, London, Macmillan.
Willis, P. *et al.* (1985) *The Social Condition of Young People in Wolverhampton in 1984*, Wolverhampton; Wolverhampton Borough Council.
Wilson, E. (1977) *Women and the Welfare State*, London, Tavistock.
Wilson, E. (1983) 'Feminism and social Policy' in Loney, M., Boswell, D. and Clarke, J. (eds) *Social Policy and Social Welfare*, Milton Keynes, Open University Press.
Winchester, D. (1983) 'Industrial relations in the public sector' in Bain, G. (ed.) *Industrial Relations in Great Britain*, Oxford, Blackwell.
Wolfenden Committee (1978) *The Future of Voluntary Organisations*, London, Croom Helm.
Wood, B. (1976) *The Process of Local Government Reform*, London, Allen & Unwin.
Wood, S. (1985) 'Work organisation' in Deem, R. and Salaman, G. (eds) *Work, Culture and Society*, Milton Keynes, Open University Press.
Wooton, B. (1983) 'Reflections on the welfare state' in Bean, P. and MacPherson, S. (eds) *Approaches to Welfare*, London, Routledge & Kegan Paul.
Wright, E. O. (1978) *Class, Crisis, and the State*, London, New Left Books.
Wright, P. (1985) *On Living in an Old Country. The National Past in Contemporary Britain*, London, Verso.
YODU (1981) *YODU Quartely Mailing*, Leicester, NYB December.
YODU (1983a) *Youth Workers' Guide to the Youth Training Scheme*, Leicester, NYB.
YODU (1983b) *Youth Service Involvement in the Youth Training Scheme: A Survey Report*, Leicester, NYB.
Youth Committee for Northern Ireland (1985) *In the Service of Youth. A Review of the Role of the Youth Worker in Northern Ireland*, Belfast, Youth Committee for Northern Ireland.
Youth Service (1975) *Youth Service Policy*, Special no. 1.
Youth and Policy (1984) 'Youth Service Report, House of Commons', *Youth and Policy*, no. 10.

Index

283